BATTLES OF THE
INDIAN MUTINY

Also available in this series

AGINCOURT *Christopher Hibbert*
THE SPANISH ARMADA *Michael Lewis*
BATTLES OF THE ENGLISH CIVIL WAR *Austin Woolrych*
BATTLES OF THE '45 *Katherine Tomasson and Francis Buist*
TRAFALGAR *Oliver Warner*
CORUNNA *Christopher Hibbert*
WATERLOO *John Naylor*
BATTLES OF THE CRIMEAN WAR *W. Baring Pemberton*
BATTLES OF THE BOER WAR *W. Baring Pemberton*
YPRES 1914: DEATH OF AN ARMY
Anthony Farrar-Hockley
THE SOMME *Anthony Farrar-Hockley*
THE IRONCLADS OF CAMBRAI *Bryan Cooper*
CORONEL AND THE FALKLANDS *Geoffrey Bennett*
THE BATTLE FOR THE MEDITERRANEAN
Donald Macintyre
THE BATTLE OF THE ATLANTIC *Donald Macintyre*
THE BATTLE OF MATAPAN *S. W. C. Pack*
THE BATTLE FOR NORMANDY
Eversley Belfield and H. Essame

By the same author in Pan Books
RAJ: The Story of British India

CONDITIONS OF SALE

This book shall not, by way of trade or otherwise, be lent, re-sold, hired out or otherwise circulated without the publisher's prior consent in any form of binding or cover other than that in which it is published and without a similar condition including this condition being imposed on the subsequent purchaser. The book is published at a nett price, and is supplied subject to the Publishers Association Standard Conditions of Sale registered under the Restrictive Trade Practices Act, 1956.

British Battle Series

BATTLES OF THE INDIAN MUTINY

MICHAEL EDWARDES

UNABRIDGED

PAN BOOKS LTD : LONDON

First published 1963 by B. T. Batsford Ltd.
This edition published 1970 by Pan Books Ltd,
33 Tothill Street, London, S.W.1

ISBN 0 330 02524 4

© Michael Edwardes 1963

Printed and bound in England by
Hazell Watson & Viney Ltd
Aylesbury, Bucks

CONTENTS

	LIST OF ILLUSTRATIONS	vii
	LIST OF MAPS	viii
	PREFACE	ix
	Introduction THE DEVIL'S WIND	
1	*The Causes of the Mutiny*	1
2	*The Company's Army*	5
	Part One DELHI	
1	*The Fall of Delhi*	11
2	*The Road Back*	13
3	*The City and the Ridge*	15
4	*The Long Wait*	17
5	*Preparations in the Punjab*	20
6	*The Battle of Najafgarh*	22
7	*Breaching the Walls*	26
8	*Storming the City*	33
9	*The Capture of Delhi*	38
10	*The Aftermath: Agra*	41
	Part Two OUDH AND ROHILKHAND	
1	*The Early Days*	47
2	*Outbreak at Cawnpore*	54
3	*Crisis at Lucknow*	58
4	*The Defeat at Chinhut*	61
5	*The Siege of the Residency*	64
6	*The Battles for Cawnpore*	67
7	*The First Campaign in Oudh*	77
8	*The Road to Lucknow*	86
9	*The Relief of the Residency*	93
10	*The Second Siege*	99

11	*The Final Relief*	102
12	*Withdrawal from the Residency*	111
13	*The Saving of Cawnpore*	114
14	*A Time of Preparation*	121
15	*The Capture of Lucknow*	126
16	*Chasing the Rebels*	137
17	*The Campaign in Rohilkhand*	143

Part Three CENTRAL INDIA

1	*The Outbreak of the Mutiny*	153
2	*The Campaign in Malwa*	157
3	*The Road to Jhansi*	161
4	*The Battle of the Betwa*	169
5	*The Storming of Jhansi*	171
6	*From Jhansi to Kalpi*	176
7	*The Victory at Kalpi*	180
8	*The Rebels at Gwalior*	185
9	*The Campaign for Gwalior*	188
10	*The Pursuit of Tantia Topi*	195

Epilogue AFTER THE MUTINY

1	*The Queen's Peace*	202
2	*The Reform of the Army*	206
	APPENDIX: *The Course of the Mutiny*	210
	BIBLIOGRAPHY	215
	INDEX	217

ILLUSTRATIONS IN PHOTOGRAVURE
(*Between pages* 108 *and* 109)

Hindu Rao's House after the Siege – from a photograph
by F. Beato
(By courtesy of the Radio Times Hulton Picture Library)

Bastion held by rebels at Delhi
(By courtesy of the Radio Times Hulton Picture Library)

Sir Henry Lawrence – from a contemporary engraving
(By courtesy of the Radio Times Hulton Picture Library)

Brigadier-General James Neill – from a
contemporary engraving
(From *The History of the Indian Revolt*, *1858*)

Lieutenant-General Sir James Outram, Bt – from a
contemporary engraving
(By courtesy of the Radio Times Hulton Picture Library)

Major-General Sir Henry Havelock, Bt – from a
contemporary engraving
(By courtesy of the Radio Times Hulton Picture Library)

Major-General Sir Archdale Wilson – from an
engraving after a photograph
(By courtesy of the Radio Times Hulton Picture Library)

Sir Hugh Rose – from a contemporary engraving
(From *The History of the Indian Revolt*, *1858*)

The Nana Sahib – from a contemporary engraving
(From *Narrative of the Indian Revolt*, *1858*)

The Rani of Jhansi – from a contemporary engraving
(From *The History of the Indian Revolt*, *1858*)

LIST OF ILLUSTRATIONS

The execution of two mutineers
(By courtesy of the Radio Times Hulton Picture Library)

The interior of the Secundrabagh and the remains of the rebels slaughtered by the 93rd Highlanders and the 4th Punjab Regiment – from a photograph by F. Beato
(By courtesy of the Radio Times Hulton Picture Library)

LIST OF MAPS

India: Theatres of war	xi
Plan of Delhi	27
Oudh and Rohilkhand	49
Central India	154

PREFACE

THE AIM of this work is to give a military appreciation of the more outstanding events of the Mutiny that broke out in the East India Company's army in May 1857, and of the campaign to suppress it which lasted until April 1859. The Mutiny has a very special place in the history of British India. On the British side, more was written about it than about any other episode in the whole period of the British connexion. Indians, during the years of nationalist agitation before freedom came in 1947, saw it as a war of independence. Consequently, the story of the Mutiny has been overlaid with a thick veneer of propaganda which, by concentrating on the social and political causes and consequences, has effectively obscured the military aspects. Out of many hundreds of works dealing with the Mutiny, only two of any importance among the shorter ones have been directly concerned with these aspects. Naturally, the social and political motives behind the rebellion are of great significance, and without some knowledge of them history would lack a dimension. Because of this, I have given the reader a brief résumé of what they were, and, should he wish to know more, he will find them dealt with in some detail in my *History of India* (1961).

From a military point of view, the scale of the campaigns was very small. Minute armies deployed against each other and there were very few pitched battles. Nor was the whole of the Company's army involved in the revolt, which was mainly confined to what was known as the Bengal Army. Many Indian soldiers fought on the side of the British, and vast areas of the country remained quiet and untroubled. Much of the campaign was fought on guerrilla lines. This was a war of movement, of tracking down, and of short, sharp engagements. The Mutiny saw the development of the 'movable column', a self-sufficient body of troops capable of rapid deployment, and some of the lessons learned were not forgotten when the Indian Army was reorganized after the Mutiny.

The course of the Mutiny falls into five distinct and separate phases; first came the outbreak and the measures taken immediately; this was followed by the capture of Delhi and the two reliefs of Lucknow; then came the reconquest of Oudh; this was followed by the suppression of the revolt in Central India; and finally, there were the mopping-up operations. At the same time, it must be understood that the Mutiny was not a homogeneous affair but a series of mutinies which militarily had very little to do with each other. The troops that mutinied in one particular area, generally speaking stayed there, the only exceptions being in the cases of Delhi and Lucknow which, for specific reasons, attracted mutineers from other places. Amongst the mutineers and their civilian allies, there was no overall leadership, no guiding hand to mould the Mutiny into a full-scale rebellion. The campaigns of the British to suppress the revolt were, consequently, without overall leadership either. The areas of military activity were quite separate and I have chosen to deal with them so, connecting them together by a detailed chronology at the end of the book which the reader can refer to when necessary.

With regard to the spelling of Indian names, I have preferred in the case of such well-known places as Cawnpore and Lucknow to retain these spellings rather than to use Kanpur and Laknao. Most other names have been modernized.

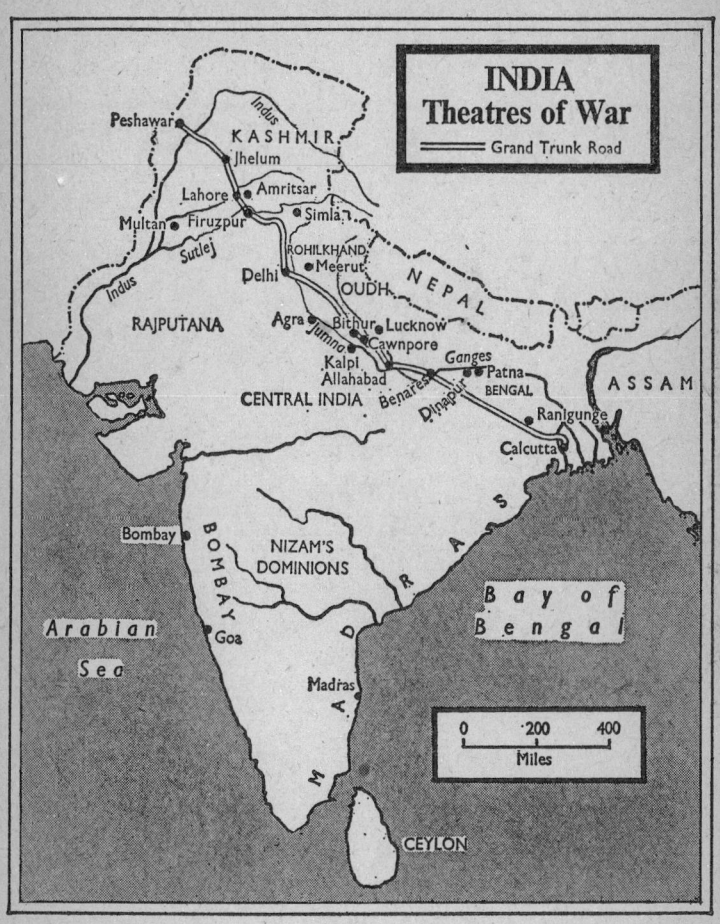

Introduction
THE DEVIL'S WIND

1

The Causes of the Mutiny

BASICALLY, THE origins of the revolt of 1857 lie in the reaction of a conservative, tradition-loving section of Indian society to the modernizing zeal of their British conquerors. As the British consolidated their power in India, they also sought to reform Indian society both morally and politically. In creating a rational and efficient administration, the British obviously threatened much of the traditional order. Princes and landowners, the principal representatives of that order, felt themselves under sentence of extinction. Under the governor-generalship of Lord Dalhousie (1848–56), both the princes and the landowners had been subjected to the heavy hand of government. Dalhousie wished to remove as many feudal states as he could, leaving only a few of the larger ones nominally independent but actually under the control of the central government. The plan was laudable, for it was designed to lead to better government and a happier situation for the peasantry, who under their feudal princes had no rights or protection from the whims of their rulers. Dalhousie first used his power to annex a state where there was no direct heir. In doing this, he refused to accept the custom that a childless ruler had the right to adopt an heir. Satara, Jhansi, Nagpur, and a number of minor states were annexed. The kingdom of Oudh, which had been grossly misgoverned for many years, was also made a part of British India. Dalhousie's second objective was to expropriate land from landlords without proper title to their estates. Some 20,000 were confiscated in the Deccan alone.

Because the government was a foreign government, and its agents foreign, too, with only a slight understanding of customary law and even of local languages, there were many cases of injustice which the government did little to remedy. The reforms were carried out ruthlessly with little or no attempt to consider the feelings of those involved. It is little wonder that those who suffered were angry or that those who might find themselves in the same position were frightened. But it was not only politically that the princes were affected. They had only to look around them to see the British interfering at every level of life. In the twenties and thirties of the nineteenth century, a number of reforms had taken place. Suttee (or widow-burning) had been abolished, infanticide suppressed, and a campaign against the Thug gangs who robbed and murdered in the name of the goddess Kali had been mounted. These excrescences on Hindu society had quite justifiably been looked upon with horror by the British, but they had also allowed themselves to view the Hindu religion as a barbaric, pagan creed, beneath contempt. Many of the officers of the Company's army held this opinion and took every opportunity of trying to persuade their men to become Christians.

Some of the sepoys felt that an attempt would be made to break their caste in such a way as to cut them off from their religion. Hinduism, unlike Christianity, is indivisibly part of the social order. Man's place in society is carefully ordered by the mechanism of caste. Break a man's caste, and not only is his place in society destroyed but he stands on the threshold of a damnation far worse than the Christian concept of hell. A Hindu believes that reincarnation continues until the highest caste – the Brahmin – is reached, after the soul has returned many times and has suffered much. When a Brahmin dies, his reward is oblivion, the heaven of the Hindus. Many of the sepoys in the Company's army were Brahmins and consequently felt they had everything to lose from the Christianizing activities of the British. In their fear, they had in fact mutinied before 1857.

In Vellore in South India, the sepoys had revolted in 1806, as they had been ordered to wear a new style of headdress, to trim their beards, and to give up wearing caste marks. This they believed to be an attempt to make them Christians. The mutiny was brutally suppressed. In 1824 a sepoy regiment ordered to Burma refused to move because it felt its caste endangered by the official refusal to supply them with special transport to carry their cooking pots, while caste usage compelled each man to have his own set. Guns opened fire on the sepoys on the parade ground where they were assembled, and next morning six of the ringleaders were hanged and hundreds condemned to 14 years' hard labour on the public roads. Five more were later executed and their bodies hung in chains as an example to their fellows. In 1852 another regiment also refused to cross the sea to Burma. This time, however, the sepoys were simply marched away to another station. A number of other mutinies and near-mutinies had taken place, all with some basis of fear that the British were trying to break their caste and make them turn Christian.

By the end of 1856 the whole of India – and particularly the north – was uneasy. Nearly every class had been shaken in some way by the reforms and political changes instituted by the administration. Only those Indians who were most westernized were unaffected by fear. The newly emerging middle class had no wish to preserve the old order untouched, and during the Mutiny they remained actively loyal. But the dispossessed were awaiting their opportunity. Those princes who had lost the territories they felt to be rightly theirs, the king of Oudh – who had been deposed in 1856 and whose kingdom had been annexed – the last sad descendants of the Mughal emperors at the twilight court of Delhi, all were awaiting an opportunity to rise in rebellion. Their agents were active among the sepoys, playing upon their fears and exciting their apprehensions, recalling the tale that 100 years after the battle of Plassey would come the day that saw the end of British rule. The fuel was ready for the fire, all that was needed was a spark. The British themselves provided it.

In 1857 it was decided to replace the old musket known as Brown Bess with the new Enfield rifle, which had a much longer range and infinitely greater accuracy. To load the new rifle entailed biting a greased cartridge. The sepoys believed, with some justification, that the grease was made from cow or pig fat – the first, from an animal sacred to the Hindus, and the second from an animal held unclean by the Muslims. The Hindu sepoys saw this as an attempt to break their caste as a preliminary to making them all Christians. Slowly at first, but with increasing momentum, sepoy regiments refused to accept the new cartridges and finally broke into open mutiny. To them rallied the disaffected. At last the opportunity had come to make a stand against the British and, with the Bengal Army at their backs, the rebels seemed to have every chance of success.

2
The Company's Army

THE ARMED forces of the East India Company had their origin in the simple necessity of guarding the goods and the persons of the first English traders in India. When the once powerful Mughal empire began its long period of decline, local rulers were quick to throw off its authority and, freed from any control from Delhi, fought among themselves and often directly threatened the tiny settlements of the Europeans. The step from armed guards to trained and disciplined troops was a short one, and soon native troops, officered by Europeans, began to play a decisive role in the struggle for empire. The British finally won domination by their superior military forces deployed against undisciplined native armies. The number of white troops was never very large. The three main centres of British rule, Bombay, Madras, and Calcutta, each had its own forces and its own commander-in-chief, but the commander of the Bengal Army was also the commander-in-chief of all British forces in India and, when necessary, supreme in all military matters.

At the beginning, recruitment for the army took place among the lower castes or from Afghan or Turkish mercenaries but, as settled government spread, a deliberate policy of involving peasants and the sons of large landowners was begun in order to give to the army a wider, more 'national' basis. Many of the new recruits came from the Brahmin caste, and in the Bengal Army, in which the mutiny was to take place, the men were almost entirely high caste.

Apart from the Company's own forces, there were also bodies of the royal army, ie, British troops stationed in India on loan to, and paid for, by the Company. In 1857 their numbers had been reduced because of the Crimean war and, at the time of the outbreak, there were no artillery or engineer units and only four regiments of cavalry and 22 infantry battalions in India. In May 1857, on the eve of the Mutiny, there were about 40,000 Europeans of the Company's and royal armies, and the immense total of around 300,000 Indians, an overwhelming majority of almost eight to one.

In the spring of 1857 the Bengal commander-in-chief, General Anson, and the whole of his headquarters staff were in the hill station of Simla. The governor-general and the civil government were in Calcutta, over 1,000 miles away. Consequently, the governor-general at the time of the crisis was cut off from his military advisers. The military area of the Bengal command, which stretched across the whole of northern India (see map, page xi) from Calcutta to the Afghan frontier at Peshawar, was organized in seven divisional commands. As appointments in the Company's army went by strict seniority, most of the generals commanding were fairly old – one, indeed, was over 70 – and all, generally speaking, were unfit for active service because of long service in bad climates. Some were men of distinction with recent experience of military action, but General Anson had in fact seen no fighting since the war against Napoleon nearly 50 years before.

The European garrison was rather thinly dispersed across the vast bulk of India. As far as the Bengal area was concerned, most European troops had been moved into the Punjab which had been conquered and annexed eight years before, and which had come accompanied by a troubled frontier with Afghanistan. At Calcutta there was one infantry battalion, and another was stationed some 400 miles away at Dinapur. One regiment was stationed at Agra and one at Lucknow. Altogether, in an area as large as France and Germany combined, there were only four battalions and a few batteries of artillery totally manned by Europeans and therefore reliable. The concentration of European troops in the Punjab, however, made it possible for the authorities there to disarm the sepoy regiments without much fuss and later to supply the troops and artillery which were to retake Delhi.

The sepoys, then, could look around them and see very little white opposition should they choose to rise. The agents of the dispossessed, who moved among them, were sure to have pointed this out. In Oudh, seething with discontent after the annexation of 1856, there were no British troops at all. The odds were obviously on the side of the sepoys.

The affair of the greased cartridges was to have its first effect on the 19th Native Infantry at Berhampur on February 26th, 1857. There were no British troops there and the regiment was marched to Barrackpur near Calcutta and disbanded, without incident, under the eyes of a British regiment hastily brought from Rangoon. But the fire was to spread, and, on March 29th, there was trouble in the 34th Native Infantry at Barrackpur when a sepoy ran amok, calling upon his comrades to join him. When he shot the adjutant and threatened other officers, the guard refused to disarm him. The sepoy finally attempted to commit suicide but was revived and later executed. The regiment, however, was not disbanded until May 6th, mainly on the insistence of the British officers that it was an isolated outbreak and that the majority of the men were not mutineers. In fact, neither the civil nor the military authorities believed in the possibility of a real revolt. The hot weather was approaching, European troops were being moved to the cool hill stations, officers were going on leave. There had been isolated mutinies before, but 'Jack' Sepoy would never openly revolt. Only one or two officers and administrators felt that the situation was grave, and they were to be proved tragically right. The Devil's Wind was soon to blow through northern India, almost sweeping the British away in its violence.

Part One
DELHI

1
The Fall of Delhi

THE FIRST real outbreak of the Mutiny took place at Meerut, some 40 miles north-east of Delhi, on Sunday, May 10th. Meerut was the most important military station in the area and had a European garrison of considerable size, consisting of one infantry and one cavalry regiment, and some artillery. The native troops were of almost equal strength. On the surface, Meerut seemed the least likely place in northern India for a mutiny, or, if one started, for a successful one. Yet both happened. In Delhi, the old imperial capital, there was a brigade of three regiments of native infantry and a light field-battery.

On April 23rd, the native cavalry at Meerut refused to use the greased cartridges. A native court martial, convened to try the mutineers, handed out long sentences of imprisonment. Then, on May 9th, the divisional commander ordered that the convicted men, shackled with leg-irons, should be paraded in front of the whole garrison. Eighty-five shuffled down the lines in the heat of a hot-weather morning. The next day the native regiments broke into open revolt at a rumour that the British troops were coming to attack them. The jail was broken open and the prisoners released, bungalows and offices were set on fire, isolated British officers and their families attacked and murdered.

The military commanders, caught off balance in a situation for which they had neither precedent nor experience, hesitated for long enough to permit the mutineers to leave the city. No one expected that they would make for Delhi, a long distance away in the gruelling Indian sun, and no cavalry was sent to pursue them. By the morning of the next day, Meerut was deserted and silent. The curtain, however, was going up on the drama at Delhi.

The capture of Delhi by the mutineers was to have a tremendous effect on the sepoys. Delhi was the former capital of the Mughal emperors and, in the recesses of the palace, the last representative of the house of Timur still kept shadowy court, a pensioner of the British. Inside the palace, too, were those who had waited long for an opportunity to do something against the British who had usurped the Mughal power and who, on the death of the present king, Bahadur Shah, had said that his heir must renounce the title of king and leave the palace. When the sepoys arrived they were welcomed as liberators, and all the romance and glamour of a once great native dynasty rising again were grafted on to their simple aims.

There was little or nothing that the few British officers and civilians in Delhi could do against the three native regiments, the mutineers from Meerut, and the retainers of the king. The arsenal, one of the largest in India, was inside the city walls and guarded only by native troops. The main magazine was some three miles outside the city, having been moved there a few years earlier for added security. That, too, was guarded by native infantry. By nightfall of the 11th, the Europeans in Delhi had been hunted down. Some had escaped, some were prisoners in the palace, many had been killed either by their own men or in the blowing up of the arsenal to prevent it falling into the hands of the mutineers. The magazine remained intact and was handed over to the mutineers by its native guard. Three thousand barrels of powder were saved to sustain the mutineers for three months against the attacks of the British.

2

The Road Back

THE NEWS of the mutiny at Delhi reached Ambala over the telegraph at three in the afternoon of May 11th. An hour later another telegram came, and then no more was heard. The telegraph wires did not go as far as Simla, where the commander-in-chief and his staff were comfortably immured, and it was not until the following day that General Anson received copies of the telegrams and sent out his first orders for troops to move in the direction of Delhi.

At Ambala a force of Europeans was assembled, consisting of two troops of Horse Artillery, Her Majesty's 9th Lancers, Her Majesty's 75th Foot, and the 1st and 2nd Bengal Fusiliers. In the station there was also the 9th Light Cavalry, the 4th Irregular Cavalry, and the 5th and 60th Bengal Infantry. The commander-in-chief refused to disarm the last two as he was assured of their loyalty by the British regimental officers. Later the 60th mutinied and went to Delhi and the 5th had to be disarmed.

When Anson arrived in Ambala on May 15th, he found telegrams urging him – rather obviously – to retake Delhi as soon as possible. Unfortunately, it was not even possible to get a force moving in the direction of the city. The reasons for this lay in the antiquated organization of the army. Firstly, Anson was without an arsenal – the only one placed to supply him was in the hands of the mutineers at Delhi. The nearest now was away to the north and it would take time for supplies to be moved. Furthermore, he had nothing to carry supplies anyway, as, after the Sikh war some nine years before, all army transport had been disbanded. Civilian contractors had to be bullied, grain and meat had to be procured. As for medical services, Anson was without drugs, equipment, or even bandages. This was not the fault of the army but of the government, whose policy it was to operate a peacetime military force with the strictest economy. General Anson's forces had fewer than 20 rounds of ammunition per man, his artillery had none at all, and there were no bullocks to pull the guns.

Despite this, the first section of troops moved off to Karnaul on May 17th and by the 30th all of Anson's little force had arrived there. On the 27th, however, Anson himself died of cholera after handing over his command to Sir Henry Barnard, who at least had seen action in the Crimea. Barnard decided without delay to march on Delhi and to meet and join up with a force from Meerut under the command of Archdale Wilson.

Wilson's forces, two squadrons of carabineers, a wing of the 60th Rifles, two 18-pounders, and some native cavalry, fought two battles on the 30th and 31st on the river Hindon, defeating mutineers from Delhi and capturing five cannon. Wilson then made for Baghpat, where Barnard's force awaited him.

Some six miles from Delhi a body of mutineers was strongly entrenched at a place called Badli-ke-serai. The mutineers numbered about 30,000 men and they had 30 guns. Against this force on June 8th Barnard threw his and Wilson's men and, after a sharp engagement, drove the sepoys from their position. Barnard then advanced to the old military cantonments outside the city on what was known as the Ridge. Rather foolishly the British burned the native troop lines as a gesture of defiance towards the city. They were to regret the shelter the buildings would have provided when the grinding sun beat down on them, as the little force hung on to the Ridge for over three months in the hottest season of the Indian year. But now the British were jubilant over the affair at Badli-ke-serai. They were on the offensive, and many thought the city would fall in a matter of days.

3

The City and the Ridge

ELATED BY the ease with which the mutineers had been driven from their positions at Badli-ke-serai, the British now began to settle in along the Ridge, occupying a number of strong points, at Hindu Rao's house, the Observatory, an old mosque, and the Flagstaff Tower (see plan, page 27). The Ridge itself, 'formed of a hard, compact, semi-crystalline quartz rock, disposed in layers, and presenting occasional natural cliffs on the city side', extended for about two miles at an average of about 40 feet above the level of the city. One end was three or four miles from the city and the other about 1,000 yards from the Kabul Gate, so near as to invite attacks 'from the moment of occupation to the close of the operations'. There was little or no soil and what there was was unsuitable for the construction of defensive works. Hindu Rao's house was substantially built and big enough to give shelter to a large number of men. Between the two extremes lay the Flagstaff Tower, a double-storeyed circular building that could be used as an observation post. Then came a ruined mosque and then the Observatory. The countryside around was full of houses and walled gardens, rice fields and malarial swamps. Beyond Hindu Rao's house lay a cluster of houses lying along the Grand Trunk Road, known as Subzimundi, the Green Market, which was held by the mutineers, and then a plain 'covered with dense gardens and thick groves, houses, and walled enclosures' bordering on the Western Jumna Canal. Further still were three villages which, being near the walls of the city, acted as cover for sorties made by the mutineers. In front of the Ridge, between it and the city, lay Metcalfe House, with extensive gardens, an old summer palace, and a mansion known as Ludlow Castle, the latter two being near to the Kashmir Gate. The view from the Ridge was of an area of lush foliage, but, as one of the British officers later recorded, it 'concealed the movement of our enemies who, creeping out of the Kashmir and Lahore

Gates, would under cover of trees and walls and houses reach unperceived almost the foot of our position.' In the rear the British were fortunate in having a wide drain running from a lake to the river Jumna; the drain, because of the heavy rains of the year before, was filled with water and remained so throughout the siege. Without it the British would have been dependent on bad water from the Jumna or the brackish wells of the old cantonment. Not only for that was the drain valuable; it also provided a good defensive line against attack from the rear.

The city itself offered a formidable aspect to the tiny force of besiegers. The walls extended for about seven miles, two of which were defended by the Jumna. The landward walls consisted of a series of masonry curtains about 24 feet high, terminating in small bastions big enough to hold between 9 and 12 guns. In front of them was a dry ditch 25 feet wide and 20 feet deep. The entrances to the city were 10 gates placed at irregular intervals. Of these, 3 were nearest to the British. The walls had been considerably strengthened by British engineers in 1804 after a siege by the Marathas, and had been kept in good repair ever since. Though they would have offered little obstacle to a siege-train of heavy artillery, they seemed powerful and threatening to Barnard's little army. Inside the city were an unknown number of mutineers, apart from the king's body-guard and a large number of police. They had plenty of guns and ammunition. The British force was made up of about 600 cavalry, 2,300 infantry, 22 field-guns, and a light siege-train.

4

The Long Wait

THE PROBLEM facing Barnard was whether, with inadequate numbers, he should attempt to capture the city – whether he should make, in fact, a dangerous gamble against unknown odds. Barnard was under great pressure, both from among his own troops – inflamed by stories of massacres throughout northern India – and from the government at Calcutta. A plan was drawn up for an assault on the city. But what if it should fail? The British position was too precarious to allow for it. Nevertheless, Barnard gave the order for an attack to take place on June 13th. Unfortunately, the quality of his staff officers was, to say the least, low, and the commander of the piquets and outposts, Brigadier Graves, was not briefed on the general's plans.

To mount an assault it was necessary to concentrate men from the outlying posts, and, on the morning of the 13th, Graves was given a verbal order to this effect. Not knowing why the order had been given, Graves declined to act without more precise instructions and rode in to headquarters to find out what was going on. By the time he arrived it was already too late to carry out a surprise attack. After a great deal of argument, some of it highly insubordinate, the assault was abandoned.

Barnard, however, still clung to the hope that the assault might yet take place, though he was very conscious of the effects of failure. 'The place is so strong', he wrote to the governor-general, Lord Canning, on June 13th, 'and my means so inadequate, that assault or regular approach were equally difficult – I may say impossible; and I have nothing left but to place all on the hazard of a die and attempt a *coup-de-main*, which I purpose to do. If successful, all will be well. But reverse will be fatal, for I can have no reserve on which to retire. But, assuredly, you all greatly under-estimated the difficulties of Delhi. They have 24-pounders on every gate and flank bastion; and their practice is excellent – beats ours five to one. We have got six heavy guns in position, but do not silence theirs, and I really see nothing for it but a determined rush; and this, please God, you will hear of as successful.'

A revised plan was drawn up and, on June 15th, the scheme was considered by a council of war. All the senior military officers, though their experience was hardly of a sort to provoke confidence in their opinions, were against the project. The question of a direct assault, without adequate reinforcements and a strong surety of success, was put aside.

Whether an attack could have been successful formed the basis for much argument for many years after the end of the Mutiny. One thing, however, was certain. The opportunity to capture Delhi by a *coup-de-main* was gone. Immense reinforcements flooded into the city. Brigades of cavalry and infantry, bands playing the well-known English marching tunes at their head, their regimental colours flying, could be seen from the Ridge as they marched in to swell the numbers opposing the British.

On the Ridge itself no one seemed in command. There was no organization, no proper system of guard and relief. If one piquet was attacked, the whole force stood to, whether it was necessary or not. If an attack was launched, no one was detailed to command it.

The mutineers made frequent sallies against the British posts, every new reinforcement feeling itself obliged to show its mettle. Hindu Rao's house was attacked on June 12th, 13th, and 15th. On the 17th the British sallied out to destroy a battery of artillery which threatened the Ridge. On the 23rd, – the centenary of Clive's victory at Plassey, and the day on which it had been forecast that British rule would be overthrown – a large body of mutineers attacked several posts on the Ridge, only to be thrown back in disorder.

Reinforcements for the British were also coming in, though slowly. The most important, perhaps, was the arrival of two officers, Neville Chamberlain and Baird Smith. The first took up the post of adjutant-general, which at that time corresponded with the modern chief of staff. Baird Smith, an engineer, brought with him a labour corps which he had raised. At the end of June there were further drafts of infantry and artillery, but there were still insufficient for a direct attack upon the city.

Casualties, in so small a force, were high. There was also cholera in the British camp. On July 5th, Barnard died of that dreaded disease and General Reed took command, though he too collapsed within a fortnight of taking over. Chamberlain, who was really in command under the nominal leadership of Reed, was wounded on July 14th and ceased to play an active part in the operations. Reed was succeeded by Archdale Wilson though, in fact, he was not the senior officer in the camp.

Wilson's personality and his actions – or rather, his lack of them – were strongly criticized by historians of the Mutiny. Much was against him. He was over 60, with some 40 years of service in the East, and his intelligence and knowledge of war were not particularly high. Nevertheless, he was not without organizational experience and the effect of his appointment was immediately noticeable. The force on the Ridge began to behave like an army.

But it was an army suffering badly and achieving nothing. It was wasting away from disease and the attacks of the mutineers. In one week in July, 25 officers and 400 men were killed or wounded. Though the force had increased to 6,600 at the beginning of the month, the drain was too heavy. But where could reinforcements be found? As other parts of the north fell to the mutineers, there was no other source but the Punjab.

5

Preparations in the Punjab

THE SITUATION in the Punjab – the Land of the Five Rivers – was fraught with danger. Only nine years before, the country had finally been annexed from the Sikhs who had ruled it. The area covered by the Punjab included the North-west Frontier with all its tribal troubles, and, over the border, Afghanistan.

As soon as the news arrived from Delhi, the administration under John Lawrence took action. The military was alerted and one of the first steps was the formation, under Neville Chamberlain, of a 'movable column', lightly equipped, and ready to move with speed against any area of disaffection. Swift action was taken at Lahore, the capital, to disarm sepoy regiments. At Peshawar, on the frontier, the disarming of the regiments had a profound effect on the local leaders. 'As we rode to the disarming', wrote Herbert Edwardes, 'a very few chiefs and yeomen of the country attended us, and I remember judging from their faces that they came to see which way the tide would turn. As we rode back, friends were as thick as summer fires.'

It was not all smooth running. At Ludhiana the local brigadier was indecisive and the town was burnt and looted by the mutineers. But, generally speaking, the situation in the Punjab was under control and the administration could set about the task of reinforcing the little garrison on the Ridge at Delhi.

The first step was to send the movable column, now commanded by John Nicholson since Chamberlain had been appointed adjutant-general, to the aid of the Delhi Field Force. The second was to prepare a siege-train. Plans were made for Nicholson to arrive at Delhi by August 15th, accompanied by the movable column and other troops numbering altogether 4,200 men. Nicholson, however, while on the way with his men, received a letter from Archdale Wilson telling him that his communications were threatened to the rear, and would Nicholson push on with all possible speed 'both to drive these fellows [the enemy] from our rear and to aid me in holding my position'. Nicholson's reply was to leave the column and go on ahead of it to Delhi.

6

The Battle of Najafgarh

WHEN NICHOLSON arrived at Delhi everyone expected the situation to take a turn for the better. His reputation, built up from his exploits in the Punjab with the movable column, had inflamed everyone's imagination – except that of his seniors. 'Nicholson', wrote one officer, 'has come on ahead and is a host in himself if he does not go and get knocked over as Chamberlain did. The camp is all alive at the notion of something decisive taking place soon.'

Very few people in the camp knew Nicholson personally, but he was soon seen moving about, 'visiting all our piquets, examining everything, and making most searching inquiries about their strength and history', as one officer noted in his diary. The same officer described the commander of the movable column: 'He was a man cast in a giant mould, with massive chest and powerful limbs, and an expression ardent and commanding, with a dash of roughness; features of stern beauty, a long black beard, and deep sonorous voice. There was something of immense strength, talent, and resolution in his whole frame and manner, and a power of ruling men on high occasions which no one could escape noticing.' There seemed to be a grave sense of purpose about him, which was really shyness, and his presence at the headquarters mess acted as rather 'a damper on the gaiety of some who sat around him'.

Nicholson was anxious to get his column into action and received permission from Wilson to use it to clear a battery which the mutineers had erected at Ludlow Castle and which was shelling the post at Metcalfe House. On the morning of August 12th, Nicholson rejoined his troops at Rhai, a short distance from Delhi, and greeted his men by telling them that General Wilson had promised the column a little job by way of getting their hands in. The 'little job', however, had already been done in the early hours of that very morning, and the

THE BATTLE OF NAJAFGARH

guns had been captured; the cost had been high, with 19 killed and 94 wounded, including Brigadier Showers.

On the 13th the movable column had arrived at Alipur within sight of the Flagstaff Tower. The air was filled with the noise of cannon and hot, foetid smells of the camp on the Ridge. The seven miles of road that led to Delhi were surrounded by devastation. Trees had been cut to supply fuel and all the leaves had been stripped to feed the camels of the supply trains. Early on the 14th, the column marched into camp, their numbers nearly doubling the force on the Ridge.

The numbers of mutineers inside the city had grown larger, too, and when they heard of the imminent arrival of a heavy siege-train, a large force sallied out to intercept it. Here was Nicholson's opportunity. In the early morning of the 25th of August, in torrential rain, a column of 2,500 men and 16 guns marched out to do battle.

The march was difficult. The roads, such as they were, had become quagmires and for the first nine miles the column had to make its way through two swamps, in which the guns were perpetually sinking. But Nicholson was determined to engage the enemy 'if possible, before night'. With the troops was the former magistrate of Delhi, Sir Theophilus Metcalfe who, knowing the countryside, had volunteered to act as guide. During a halt at the village of Nanglui, Metcalfe rode on ahead and found enemy outposts some five miles on.

By 5 PM the column had crossed a deep stream and was preparing to face the enemy. While they were crossing, Nicholson was out reconnoitring. The enemy's line, he found, extended for about two miles from the town of Najafgarh to a bridge over a canal. 'Their strongest point', wrote Nicholson in his report, 'was an old serai [travellers' resting place] on their left centre, in which they had four guns; nine more guns were between this and the bridge.' Nicholson's plan was 'to force the left centre, and then changing front to the left, sweep down their line of guns towards the bridge'.

The column formed for this attack. The two European regiments, the 61st Queen's and the 1st Bengal Fusiliers, with

Green's Punjab Infantry would attack the serai, leaving 100 men from each to act as rearguard and reserve. Four guns were to cover the force's right and ten the left, while the 9th Lancers and the Guides' Cavalry would support the line. The 2nd Punjab Cavalry and Lind's Multani Horse, with two guns, remained behind to guard stores and ammunition.

The mutineers' artillery was already shelling the attacking force and the infantry lay down in the mud to allow their own guns to answer. Soon the bugles sounded the advance and, with Nicholson at their head, the infantry swept across the 200 yards of mud that separated them from the enemy. In a few minutes the serai was captured and the infantry formed up to the left and drove the mutineers into a swift retreat across the bridge, capturing all their guns.

Meanwhile, the Punjabis had driven the mutineers out of Najafgarh itself, but in attacking another body of mutineers they came up against stiff opposition. Their commander was killed as well as many of his men, and the 61st had to go to their assistance before the mutineers could be routed. But for this, the battle had been almost bloodless. Over difficult terrain, Nicholson had defeated in little over an hour some 5,000 or 6,000 mutineers, had captured all their guns and stores, and had killed 800. British losses were two officers and 23 men killed and two officers and 68 men wounded.

There was, however, no comfort for the victors apart from the happiness of success. The force, without food or shelter, was compelled to bivouac for the night. Fortunately, the night was warm and next day the column formed up to march the 18 miles back to Delhi.

On the Ridge there was great rejoicing at the first victory since Badli-ke-serai. But Najafgarh was really only half a success for, at a village only a few miles away, another brigade of mutineers was waiting. Nicholson, when he learned of this too late to do anything about it, complained bitterly. 'Had I had a decent political officer with me', he wrote to John Lawrence, 'to get me a little information, I might have smashed the Bareilly brigade at Palam the next day. As it was, I had no information, not even a guide that I did not pick up for myself on the road.' Nevertheless, the mutineers were quiet, shocked by their defeat.

Inside the city, according to the spy system that William Hodson had organized, there was great fear and anxiety, and feelers were being put out for a truce. On August 30th Hodson records that a messenger came in from Delhi 'with much assurances and great promises; but he was sent back rather humbler than he came, for he fancied he should make terms and could not get a single promise of even bare life for any one, from the king downwards'.

As September came in, Hodson speaks of everything as 'stagnant, save the hand of the destroying angel of sickness. We have at this moment 2,500 in hospital, of whom 1,100 are Europeans.' But the siege-train was nearing Delhi and the air was alive with expectation.

7

Breaching the Walls

ON SEPTEMBER 4th, in the early morning, the siege-train arrived. The great guns drawn by elephants were accompanied by a vast number of carts carrying sufficient ammunition 'to grind Delhi to powder'. The problem now was to plan its use. Inside the city it was believed that there were over 40,000 mutineers and 40 pieces of field artillery, with plenty of ammunition for them and for the 114 guns which were mounted on the walls. Wilson was unwilling to hazard an attack against such odds. On August 20th, Wilson had written his opinion in a letter intended for the governor-general. Even with the arrival of the siege-train he felt that he could not 'hold out any hope of being able to take the place' without a larger force. Before sending the letter, Wilson submitted a draft to Baird Smith for his comments. Smith's reply was simple – take the risk now – and he supported his statement with telling arguments. Wilson, reluctantly, accepted them, and placed the whole responsibility for their success or failure on Baird Smith. 'It is evident to me', he pencilled on Baird Smith's memorandum, 'that the results of the proposed operations will be thrown on the hazard of a die; but under the circumstances in which I am placed, I am willing to try this hazard – the more so as I cannot suggest any other plan to meet our difficulties. I cannot, however, help being of the opinion that the chances of success under such heavy fire as the working parties will be exposed to, are anything but favourable. I yield, however, to the judgement of the chief engineer.'

In fact, Wilson's agreement came just in time. Some of the younger and more dynamic officers were planning to have him superseded. Frederick Roberts, later Lord Roberts, records in his memoirs a council of war being called to decide definitely whether the assault should take place or not. Nicholson 'had been talking to me in confidential terms of

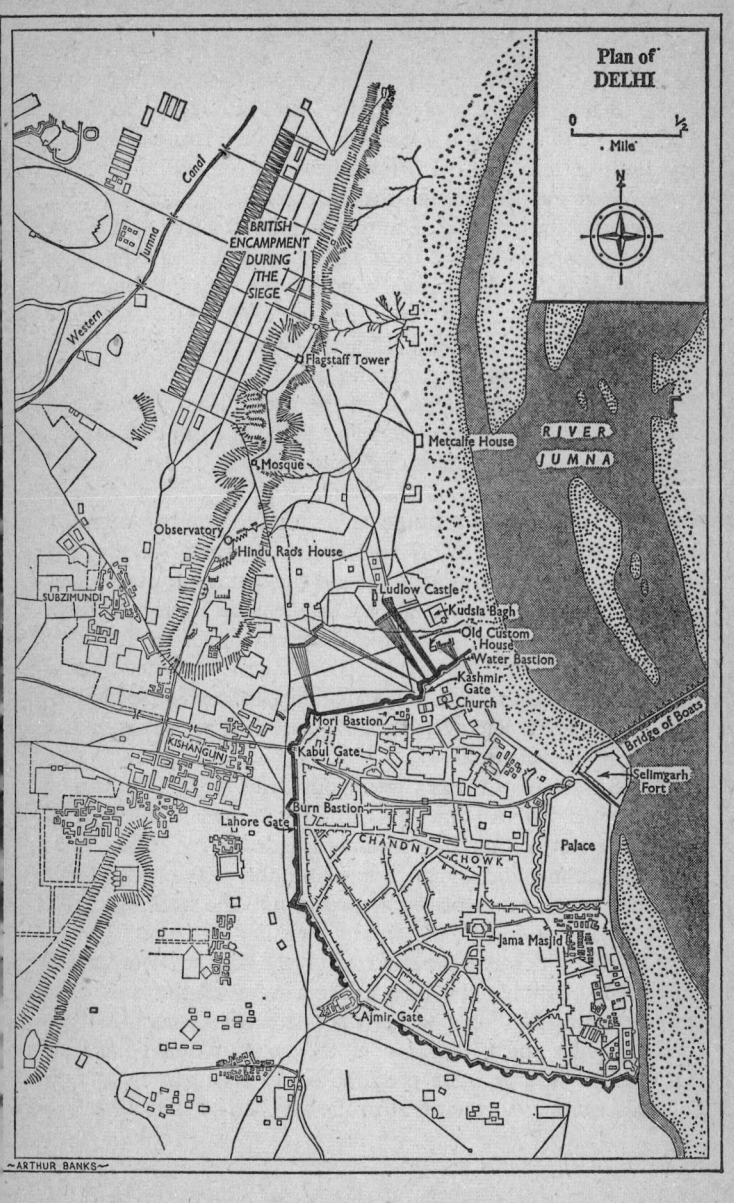

personal matters, and ended by telling me of his intention to take a very unusual step should the council fail to arrive at any fixed determination regarding the assault. "Delhi must be taken", he said, "and it is absolutely essential that this should be done at once; and if Wilson hesitates longer I intend to propose at today's meeting that he should be superseded." I was greatly startled, and ventured to remark that, as Chamberlain was *hors de combat* from his wound, Wilson's removal would leave him, Nicholson, senior officer with the force. He smiled as he answered: "I have not overlooked that fact. I shall make it perfectly clear that, under the circumstances, I could not possibly accept the command myself, and I shall propose that it be given to Campbell, of the 52nd; I am prepared to serve under him for the time being, so no one can ever accuse me of being influenced by personal motives."' Fortunately, such strong action was unnecessary.

The plan drawn up by Baird Smith and another engineer officer, Alexander Taylor, was for the breaching of the city walls with batteries of artillery and the laying of mines. The section chosen was that nearest to Metcalfe House, because this was the only part of the walls directly opposite the camp, and the gardens supplied some cover for the engineers. Siege materials – gabions, fascines, and scaling-ladders – had already been prepared, and all that now remained was to site the batteries of siege-guns.

The first heavy battery was brought up on the evening of September 7th. All through the night, camels and bullocks carrying stores, then heavy guns each drawn by 40 bullocks, made a tremendous noise. For a time the guns on the Mori Bastion poured well-placed grapeshot into the working party, but the fire soon subsided and by morning the battery was in position; by the time the sun rose on the 8th, however, it had not been possible to fix the platforms on which the guns were to be mounted. For a while it seemed that General Wilson might order the withdrawal of the guns. When Nicholson heard this he was quite prepared – as he said in a letter to John Lawrence – 'to appeal to the army to set him [Wilson]

BREACHING THE WALLS

aside and elect a successor'. But the order was not given and, under fire from the city, the platforms were fixed. The battery, known as No 1, was about 700 yards from the Mori Bastion, about halfway between Hindu Rao's house and the city. It was divided into two parts, one of five heavy guns and a howitzer designed to destroy the Mori Bastion, and a second, of four guns, to hold the enemy's fire from the Kashmir bastion. By the afternoon of the 8th, despite attacks and heavy fire from the walls, No 1 battery had demolished the Mori Bastion.

The British now prepared to site No 2 battery. First they occupied Ludlow Castle and the Kudsia Bagh, then the guns were moved up to batter the Kashmir bastion and make a breach in the curtain between it and the Water Bastion. By 8 AM on the 11th, this battery too was hammering at the walls. Under cover of fire from No 2, the engineers and sappers pressed forward with No 3. This was sited behind one of the buildings of the old Custom House, about 160 yards from the Water Bastion. A mortar battery was also sited in the Kudsia Bagh. The work was carried out under heavy fire and mainly by Indian pioneers. Many were killed but the work was barely interrupted. 'As man after man was knocked over', wrote the commander of No 3 battery, 'they would stop a moment, weep a little over a fallen friend, pop his body in a row along with the rest, and then work on as before.' Soon the guns were firing and, to the watchers on the Ridge, the walls of Delhi like some Indian Jericho appeared to tumble down.

On September 13th arrangements were made to carry the assault through the breaches in the wall and into the city. A daring reconnaissance on the night of the 13th showed that the breaches were large enough. Orders were issued for the assault to begin next morning. Five columns – very weak in numbers, as casualties had been high during the siting of the batteries – were to make the assault. Most of the men who were not sick had been on duty continuously for nearly a week. The first three columns, under Nicholson's command, were to take the Water Bastion and the Kashmir Gate; the fourth, under Major

Reid, was to capture the suburb of Kishangunj, thus covering the right of Nicholson's force, and then to enter by the Kabul Gate when it was opened for them by Nicholson; the fifth column was to remain in reserve near Ludlow Castle. The camp on the Ridge was to be covered by the cavalry brigade which could be called up should it be necessary.

The following was the composition of the five columns:

1st column : Brigadier-General Nicholson
    75th Foot   300
    1st Bengal Fusiliers   250
    2nd Punjab Infantry   450
                                       1,000

2nd column: Brigadier Jones
    8th Foot   250
    2nd Bengal Fusiliers   250
    4th Sikhs   350
                                       850

3rd column: Colonel Campbell
    52nd Foot   200
    Kumaon Battalion   250
    1st Punjab Infantry   500
                                       950

4th column: Major Reid
    Sirmur Battalion   } 850 with 1,000 men of
    Guides' Infantry   } Kashmir Contingent
    Collected piquets } in reserve

5th column: Brigadier Longfield
    61st Foot   250
    4th Punjab Infantry   450
    Baluch Battalion   300
                                       1,000

Each column included a detachment of artillerymen to operate captured guns, and a party of engineer officers.

BREACHING THE WALLS

During the night, preparations went on unceasingly. One officer, Richard Barter, recorded in his diary:

> In the evening the order was published for the storming of Delhi a little before daybreak the next morning, September 14th, and we each of us looked carefully to the reloading of our pistols, filling of flasks, and getting as good protection as possible for our heads, which would be exposed so much going up the ladders. I wound two puggris or turbans round my old forage cap, with the last letter from the hills in the top, and committed myself to the care of Providence. There was not much sleep that night in our camp. I dropped off now and then, but never for long, and whenever I woke I could see that there was a light in more than one of the officers' tents, and talking was going on in a low tone amongst the men, the snapping of a lock or springing of a ramrod sounding far in the still air, telling of preparation for the coming strife. A little after midnight, we fell in as quietly as possible, and by the light of a lantern the orders for the assault were then read to the men. They were to the following purport: Any officer or man who might be wounded was to be left where he fell; no one was to step from the ranks to help him, as there were no men to spare. If the assault were successful he would be taken away in the doolies, or litters, and carried to the rear, or wherever he could best receive medical assistance. If we failed, wounded and sound should be prepared to bear the worst. There was to be no plundering, but all prize taken was to be put into a common stock for fair division after all was over. No prisoners were to be made, as we had no one to guard them, and care was to be taken that no women or children were injured. To this the men answered at once, by 'No fear, sir'. The officers now pledged their honours on their swords to abide by these orders and the men then promised to follow their example. At this moment, just as the regiment was about to march off, Father Bertrand came up in his vestments, and, addressing the Colonel, begged for permission to bless the regiment, saying: 'We may differ some of us in matters of religion, but the blessing of an old man and a clergyman can do nothing but good.' The Colonel at once assented, and Father Bertrand, lifting his hands to Heaven,

blessed the regiment in a most impressive manner, offering at the same time a prayer for our success and for mercy on the souls of those soon to die.

At three o'clock on the morning of September 14th, some 3,000 men waited between the Ridge and Ludlow Castle for the order to advance.

8

Storming the City

THE GENERAL plan of attack was firstly, with the aid of scaling-ladders, to cross the ditch in front of the walls and then to take possession of defensible positions at the wall itself. This achieved, the next stage was to be left to the commanders themselves to decide, whether 'dependent upon the circumstances of the moment and the resistance of force' the column should penetrate into the narrow streets of the city itself and make for the king's palace. It was thought that the mutineers would probably break and flee the city. As Nicholson had put it, 'Don't press the enemy too hard. Let them have a golden bridge to retire by.'

The morning of the 14th was fine. As the columns took up their positions the siege-guns were still battering the walls. On the left of the Kudsia Bagh was Nicholson's column; next to it, that commanded by Brigadier Jones. As the mutineers had repaired some of the gaps in the walls during the night, the guns were still shelling them. This delayed the advance, and the sun was high before the order came to move.

Nicholson, after consulting Jones, gave the signal and, with himself leading, the 60th Rifles swept forward to the glacis and the three columns moved out of the Kudsia Bagh. The men carrying the scaling-ladders rushed forward through a tremendous fire from the defenders. 'Man after man was struck down and the enemy, with yells and curses, kept up a terrific fire, even catching up stones from the breach in their fury and, dashing them down, dared the assaulters to come on.' Come on they did. Soon the breach in the Kashmir curtain was taken.

Meanwhile, the second column advanced towards the breach in the Water Bastion and took it. The mutineers now retired, and the two columns began to pour into the space between the Kashmir Gate and the church (see plan, page 27). As the columns advanced towards the breaches an explosives party, consisting of two lieutenants, Home and Salkeld, with British and Indian sappers carrying gunpowder and sandbags, made for the breach leading to the Kashmir Gate. With them was a bugler to sound the 'advance' as soon as the gate had been blown in. Under heavy fire the party managed to place the charge against the gate and set the fuse. With a shattering roar the massive gate was blown. Home ordered the bugler to sound the 'advance' but, in the din of the assault, it was not heard. Nevertheless, the commander of the 52nd Foot, Colonel Campbell, heard the explosion and pressed on to the gate and through it to join men of the first column who came scrambling over the bastion. 'The sight at this moment', wrote an eye-witness, 'was beautiful. We could see the two columns . . . like a swarm of bees . . . then like hounds topping the fence into gorse cover they disappeared into the town.'

The plan was now for Nos 1 and 2 columns to turn right, move along to the Kabul Gate, where the fourth column was supposed to be waiting for admittance, and then to attack the heavily fortified Burn Bastion. No 3 was to make for the Jama Masjid.

Unfortunately, No 4 column was not doing so well. Reid's column had been delayed in starting because the four guns that were to support it did not arrive on time and, when finally they came up, it was found that there were only sufficient gunners to man one gun. The signal for Reid's advance was to be the blowing of the Kashmir Gate, but before this took place an outlying part of Reid's reserve force, which had been sent to create a diversion, came in contact with the enemy. Reid therefore decided to move, without his guns and half an hour *in advance* of the other columns. He soon discovered that the mutineers had reoccupied defensive positions in front of Kishangunj. Without guns, Reid was in a difficult position. With grapeshot, he could have cleared his way, but without it his little force was faced by some 15,000 well-trained men. His own regular troops were good, but he had with him the untrained Kashmir Contingent.

As Reid was preparing to launch an attack, he was severely

wounded in the head by a musket ball, and there was some confusion as to who should succeed him in command. Captain Richard Lawrence, in charge of the Kashmir Contingent, was senior but was thought of as a political officer and not a military one. Captain Muter of the 60th Rifles therefore assumed command. Both officers issued conflicting orders. Lawrence began to retire on Hindu Rao's house as the force was still without artillery and he felt himself threatened. Muter also fell back. The part of the Kashmir Contingent which had been first in action broke under enemy pressure and retired in considerable disorder and with the loss of four guns. In the chaos it seemed possible for a time that the enemy might even break into the camp on the Ridge or move against the flank of the columns storming the walls. Fortunately, the batteries at Hindu Rao's house, by hurling shrapnel at the advancing mutineers, managed to hold them off until the cavalry brigade, commanded by Hope Grant – which had been covering the assaulting columns – came up. Grant moved up horse artillery and some 400 troops on to the broken ground between the Mori Bastion and Kishangunj. For two hours they remained under heavy fire until the cavalry was reinforced by some infantry. When the news came that the assaulting columns had established positions inside the city, the cavalry withdrew to Ludlow Castle. Casualties were heavy but the fourth column had been protected in its retirement and an attack upon the camp had been prevented.

When No 2 column reached the Kabul Gate the expected reinforcement from Reid was, of course, not there. Brigadier Jones therefore moved on round the walls and his advance guard actually reached the Burn Bastion where, however, they were driven back. The failure of No 4 column had released many of the enemy, who had returned to the city, and Jones found himself under heavy fire from the houses near the walls. Nicholson, after ordering Colonel Campbell to move on the Jama Masjid, reformed No 1 column at the Kabul Gate. Despite the retreat of Reid's column and the increased fire from the enemy, Nicholson was determined to push on and capture the Lahore Gate. This gate was commanded by a bastion about two-thirds of the way between it and the Kabul Gate. But to reach the bastion it was necessary to go through very narrow lanes exposed to heavy fire from the houses.

Those with Nicholson pressed him to establish his position and wait for further information before attempting to run the gauntlet of enemy fire. Nicholson, however, was determined to push on in order to re-establish the initiative lost by the failure of the fourth column. Beyond the Kabul Gate ran a lane about 10 feet wide which skirted the walls leading up to the Burn Bastion. The left side, as it faced the column, was lined by houses with flat roofs and parapets. On the right side, protecting buttresses reduced the width at these points to about three feet. The houses were strongly held by the mutineers and about 160 yards from the entrance was a brass cannon and, 100 yards behind it, another. Behind these again was the wall of the bastion protecting the Lahore Gate, and on this were mounted several heavy guns.

It was into this that Nicholson decided to penetrate against all the advice to the contrary.

The first attempt was thrown back by the fire of grapeshot, musket balls, and showers of stones. The men – of the 1st Fusiliers – reformed and again attacked, this time capturing the first gun, and made for the second. Again they were forced to withdraw. This time Nicholson himself rushed forward. In a moment he was shot down. Finally, it was decided to retire – after the deaths of eight officers and 50 men. Nicholson – still alive – was removed to his tent in the camp. He died eight days later.

Meanwhile, Colonel Campbell had made his way down the Chandni Chowk to the Jama Masjid. There he found the great mosque sandbagged and its gates and arches bricked up. Without artillery or gunpowder he could do nothing. After half an hour under heavy fire he retired to a large enclosure, known as the Begum Bagh, where he waited for assistance from the other column. But Nicholson's failure to take the lane leading to the top end of the Chandni Chowk had left Campbell in an unsupported position in advance of the other columns and without communication with them. Campbell held the Begum Bagh for an hour and a half before he heard that the first and second columns had been unable to advance beyond the Kabul Gate. He then fell back on the church, occupied Skinner's house and posted men at the ends of the two streets leading into the heart of the city from the open space round the church.

The situation of the British on the night of the 14th was not altogether comfortable. Losses had been heavy – 66 officers and 1,104 men killed and wounded – and though they were inside the city they were, because of the repulse of No 4 column, still threatened on their flank. It was decided that the best plan was to fortify the advanced positions and throw out piquets to maintain communications between the columns.

General Wilson, the nominal commander of the attack, now established his headquarters in the church. Hearing the bad news of heavy casualties, the repulse of No 4 column, the mortal wounding of Nicholson, and that the assaulting force was apparently lost in the maze of the city, Wilson almost gave the order for withdrawal. But he was surrounded by men less easily depressed, and under their pressure – and particularly that of Baird Smith – he, 'fairly broken down by fatigue and anxiety', decided to hold on to what had been gained and to prepare for an advance.

9
The Capture of Delhi

THE NIGHT of September 14th was quiet except for the search for loot which spread into the next day. Close to the Kashmir Gate was that part of the city occupied by merchants of European liquor. Most historians of the Mutiny have stated that the mutineers deliberately left large quantities of liquor in open view in order to demoralize the British soldier, who was well known as liking, and over-liking, his drink. One historian, J. W. Kaye, wrote 'A black or a green bottle filled with beer or wine or brandy was more precious [to the soldiers] than a tiara of diamonds. The enemy knew this too well; and with the subtlety of their race had purposely left the immense supplies of intoxicating liquor stored in the city, open to the hand of the spoiler.' The liquor was, in fact, stored in cellars which were broken into by the soldiers in search of plunder. If the mutineers had been subtle enough to think of such a piece of sabotage, they should have been clever enough to have taken advantage of it – for the assaulting force spent two days in an orgy and were, as Hodson recorded, 'demoralized by hard work and hard drink'. But the enemy left them alone. Rather late, Wilson ordered the liquor stores to be destroyed, an order regretted by at least one officer present. 'It was deplorable to see hundreds of bottles of wine and brandy, which were sadly needed for our sick, shattered and their contents sinking into the ground. Wine which had fallen to threepence a bottle soon rose again to six shillings.'

The morning of September 16th brought little comfort to the still depressed and anxious Wilson. The mutineers evacuated the suburb of Kishangunj, and a breach had been made in the walls of the magazine. The place was soon captured; inside were 171 guns and howitzers and a large quantity of ammunition. But this did not revive Wilson's spirits. 'We took possession of the magazine this morning', he wrote on the afternoon of the 16th, 'with the loss of only three men wounded.

This advances us a little but it is dreadfully slow work. Our force is too weak for this street fighting, when we have to gain our way inch by inch; and of the force we have, unfortunately, there is a large portion, besides the Jammu [Kashmir] troops, in whom I place no confidence . . . I find myself getting weaker and weaker every day, mind and body quite worn out. The least exertion knocks me down. I walk with difficulty, and fully expect in a day or two to be laid altogether on my bed . . . We have a long and hard struggle still before us; and I hope I may be able to see it out.'

The advance through the narrow streets was very costly, each house having to be cleared of mutineers. But soon the houses were evacuated and movement was fairly easy. Artillery was now beginning to shell the palace itself. The mutineers' resistance was continuous, though many had fled the city. But the British troops were still reeling from their rape of the liquor shops and many refused to follow their officers. On the 18th an attack on the Lahore Gate was repulsed because the men refused to fight.

On the 19th, however, the Burn Bastion fell, and this was the beginning of the end. Early the following morning Jones captured the Lahore Gate and then divided his force in two, sending one detachment under Major Brind up the Chandni Chowk to the Jama Masjid and taking the other himself towards the Ajmir Gate. Brind's detachment took the mosque without much difficulty, and Jones also reached his objective. Brind, on capturing the Jama Masjid, sent General Wilson a note urging him to attack the palace immediately. The order was given and, one of the gates having been blown in, the palace was occupied. The old king and his followers had evacuated the place on the 18th, and all that was found were vast quantities of carriages, palanquins, cannon, and plunder brought in by the mutineers. General Wilson now moved his headquarters into the palace. It was a sorry sight that Wilson saw from the ramparts. 'The demon of destruction', wrote one of his staff, 'seemed to have enjoyed a perfect revel. The houses in the neighbourhood of the Mori and Kashmir bastions were a mass of ruins, the walls near the breaches were cracked in every direction, while the church was completely riddled by shot and shell ... In the Water Bastion the destruction was still more striking. Huge siege-guns, with their carriages, lay about seemingly like playthings in a child's nursery.'

With the capture of the palace, the Jama Masjid, and the Selimgarh Fort by the bridge of boats (see plan, page 27), the city was virtually in the hands of the British. The situation, however, was still dangerous. Many thousands of mutineers lurked around the city and gangs of sepoys still remained concealed in the narrow lanes and twisting streets. But on the 21st a salute of guns was fired to announce the formal capture of the city.

10

The Aftermath: Agra

As the salvo rang out from the ramparts of the palace, a tragedy was playing itself out at the tomb of Humayun, some six miles from Delhi. The old king and his followers had taken up residence there after they evacuated the palace. On the 20th, refusing to accompany the rebel commander-in-chief, Bakht Khan, and his men, the king surrendered to William Hodson on a promise that his life would be spared. The king, with his favourite wife and son, was brought to a house in the Chandni Chowk. Roberts described him as looking 'most wretched'. On the 21st of the month, Hodson once again returned to Humayun's tomb, having heard that three of the princes – whom everyone believed had been directly involved in the murder of the English in Delhi – were hiding there. The princes, hoping for the same clemency as had been shown to the king, attempted to extort a promise from Hodson which he refused to give. The princes finally surrendered without a guarantee of any sort and, on their way to the city, were killed by Hodson on the pretext that the mob which accompanied them was threatening to rescue them. The pros and cons of Hodson's action were the subject of much controversy throughout the remainder of the nineteenth century. Hodson himself was to be killed six months later at the capture of Lucknow.

Hodson's act differed only in the importance of his victims from what was happening to the other citizens of Delhi inside the city. The population had been almost entirely driven out into the surrounding countryside. Delhi was a city of the dead. Houses were destroyed, and a proposal was put forward that the whole city should be razed to the ground. Prize agents were busy digging up treasure and valuables, summary courts martial were sentencing soldiers and civilians alike to death, without much pretension to the proper laws of evidence. A bloody vengeance for the murder of English men, women, and children, was to have full and horrifying rein.

The day after the final occupation of the city, plans were made to equip a column to relieve Agra, some 160 miles from Delhi along the river Jumna, and then to move on to Cawnpore. The column, of 750 British and 1,900 troops under Brigadier Greathed, left Delhi on September 24th, no mean achievement considering the condition of the troops after the capture of the city.

Agra was the headquarters of the civil government in what was then known as the North-west Provinces (not to be confused with the much later North-west Frontier Province). Agra was a large Mughal fortress. The garrison at Agra consisted of the 3rd Bengal Fusiliers, a British regiment recently raised and totally inexperienced, and a battery of European artillery. Many of the Fusiliers were away on sick leave in the hills. Two native infantry battalions, who had made up the remainder of the garrison, had been successfully disarmed on May 31st. Public opinion in Agra had demanded that the fort be made ready as a place of refuge for the British as the outlying districts passed out of civil control. Very little was done to prepare the fort for occupation, and when in June it was heard that a force of mutineers was advancing towards Agra and some 6,000 people moved into the fort, it had neither adequate stores nor sanitary arrangements.

The lieutenant-governor of the province, John Colvin, though an able and intelligent administrator, was unfortunately easily influenced by those surrounding him who believed that, though the sepoys had mutinied, everyone else was loyal to the British. Better and more informed advice was ignored. There were, however, one or two men who could act decisively when necessary, and the fort was soon fully provisioned. But the military leaders were not particularly outstanding, and a foolish attempt to attack an approaching force of mutineers ended in a defeat, which, in turn, was followed by a rising in the city. The British were now confined to the fortress where they were, in fact, safe from anything short of an all-out attack. Nevertheless, as Greathed moved towards the city, he was bombarded with appeals for help, and the column entered the

THE AFTERMATH: AGRA

city on October 11th without opposition. The vast rebel force which Greathed had been told was threatening Agra seemed to be a figment of the imagination.

Those inside the fort had, apparently, suffered very little from their privations. The soldiers were smartly dressed, with scarlet and pipe-clay, the women elegant in fashionable dresses. Not so the relieving force. One who saw it come in wrote: '"Those dreadful-looking men must be Afghans", said a lady to me, as they slowly and wearily marched by. I did not discover they were Englishmen till I saw a short clay pipe in the mouth of nearly the last man. My heart bled to see these jaded, miserable objects, and to think of all they must have suffered since last May, to reduce fine Englishmen to such worn, sun-dried skeletons.'

The weary troops were told that the enemy had taken themselves off as soon as the approach of Greathed's column was known. The local intelligence officers informed Greathed that 'they had no doubt whatever that their information was correct and that there was no need to follow up the enemy until our troops were rested and refreshed'. Greathed foolishly accepted this advice – and, without warning, as they were making camp, the column was attacked. It rallied, however, and the mutineers were routed and pursued for some miles, losing all their guns and baggage.

Greathed's orders, however, were to push on to Cawnpore where the situation – as at Lucknow, where the British were besieged in the Residency – was serious. On the way to Agra, Greathed had come across an appeal from General Havelock in a rather unlikely place. Frederick Roberts, who was there, recorded the incident in his memoirs:

> Some excitement was caused on reaching camp by the appearance of a fakir seated under a tree close to where our tents were pitched. The man was evidently under a vow of silence, which Hindu devotees often make as a penance for sin, or to earn a title to more than a fair share of happiness in a future life. On our addressing him, the fakir pointed to a small wooden platter, making signs for us to examine it. The

platter had been quite recently used for mixing food in, and at first there seemed to be nothing unusual about it. On closer inspection, however, we discovered that a detachable square of wood had been let in at the bottom, on removing which a hollow became visible, and in it lay a small folded paper, that proved to be a note from General Havelock, written in the Greek character, containing the information that he was on his way to the relief of the Lucknow garrison, and begging any commander into whose hands the communication might fall to push on as fast as possible to his assistance, as he sorely needed reinforcements, having few men and no carriage to speak of.

On October 14th, the column moved out of Agra along the road to Cawnpore.

Part Two
OUDH AND ROHILKHAND

1
The Early Days

AS REFERENCE to a map will show (see page 49), the newly annexed province of Oudh lay across British communications from Calcutta to Delhi and the north. The river Ganges, with its tributary the Jumna, was the main highway for supplies, and along its banks lay the great cities and the British cantonments. The railway from Calcutta only reached out for about 120 miles and the Ganges and other navigable waterways were life lines to be preserved at all costs. Oudh bordered the Ganges for many miles and already, before the outbreak in May, bad administration had brought the province to the edge of rebellion.

The headquarters of the military command for Oudh and the area known as the Doab was at Cawnpore. In charge was Major-General Sir Hugh Wheeler, an old man with 54 years' service in India behind him. The garrison at Cawnpore was large but, as at other stations, recent annexations in Sind and the Punjab had heavily reduced the number of Europeans. In fact, the only European units in Oudh were the 32nd Foot at Lucknow, and a battery of the Bengal Artillery at Cawnpore and Lucknow. Native troops in the area were overwhelmingly superior in numbers.

In Lucknow, a week before the outbreak at Meerut, the 7th Oudh Irregulars refused to accept the greased cartridge and were disarmed. The chief commissioner of Oudh, Sir Henry Lawrence, brother of John, took this as a warning of the mutiny he had himself foretold some years before. Lawrence began to make preparations, moving stores into the Residency area and, when news came of the outbreak at Delhi, asking for and receiving military command of all troops in Oudh. This meant that Wheeler at Cawnpore was now deprived of most of his command and of all his European troops apart from 60 artillerymen. Except by telegraph and letters, the two men were not in communication with one another, despite the fact that Cawnpore was only 48 miles from Lucknow. Sir Hugh was old and Sir Henry was ill, a combination which, despite Lawrence's determination, was to lead to tragedy.

While Lawrence was preparing for the worst yet keeping up a bold front as if nothing were the matter, the situation in Cawnpore was deteriorating rapidly. The civil and military station there was spread out for some six miles along the southern bank of the Ganges (see plan, page 49). About the centre and some three-quarters of a mile away from it, lay the native city covering a large area and thickly populated. Living near Cawnpore, at Bithur, was the Nana Sahib who was to play an important role in the coming rebellion. Wheeler's wife, an Indian, was said to be of the same caste as the Nana and she and the general were on intimate terms with him.

At Cawnpore there were large European and Eurasian populations, business men and their families and a staff of railway engineers preparing embankments for the extension of the track from Calcutta. Wheeler's problem was to protect them. He thought that he knew what was going on in the minds of the sepoys and believed he was in a position to outwit them.

Between May 10th and 30th, Wheeler was busy making preparations to shelter non-combatant Europeans at some fortified place near the river where they could be embarked on steamers down river to Allahabad or Calcutta. There were two possible places which could be adequately defended. One was the Magazine, some miles north of the military station. This was defensible and contained large stocks of weapons and ammunition, but it was rather hard to get to and lay some distance from the river, though this distance in fact disappeared when the river rose in the rainy season. The other possible site was two large barrack buildings, one of masonry and the other with a thatched roof, out in the open close to the road from Allahabad. The latter site was the one chosen. The reason for the choice is not known, but it is reasonable to believe that the Nana Sahib had assured Lady Wheeler that, should the sepoys mutiny, they would immediately make for Delhi and there would be no attack upon the Europeans at Cawnpore.

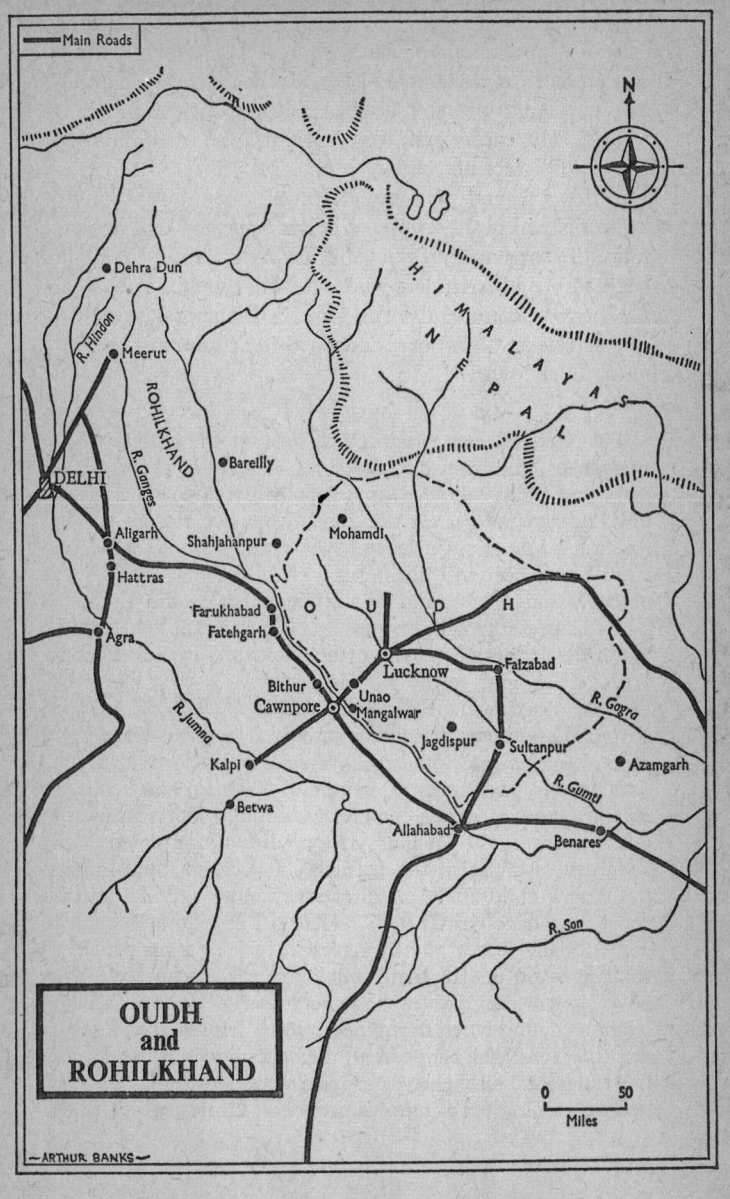

Whatever the reason, Wheeler ordered a parapet and gun emplacements to be erected around the barracks. Though there was plenty of water near by, insufficient supplies were moved in. The earthworks were built of loose earth only four feet high and were not bullet-proof.

Towards the end of May, expecting an outbreak on the Muslim festival of Id-ul-fitr, Wheeler appealed to Lawrence to send him some men of the 32nd. Lawrence sent 84 men and two squadrons of irregulars who were still thought to be loyal. With them in command went Captain Fletcher Hayes who, on his arrival at Cawnpore, described the situation there in a letter to Lucknow.

> The General was delighted to hear of the arrival of the Europeans, and soon from all sides, I heard of reports of all sorts and kinds which people kept bringing to the General until nearly one AM on the 22nd, when we retired to rest. At six AM I went out to have a look at the various places, and since I have been in India never witnessed so frightful a scene of confusion, fright, and bad arrangement as the European barracks presented. Four guns were in position loaded, with European artillerymen in nightcaps and wide-awakes and side-arms on, hanging to the guns in groups – looking like melo-dramatic buccaneers. People of all kinds, of every colour, sect, and profession, were crowding into the barracks. While I was there, buggies, palki-gharrees, vehicles of all sorts, drove up and discharged cargoes of writers, tradesmen, and a miscellaneous mob of every complexion, from white to tawny – all in terror of the imaginary foe; ladies sitting down at the rough mess-tables in the barracks, women suckling infants, ayahs and children in all directions, and – officers too! In short, as I have written to Sir Henry, I saw quite enough to convince me that if any insurrection took or takes place, we shall have no one to thank but ourselves, because we have now shown the natives how very easily we can become frightened, and when frightened utterly helpless. During that day (the 22nd) the shops in all the bazaars were shut, four or five times, and all the day the General was worried to death by people running up to report improbable stories, which in ten

THE EARLY DAYS

minutes more were contradicted by others still more monstrous. All yesterday (23rd) the same thing went on; and I wish that you could see the European barracks and the chapel close to it – and their occupants. I believe that if anything will keep the sepoys quiet, it will be, next to Providence, the great respect which they all have for General Wheeler, and for him alone. He has all his doors and windows open all night, and has never thought of moving or of allowing his family to move. Brigadier Jack, Parker, the cantonment magistrate, and Wiggins, the judge advocate-general, are, I believe, the only people who sleep in their houses.

A few days later, Hayes, having taken his squadron of irregulars out to attempt to pacify a district, was murdered by his men when they mutinied.

Wheeler was now left with a tiny force of 60 European artillerymen with six guns, 84 men and 70 invalids of the 32nd Foot, 200 unattached officers and civilians, and 40 drummers. There were about 330 women and children. In order to try and swell his miserable force, Wheeler actually asked the Nana Sahib for aid! The Nana sent 200 horse and 400 foot with two guns. These were posted at Nawabgunge near the treasury and the Magazine.

Wheeler, of course, hoped for reinforcements from the south and, on June 15th, bullocks and elephants were sent down towards Allahabad to help establish a system of convoys. The European troops at the disposal of the government in Calcutta were few, and far away from Cawnpore and Lucknow. The 53rd Foot was in Fort William, Calcutta, and the 10th Foot at Dinapur. The 84th Foot, brought back from Burma, was at Barrackpur and orders had gone out to send the Madras Fusiliers from Fort St George, Madras, half of the 37th Company of Royal Artillery from Ceylon, and the 37th Foot from Burma, while the 64th and the 78th, returning from service in Persia, were to come to Calcutta directly by sea. The government sent the 84th up-country, to be followed by the Madras Fusiliers. The Fusiliers, under the command of Colonel Neill, arrived at Calcutta on May 24th; Neill immediately moved up-country with orders to take command at Allahabad on his arrival. Some of his men went by river-steamer, others went to the end of the railway track at Ranigunge and then on by bullock and elephant.

From Ranigunge, the route lay along the Grand Trunk Road which crossed the Ganges at Benares. Neill arrived there on July 3rd and insisted that the native troops in the cantonment should be disarmed. The disarming was completely mishandled and the matter was settled only when artillery was turned upon the sepoys. From Benares, Neill pushed on to Allahabad on July 9th.

Allahabad represents yet another failure in this period of failures, inefficiency, and incompetence, and one which had appalling consequences for the British at Cawnpore and Lucknow. Allahabad, a holy city to the Hindus, stands at the junction of the Jumna and the Ganges. Between the city and the actual meeting point of the two rivers stands a vast Muslim fort which dominated the river and the roads to Delhi and into Oudh. Allahabad, despite its strategic position, had no British garrison. Towards the end of May, European families moved into the fort and about 100 civilians were formed into a volunteer corps. Some 60 military pensioners were brought in from Chunar. Nothing else was done.

When the advance reinforcements – 110 men of the 84th and 15 of the Madras Fusiliers – passed through Allahabad on their way to Cawnpore, all was quiet. One of the native regiments, the 6th Native Infantry, had even asked to be sent to Delhi with what appears to have been a genuine desire to fight for the British against the mutineers. Until June 4th, everything remained quiet, but then the news reached Allahabad of the disarming at Benares. On the evening of June 6th, the men of the 6th Native Infantry were paraded to hear a letter from the governor-general thanking them for their offer to go to Delhi. Within a few minutes of the end of the parade, the 6th had mutinied. Several officers were killed as they hurried to the lines and six cadets recently arrived from England were also murdered as they left the mess-house.

THE EARLY DAYS

Inside the fort, a company of the 6th was successfully disarmed and marched out. The city itself was soon in the hands of the mob. The jail was broken open and the prisoners released, and any European found outside the fort was killed; the European quarter was looted and burnt. One of the principal losses was that of 1,600 bullocks of the transport-train.

Reinforcements, however, continued to arrive from Benares and on June 11th Neill himself reached Allahabad. He brought with him – cholera. The countryside around was now disturbed with revolt; Fatehpur, 40 miles away on the road to Cawnpore, had murdered its Europeans. No longer was it possible to send up reinforcements in small numbers. Some had already arrived at Cawnpore where Wheeler, assured that more were on the way, sent them on to Lucknow. No more came. The débâcle at Allahabad led inevitably to the fall of Cawnpore and the siege of the Lucknow Residency, and it was not until the end of June that it became possible to make a move in the direction of Cawnpore.

Meanwhile, in Allahabad and in the districts surrounding the city, Neill's men were carrying out what they believed to be a 'righteous retribution'. Neill's method of re-establishing order was ruthless and horrible, and understandably had the most dangerous effect upon those sepoys who wavered between revolt and loyalty to the British.

2

Outbreak at Cawnpore

AFTER THE excitement and fear of May 24th, the little force inside the entrenchment at Cawnpore had settled down to await reinforcements. These arrived as May drew to a close. Assured of 'more behind', Wheeler sent them on to Lucknow. With the air full of rumours, some of the sepoys wanted to wait, others called for immediate revolt. 'The chief obstacle', wrote Hayes on May 26th, 'to a rise and insurrection of the sepoys is, that they are undecided as to who should commence it. They have been wrangling among themselves for some days. An attempt was made by a native officer to make the cavalry seize their arms and turn out. He made a trumpeter take his trumpet and commence with the signal, but the trumpet was seized and snatched away by another native officer. Last night there was an alarm, and the gunners stood to their guns, but everything passed over quietly.'

But things were not to remain quiet for long. On the night of June 4th, the 2nd Native Cavalry and the 1st Native Infantry mutinied although they did not injure their officers. The two regiments then joined the Nana Sahib's men in seizing the treasury. All the sepoys were not ripe for mutiny and a company of the 53rd Native Infantry actually defended the treasury for some time against their comrades. Thinking, however, that the 53rd and the 56th had followed the cavalry and the 1st Native Infantry in rebelling, Wheeler had artillery turned on their lines. Even in face of this proof that the British did not trust them, all the native officers and many men of the 56th joined Wheeler and the others inside the entrenchment. The rest of the sepoys did just as the Nana Sahib had said they would, and marched off towards Delhi, having murdered no one nor damaged property to any extent. Wheeler felt that all he had to do was wait for reinforcements. He was soon disillusioned. The sepoys had gone no further along the road to Delhi than the town of Kullianpur. On

OUTBREAK AT CAWNPORE

June 6th, Wheeler received a letter from the Nana Sahib telling him that he was about to be attacked. Hurriedly, those who had left the entrenchment returned. Within a few hours the entrenchment was surrounded, the guns from the Magazine which Wheeler had not destroyed were brought up, and the first round-shot dropped near a party of women and children gathered outside one of the barracks. The siege had begun.

The actual garrison at the time of the siege was only 240 men. The number of women and children had increased to 375. The sun was at its hottest, like 'a great canopy of fire', gun-barrels burned the hand, and there was little or no protection, though it was discovered some 60 years later that there was a huge underground room beneath one of the barracks that would have given cool and bullet-proof shelter. The garrison, however, did not know that it existed.

The sepoys concentrated their efforts on shelling the entrenchment with the wide variety of artillery they had acquired from the Magazine. The death roll among the defenders grew steadily. About a week after the siege began, one of the barracks was burnt down. On the anniversary of the battle of Plassey, June 23rd, a great assault had to be beaten off. But food and water were scarce, as the route to the well was open to heavy fire from the sepoys.

By June 25th, the ammunition was almost gone and starvation stared the garrison in the face. Their hope of reinforcement was finally shattered. To evacuate the entrenchment with the women and children was impossible. On that day, a letter from the Nana Sahib was brought into the entrenchment by a half-caste woman. It offered terms of surrender: 'All those who are in no way connected with the acts of Lord Dalhousie [the former governor-general] and are willing to lay down their arms, shall receive a safe passage to Allahabad.'

Wheeler himself was against surrender, but others thought they should at least attempt to save the women and children. Next morning a meeting was arranged and the Nana's representatives proposed that the British should surrender their guns and treasure and that they should march out of the entrenchment with their hand-arms and 60 rounds of ammunition for each man. In return, the Nana would provide transport for the women and children and the sick, and boats with supplies aboard would be waiting at the Sati Chaura Ghat. On these terms, a written treaty was drafted and accepted. The Nana then demanded that the garrison should evacuate that very night but finally agreed, when faced with a threat that the British would fight to the last man, to wait until the following day.

On June 27th, what remained of the garrison marched out towards the river. The sick and the women were carried down in palanquins, the children were, ironically enough, many of them carried by some of the sepoys who a day or two before had been trying to kill them. At 8 AM the survivors were piling into the boats, large clumsy vessels with thatched roofs 'looking at a distance rather like floating haystacks'. By nine o'clock, all were embarked and waiting to move off. What happened next was believed at the time, and later, to be 'so foul an act of treachery the world had never seen'. But it is more likely that it was one of those ghastly accidents that spatter the pages of history and on which any interpretation suitable to the needs of the occasion can be imposed. Probably a musket shot was heard and the British, fearful of treachery and with nerves tattered by three weeks of constant siege, immediately opened fire. Soon raked with grapeshot and ball, the little fleet was on fire and attempts to push the unwieldy vessels into midstream were unsuccessful. One boat, however, did get away and four of its occupants, after an adventurous journey which included swimming down-river under fire, finally reached safety.

Of those who survived the attack at the Sati Chaura Ghat, the men, 60 in number, were killed by the Nana's troops, and the women were imprisoned in a large house at the edge of the cantonment. Later they were moved to a small house originally built by an English officer for his native mistress and still known, for that reason, as the Bibighur – the 'Lady's House'. There they were joined by survivors from Fatehgarh, who had been captured whilst attempting to escape by river. On July 15th, when news reached Cawnpore that the British under General Havelock were approaching the city, the women and children were murdered and their bodies thrown down a well.

This massacre was to inflame the British into becoming even more ruthless than they had already been. As they moved through the countryside, they carried with them a Bloody Assize, without in many cases even a pretence of the forms of justice. The massacre of the women and children was instantly blamed upon the general evil of the Nana Sahib and his associates. Just as reasonable an explanation was given in a contemporary statement – that the savagery of the British 'left their foe without inducement to show mercy, since he received none, and made even women valueless as hostages'.

3

Crisis at Lucknow

LAWRENCE'S preparations for the worst had continued at Lucknow with the fortification of the Residency area and the levelling of as much of the surrounding buildings as was possible. From May 23rd, 'one incessant stream of store carts, conveying grain supplies, necessities of war, etc' lined the principal streets on their way to the Residency. The situation in the city and the surrounding country was tense. On the evening of May 30th fell the long awaited blow.

Colonel Inglis, commanding HM 32nd Foot, later stated that Lawrence had been warned by a native that the mutiny would start at 9 PM. As Lawrence sat down to dinner at his house in the cantonment, the 9 PM gun was fired as usual. He said with a laugh to Inglis, 'Your friends are not punctual.'

I had hardly replied, when we heard the musketry in the lines, and some chuprassis [messengers] came and reported the firing. The horses were at once ordered, and Sir Henry stood outside in the moonlight, on the steps of the Residency, impatiently awaiting his horse. There was a guard of a native officer and sixty sepoys on duty in the Residency, and immediately on the alarm, the native officer had drawn them up in a line about thirty yards distant, directly in front of where Sir Henry Lawrence stood. And now the subadar came to me and, saluting, said, 'Am I to load?' I turned to Sir Henry and repeated the question; he said, 'Oh yes, let him load'. The order was at once given, and the ramrods fell with that peculiar dull sound on the leaden bullets. I believe Sir Henry was the only man of all that group whose heart did not beat quicker for it. But he, as the men brought up their muskets with the tubes levelled directly against us, cried out: 'I am going to drive those scoundrels out of the cantonment: take care while I am away that you all remain at your posts, and allow no one to do any damage here, or enter my house, else when I return I will hang you.' Whether through the effect of this speech and Sir Henry's bearing, I know not, but the guard remained steadily at its post, and with the bungalows blazing and shots firing all round, they allowed no one to enter the house, and the residence of Sir Henry was the only one that night in the cantonment that was not either pillaged or burnt.

Forewarned, a massacre was averted, though three British officers were murdered. The 32nd saved the day and proved once again that *resolute* leadership, so sadly lacking at this time, could prevent serious trouble. Lawrence himself went off the next day in pursuit of the rebels, chasing them 10 miles and taking 60 prisoners. 'We are', he wrote in a footnote to a letter to the governor-general, 'now positively better off than we were, for we now know our friends and enemies. The latter have no stomach for a fight . . .' But events in Lucknow were to be altered by what was going on in the rest of Oudh. On May 31st, risings at Bareilly and Shahjahanpur in Rohilkhand, away to the north-west, took place. Between June 3rd and 6th, to the south and east, the same thing happened at Azamgarh, Benares, Jaunpur, Cawnpore, and Allahabad. On June 3rd, to the west, the 41st Native Infantry mutinied at Sitapur, and of the white population that survived a few reached Lucknow. On and after June 8th, Faizabad and Sultanpur fell to the mutineers, and local detachments of sepoys mutinied throughout the province. 'Every outpost', wrote Lawrence on June 12th, 'I fear has fallen, and we daily expect to be besieged by the confederated mutineers and their allies.'

June was the prelude. Fortification of the Residency continued rapidly. Non-combatants, particularly women and children, were now concentrated in the Residency area. During June a police battalion mutinied and was chased into the countryside, and the sad news from Cawnpore came in as well as a false rumour that Delhi had been recaptured. As late as June 21st, Lawrence believed that if Delhi was taken and Cawnpore could hold out he would not be besieged in Lucknow. But he did not slacken the work of preparing the Residency. At least at Lucknow, foresight was to pay off.

But before the retirement into the Residency area, Lawrence was to lose an unnecessary battle. Towards the end of June, news came in of a concentration of mutineers at Nawabgunge, 25 miles north-east of Lucknow. This news arrived the same day as that of the fate of the garrison at Cawnpore. Lawrence expected to be besieged in two or three days, but under pressure from those who surrounded him and who were calling for an aggressive gesture against the mutineers, he agreed to move out against the concentration at Nawabgunge. The action was not only ill-advised but mishandled, and from it undoubtedly stemmed the difficulties and troubles of the siege that soon followed.

4

The Defeat at Chinhut

ON JUNE 29TH, news came that the mutineers' advance guard was now at Chinhut, some 10 miles from Lucknow. The report stated that there were about 500 foot, 50 cavalry, and one small gun. This information was not trustworthy, and Lawrence believed the numbers to be greater. Nevertheless, arrangements were made for an expedition. The force assembled consisted of 300 men of the 32nd Foot, 170 Native Infantry, 36 Volunteer Horse, 84 Oudh Irregular Cavalry, with 10 guns and a howitzer drawn by an elephant. Lawrence, who was ill with overwork and strain, foolishly decided to command the troops himself. His military experience was limited and there were more competent men to hand.

It was decided that the force would move off at dawn on June 30th, but because of inefficient organization the sun was already hot when it marched off – without breakfast. After a three-mile march, the force reached the bridge over the Gumti river at Kokrail. Here a halt was called, and the 32nd were ordered to have breakfast. Unfortunately, they had not brought it with them. Lawrence, reconnoitring forward and seeing no enemy, gave the order to return to Lucknow, the wisest course to follow. Then he made his second error – the first had been to order the expedition at all – for while the orders were being given to countermarch he received news from some 'native travellers' that there was no enemy force in Chinhut at all, and changed his mind and ordered an advance.

Everything went wrong. The heat of the day was tremendous and the water-carriers seem to have deserted. The troops had had no food and there was some doubt about the loyalty of the native gunners. No proper forward reconnaissance took place, for one who was there recorded that 'a turn in the road showed us the enemy drawn up with their centre on the road and their left resting on a lake'. The Lucknow force never had a chance, for the enemy's numbers were later estimated at some 5,500 foot, 800 horse, and 12 or 16 good pieces of artillery. In command was one Barhat Ahmad, who was quite obviously a much better soldier than Lawrence. As the force moved forward, round shot smashed into them. A party of the 32nd, who had occupied the small village of Ismailganj, was thrown out of it by a party of the enemy. On the other side, the mutineers attacked a party of loyal sepoys. At this stage, Lawrence's native gunners and cavalry deserted. The 32nd tried to retake Ismailganj but, weakened by the heat and lack of food, failed to do so. Lawrence's column was now in danger of being encircled. The enemy's horse artillery was now on each flank and their cavalry had now moved in and taken the bridge at Kokrail, cutting the British off from Lucknow.

A force of volunteer cavalry charged the enemy at the bridge and broke through followed by the rest of the force, now reduced to pretty much of a rabble. Lawrence, rather too late, handed over the command of the column to Colonel Inglis and rode at full speed to the Residency, realizing that his defeat would mean an immediate attack upon the fortification. Behind him, he left almost half of the 32nd dead or wounded and some of the best of the garrison's commissioned and non-commissioned officers.

To those left in the city, the return of the defeated force could only bring fear and anxiety. Lady Inglis, watching from the Residency, wrote in her journal: 'You may imagine our feelings of anxiety and consternation. I posted myself and watched the poor men coming in; a melancholy spectacle indeed – no order, one after the other; some riding; some wounded, supported by their comrades; some on guns; some fell down and died from exhaustion not half a mile from our position. The enemy followed them to the bridge close to the Residency . . . I could see the smoke of the musketry and plainly discerned the enemy on the opposite bank of the river.' The loss of prestige was even worse. The siege of the Residency was precipitated when more fortification was necessary. All of Lawrence's careful preparations were put in jeopardy by

THE DEFEAT AT CHINHUT

his own bad leadership and inept organization. That night from inside the Residency, he wrote to Havelock:

> This morning we went out to Chinhut to meet the enemy, and we were defeated, and lost five guns through the misconduct of our native artillery, many of whom deserted. The enemy have followed us up, and we have now been besieged for four hours, and shall probably tonight be surrounded. The enemy are very bold, some Europeans very low. I look on our position now as ten times as bad as it was yesterday; indeed it is very critical. We shall have to abandon much supplies and to blow up much powder. Unless we are relieved quickly, say in fifteen or twenty days, we shall hardly be able to maintain our position. We lost three officers killed this morning and several wounded.

5

The Siege of the Residency

As THERE was no single leadership among the mutineers, it was some time before definite plans were put into action. Inside the Residency, however, Lawrence was hard at work making final preparations to hold out against a siege though on the day of Chinhut, as he wrote to Havelock, he did not expect to be able to hold out for long. On the night of June 30th, the garrison at the Machchi Bhawan was instructed to come into the Residency. They did so, to the roar of 240 barrels of gunpowder and over 5,000,000 rounds of ball and gun ammunition blown up in the fort by a slow match lit when they left. Despite Lawrence's efforts, the Residency was not ideal as a place of refuge. The Residency area was not a fortress but a series of strongpoints, many of which were overlooked by buildings in control of the mutineers. Inglis reported that these buildings had been deliberately spared from destruction by Lawrence's express orders. 'Our heaviest losses', he wrote, 'have been caused by the fire from the enemy's sharpshooters stationed in the adjoining mosques and houses of the native nobility, the necessity of destroying which had been repeatedly drawn to the attention of Sir Henry Lawrence by the staff of engineers. But his invariable reply was, "Spare the holy places and private property too as much as possible"; and we have consequently suffered severely from our very tenderness to the religious prejudices and respect to the rights of our rebellious citizens and soldiery.'

The Residency area consisted of a kind of plateau, its greatest height at the Residency buildings themselves from which it sank down rapidly to low grounds on the right or southern bank of the river Gumti. To the north, where the area was comparatively narrow and formed an irregular projection, it was enclosed by a ditch and a bank of earth about four feet high, heightened at the most exposed spots by sandbags loop-holed for muskets. The other side of

THE SIEGE OF THE RESIDENCY

what formed an irregular pentagon was bounded by the walls of various buildings and enclosures. Access to the position was by two gates, one, the Water Gate, immediately north of the Residency, and the other, the Bailey Guard, on the east. These two gates were defended by barricades and artillery. The other defences consisted of a series of batteries at the most commanding points. Two were placed on the left of the Water Gate, and above the Residency there were another two, known as Evans' and the Redan, with a mortar battery between them. At the southern extremity lay the Cawnpore battery, and at the south-west, Gubbins'. Two more batteries on the west side were unfinished at the time the siege began and were left outside the defences.

The Residency itself, an imposing building of three storeys and a tower, was not much use as a defensive position. Its windows were large and open to the enemy's shot. The upper storeys were abandoned, the ground floor occupied by soldiers, and women and children found shelter in the deep cellars. A short distance from the Residency stood the banqueting hall of two storeys, which was converted into a hospital by filling up the tall windows. Further east lay the treasury, near the Bailey Guard. Opposite was Dr Fayrer's, a large low house with a flat roof and cellars. South from Fayrer's were three other buildings, known as the Financial garrison, Sago's and the Judicial, overlooked by the post office from the west and Anderson's and Duprat's, the last-named next to the Cawnpore battery.

This description gives the impression of a well-fortified defensive position, but such was not in fact the case. The two strongest batteries – the Redan and the Cawnpore – had only three guns each, and the earthworks were in many places too weak to resist a determined assault. To defend the area, there were about 3,100 people, of whom 1,600 or so were combatant.

The defenders received a severe blow on July 2nd when a shell burst in a room, mortally wounding Sir Henry Lawrence who died two days later. The command was now divided,

Inglis taking over military responsibility and Major Banks the civil. Against constant shelling and mining, with disease and starvation taking their steady toll, the garrison held out against overwhelming odds until the first relief came in September.

6

The Battles for Cawnpore

WHILE OUDH and Lucknow slipped into revolt, Neill, having 'pacified' Allahabad, was by the end of June ready to move to the relief of the garrison at Cawnpore – which had, in fact, though Neill did not know it, already surrendered. On June 30th, 200 of the 84th Foot, 200 Fusiliers, 300 Sikhs, two guns, and a party of Irregular Horse moved off under the command of Major Renaud. Another 100 Fusiliers and one gun were to move up-river in a steamer. As Renaud marched out, a new commander arrived, General Havelock, whose name was to become a byword to Victorian children for heroism and sacrifice.

Havelock had come from Persia, where an expedition under Sir James Outram had been recalled to India. Havelock, a Queen's officer, had spent most of his service in India and had considerable experience of the demands of war. His arrival brought the first commander of any real merit to the scene of operations. His instructions from the government were simple. 'After quelling all disturbances at Allahabad, he should not lose a moment in supporting Sir Henry at Lucknow and Sir Hugh Wheeler at Cawnpore, and should take prompt measures for dispersing and utterly destroying all mutineers and insurgents'!

At Allahabad, Havelock approved all Neill's dispositions and began to make preparations for an advance. Four British battalions were to be at his disposal, the Madras Fusiliers and the 84th Foot – already at Allahabad and on the march – and the 64th Foot and 78th Highlanders, then on their way to Calcutta from Persia. But an early move was not possible. The same problems as had delayed Anson were now to affect Havelock – carriage and supplies were scarce. It was not until July 7th that Havelock was able to march.

While preparations were going on, a native runner arrived from Lucknow with the news that Wheeler and his men had surrendered at Cawnpore on June 27th and had subsequently been murdered. This was confirmed the next day, July 3rd. Havelock immediately ordered Renaud to 'halt . . . at Lohunga and keep a good lookout to rear, front, and flanks. I will then strongly reinforce you with the column that is to march tomorrow, the 4th instant. Burn no more villages, unless occupied by insurgents, and spare your European troops as much as possible.' Neill now took the first step in causing a breach between himself and Havelock. He telegraphed the commander-in-chief saying that it was his opinion that Renaud should keep on.

Havelock was, however, still unable to leave as there were still insufficient bullocks to pull his supply train. A delay of three days brought him a small reinforcement from the 78th Highlanders. On July 7th, organization was complete and they were ready to move. Paraded and waiting for transport were about 1,000 men of the four British battalions, the 64th and 84th Foot, the 78th Highlanders and the Madras Fusiliers, with 130 Sikhs, about 18 Volunteer Cavalry, and six guns. At four o'clock in the afternoon of a dull and dismal day the force moved off. Barely a quarter of a mile had been covered when there was a heavy downpour of rain and after about three hours' march, the column halted for the night. As the baggage train was very slow-moving, most of the tents had not arrived. The men were forced to spend an uncomfortable night on the damp earth without shelter.

After three days of leisurely marching – leisurely because many of the men were untrained and soon disabled and footsore – Havelock joined up with Renaud about four miles from Fatehpur. Renaud had not remained, as originally ordered, at Lohunga, because Neill's telegram to the commander-in-chief had resulted in an order to Havelock that Renaud should proceed. Havelock's intelligence, which was good, now reported that a large body of about 3,000 mutineers was rapidly approaching Renaud's tiny force. As Havelock's men were suffering badly from fatigue and exposure, he decided to rest on the 12th. But when the troops were waiting

THE BATTLES FOR CAWNPORE 69

for breakfast, a 24-pound shot landed in the camp and a body of rebel cavalry was seen approaching. The enemy obviously thought that they had only Renaud's little detachment to deal with, and they must have been unpleasantly surprised to find five regiments and eight guns awaiting them.

Havelock, in his dispatch, described the battle that followed.

> They [the enemy] insolently pushed forward two guns, and a force of infantry and cavalry cannonaded our front, and threatened our flank.
>
> I wished earnestly to give our harassed soldiers rest, and so waited until this ebullition should expend itself, making no counter-disposition beyond posting a hundred Enfield riflemen of the 64th in an advanced copse. But the enemy maintained his attack with the audacity which his first supposition had inspired, and my inertness fostered. It would have injured the morale of my troops to permit them thus to be bearded; so I determined at once to bring on an action.
>
> Fatehpur constitutes a position of no small strength. The hard and dry Grand Trunk Road subdivides it, and is the only means of convenient access, for the plains on both sides are covered at this season by heavy lodgements of water, to the depth of two, three, and four feet. It is surrounded by garden enclosures of great strength, with high walls, and has within it many houses of good masonry. In front of the swamps are hillocks, villages, and mango groves, which the enemy already occupied in force.
>
> I estimate his number at 3,500, with twelve brass and iron guns.
>
> I made my dispositions. The guns, now eight in number, were formed on the close to the chaussée in the centre, under Captain Maude, RA, protected and aided by one hundred Enfield riflemen of the 64th. The detachments of infantry were, at the same moment, thrown into line of quarter distance columns, at deploying distance, and thus advanced in support, covered at discretion by Enfield skirmishers. The small force of volunteers and irregular cavalry moved forward on the flanks on harder ground.
>
> I might say that in ten minutes the action was decided, for in that short space of time the spirit of the enemy was entirely

subdued. The rifle fire, reaching them at an unexpected distance, filled them with dismay; and when Captain Maude was enabled to push his guns through flanking swamps, to point blank range, his surprisingly accurate fire demolished their little remaining confidence. In a moment three guns were abandoned to us on the chaussée, and the force advanced steadily, driving the enemy before it at every point.

Major Renaud won a hillock on the right in good style, and struggled on through the inundation. The 78th in extension kept up his communication with the centre; the 64th gave strength to the centre and left; on the left, the 84th and regiment of Ferozepur pressed back the enemy's right.

As we moved forward, the enemy's guns continued to fall into our hands, and then in succession they were driven from the garden enclosures, from a strong barricade on the road, from the town wall, into, and through, out of, and beyond the town. They endeavoured to make a stand a mile in advance of it. My troops were in such a state of exhaustion that I almost despaired of driving them further. At the same time, the mutineers of the 2nd Cavalry made an effort to renew the combat by charging, with some success, our irregular horse, whose disposition throughout the fight was, I regret to say, worse than doubtful. But again our guns and riflemen were with great labour pushed to the front. Their fire soon put the enemy to final and irretrievable flight, and my force took up its present position in triumph, and parked twelve captured guns.

Casualties were light. 'Twelve British soldiers were struck down by the sun and never rose again. But our fight was fought, neither with musket nor bayonet, nor sabre, but with Enfield rifles and cannon; so we lost no men.'

Havelock, however, was unable to carry on a pursuit as the Irregular Cavalry had refused to fight and were next day disarmed. This left him only with the few men of the Volunteer Horse, who were 'new to the country, new to the service, unaccustomed to roughing it' but made up for such disadvantages by enthusiasm and determination.

Fatehpur was occupied, but without the ruthless vengeance

of Neill at Allahabad. In the latter, Neill, fearful of an attack upon a city seething with hatred for the man who had ordered so many executions, now asked Havelock to send him some artillerymen and the Sikhs. This Havelock was unwilling to do, especially as further reinforcements were known to be on their way up-country from Calcutta. He did however send back 100 Sikhs, 50 of whom he ordered to garrison Lohunga.

On the 14th, Havelock moved out of Fatehpur leaving the remaining Sikhs to set fire to the town. On the following day, the British arrived in front of the village of Aong, where they found the enemy dug in with two 9-pounder guns. The Volunteer Cavalry moved forward and the guns opened fire. About a third of the force, under Colonel Tytler, moved round to encircle the position while Havelock and the remainder of the force stood fast to protect the baggage from two bodies of the enemy's cavalry which were moving on their flanks. While the dispositions were being made, the enemy advanced to a village some 200 yards in front of the guns. A body of the Fusiliers under Renaud drove them out, though Renaud was mortally wounded in the engagement and died three days later. Tytler now moved forward under artillery cover and drove the enemy infantry before him. The cavalry, seeing the infantry routed, immediately withdrew, leaving their baggage and military stores strewn over the countryside. Again, Havelock's shortage of cavalry prevented a pursuit and the troops were ordered to rest and have breakfast.

Six miles further on was the Pandu Nadi, a river normally fordable but now swollen by the rains. At this point, there was a masonry bridge and Havelock was determined to capture it. The river was not only swollen, but ran at the bottom of a deep ravine and without a pontoon or boats it was practically impassable. While the troops were preparing their food, news was brought by spies that the mutineers were intending to blow the bridge. Havelock immediately ordered an advance and, still breakfastless, the troops after a march of two hours came under fire from artillery entrenched by the bridge. After a bombardment by artillery and small arms, and an unsuccessful attempt on the part of the enemy to blow it up, the bridge was taken. Soon the first of Havelock's men were crossing to the other side.

The bridge, however, was very narrow and it was nightfall before the supply waggons had crossed. The men, weary and hungry, were too tired to cook the meat butchered for them and ate only hard biscuit washed down with beer. The night was extremely hot, and by morning the meat was bad. As they lay down to sleep, the news of Havelock's victories reached Cawnpore and the women and children were murdered in the Bibighur. Havelock, of course, knew nothing of this and he and his men were anxious to move on and save them.

Havelock believed that he would have to face a really large body of rebels before he could cover the 23 miles that separated him from Cawnpore. He had already asked Neill, now a brigadier-general, to send him at least 200 Europeans, for he intended to press on to Lucknow as soon as he had disposed of Cawnpore and he needed men to garrison that city. He was also running short of ammunition for his Enfield rifles, whose superiority had been demonstrated at every turn. Stores of rum were also low.

On the 16th, under a blazing sun, Havelock and his men marched 16 miles to Maharajpur where they rested and had a meal – again hard biscuit and beer. While they were bivouacked there, a reconnaissance party of the Volunteer Cavalry sent in two Indians, sepoys of the Bengal Army who had remained loyal. One of them had come from Delhi and reported the progress of the siege, and both had been with the rebel force the day before and knew the disposition of the defences at Cawnpore.

The Nana Sahib, with 5,000 men and eight guns, had chosen a formidable position some seven miles from Cawnpore. His left was covered by the river Ganges and the high ground that sloped towards it. The road to the cantonment divided his left from his centre which was at a small village. There a 24-pounder and a 6-pounder were dug in. The Grand Trunk Road ran between the centre and the right which lay behind a

THE BATTLES FOR CAWNPORE 73

village surrounded by a mud wall and defended by two 9-pounders. On the right lay the railway embankment. The two roads met about 800 yards in front of the enemy's position, which formed a crescent about a mile and a quarter in length.

The Nana believed that Havelock would move up the Grand Trunk Road, and his artillery was disposed to sweep it with shot. Behind the guns was ranged the infantry, and cavalry was available at the rear. The position was extremely strong, and a frontal attack by so small a force as Havelock's would be doomed to failure. Havelock therefore decided to turn the position by a flanking movement. The Volunteer Cavalry was sent out to bring in informers, and from the information obtained it was decided that the enemy's left was the weakest held.

Havelock now made the potentially dangerous decision to leave his hospital, baggage, and camp followers behind with two guns and some infantry at Maharajpur. This meant that, should things go wrong, he would be cut off from his supplies. A column of subdivisions was formed, with a wing of the Madras Fusiliers heading it, and the Highlanders, the 64th, 84th, and the Sikhs behind. The Volunteer Cavalry was ordered to move up the road until it divided in two, then to continue in the hope of persuading the enemy that a frontal attack was imminent. The remainder of the force would then proceed to the right and move unseen under cover of a line of dense mango groves. The main body moved through the groves for about 1,000 yards, and then a gap revealed them to the enemy. Though the enemy attempted to reform their line, it was now too late and under steady artillery fire the British rapidly advanced against the enemy's left. The rebel artillery at the centre and right could not fire for fear of hitting their own comrades. The 24-pounders on the left, however, were causing casualties among Havelock's men and it was necessary to make a bayonet charge in order to take the guns. 'The opportunity had arrived', wrote Havelock in his dispatch after the battle, 'for which I have long anxiously waited, of developing the prowess of the 78th Highlanders. Three guns of the enemy were strongly posted behind a lofty hamlet well entrenched. I directed this regiment to advance, and never have I witnessed conduct more admirable. They were led by Colonel Hamilton, and followed him with surpassing steadiness and gallantry under a heavy fire. As they approached the village, they cheered and charged with the bayonet, the pipes sounding the pibroch. Need I add that the enemy fled, and the village was taken and the guns captured?'

The enemy's left was now crushed and their infantry, in flight, broke in two, one body retiring up the road towards the cantonments and the other rallying near the gun at the centre. Havelock reformed the line, called out 'Now, Highlanders! Another charge like that wins the day!' and aided by the 64th they took the village and the gun.

Meanwhile, the 18 men of the Volunteer Cavalry were still pressing on up the road until, seeing a party of the enemy, they charged and lost a third of their men. The 64th, the 84th, and the Sikhs had now pushed forward to the enemy's right and had driven the sepoys into retreat. But all was not yet over, for, as the columns were re-forming, heavy fire was opened from a village in which the fugitives had rallied. 'The General', recorded Major North of the Highlanders, 'who seemed to be gifted with ubiquity, and the clear tone of whose voice raised to the highest pitch the courage of the men, hurried towards the Highlanders, and said "Come, who'll take the village, the Highlanders or the 64th?" There was no pause to answer. The spirit of emulation was a flame in every breast, kindled by his calm words. We (the Highlanders), eager for approval, went off quickly in the direction indicated, moving onward in a steady compact line, our front covered by the Light company, and pushing the enemy's skirmishers through the village, from whence they were compelled to fly. The Madras Fusiliers drove them from the plantation.'

The Nana, however, was determined to make a last stand. Fresh reinforcements had been called out from the city, and two light guns and a 24-pounder opened up on the tired British, who were now about a mile ahead of their own artillery. 'My artillery cattle', wrote Havelock, 'wearied by the length of the march, could not bring up the guns to my assistance, and the Madras Fusiliers, the 64th and 84th, and 78th detachments, formed in line, were exposed to a heavy fire from the 24-pounder on the road. I was resolved this state of things should not last; so calling upon my men, who were lying down in line, to leap on their feet, I directed another steady advance. It was irresistible. The enemy sent round shot into our ranks until we were within three hundred yards, and then poured in grape with such precision and determination as I have seldom witnessed. But the 64th, led by Major Sterling and by my aide-de-camp, who had placed himself in their front, were not to be denied. Their rear showed the ground strewed with wounded; but on they steadily and silently came, then with a cheer charged and captured the unwieldy trophy of their valour. The enemy lost all heart, and after a hurried fire of musketry gave way in total rout. Four of my guns came up, and completed their discomfiture by a heavy cannonade; and as it grew dark the roofless barracks of our artillery were dimly descried in advance, and it was evident that Cawnpore was once more in our possession.'

The first real battle of the mutiny had been fought and won. That night the rebels blew up the Magazine that Wheeler had failed to destroy, while the British bivouacked outside the city, once again without food or tents. The baggage left behind at Maharajpur might have been attacked by the large numbers of enemy cavalry still lurking around the city, but it was not. On the following day, after hearing from spies sent into the city of the massacre of the women and children, and that the mutineers had left the city, Havelock and his men entered Cawnpore. Sickened by the sights at the Bibighur, the troops settled down to an orgy of drinking, having discovered huge stores of European liquor in the town. On the empty stomachs of the soldiers, it had a maddening effect. Havelock issued orders to the commissariat officers to buy up without delay all the wine, beer, and spirits that could be found in the town. 'If it [the liquor] remained in Cawnpore', he said in a telegram to the commander-in-chief, 'it would require half my force to keep it from being drunk up by the other half, and I should scarcely have a sober soldier in camp.'

Sunstroke, too, had taken its toll and cholera had broken out in the force. There was also trouble with looters, both British and Sikh, and though the death penalty was brought in for those detected in plundering it still went on until Havelock ordered the provost-marshal 'to hang up, in their uniform, all British soldiers that plunder' and made all commanding officers responsible for their men. Meanwhile, boats had to be acquired for crossing the river before the force could press on to Lucknow. On July 20th, the party that had set off by river steamer from Allahabad came in, and Neill arrived by road with a small body of reinforcements.

7

The First Campaign in Oudh

HAVELOCK WAS anxious to move on to the relief of Lucknow. He had now heard of the death of Sir Henry Lawrence and had been both saddened and determined by the news. But he was still in a dangerous position with his small body of men, weary and sick, and an unknown number of mutineers between him and the Residency. He had already selected, on arriving at Cawnpore, a spot to fortify as a strongpoint, as there was no hope of garrisoning the city with the men at his disposal. To leave the city totally undefended would be an open invitation to the Nana Sahib to return and, by doing so, to cut Havelock's communications with Allahabad and Calcutta. Havelock decided that he could only spare 300 men for the defence of Cawnpore. The site he chose for a defensive position was at a little distance from the ferry across the Ganges, on an elevated plateau about 200 yards long and 100 yards wide. This post, situated as it was on the banks of the river, could command both it and the surrounding countryside. With the aid of about 4,000 labourers, an earthwork was constructed in two days, and Havelock decided to move on into Oudh on July 20th.

Havelock was still faced with the problem of getting his force across the Ganges – at this point some 1,600 yards wide and very swift-running because of the rains. The bridge of boats which had stood there had been destroyed by the rebels and all boats had been removed or destroyed. However, by diligent searching 20 were found and, with the addition of the little steamer that had brought up troops from Allahabad, Havelock began to ferry his men across the river. The native boatmen who had gone into hiding were induced, by a promise to overlook their support of the mutineers, to return to work. With great difficulty, and in torrential rain, the force crossed the river, but it was not until the 25th that Havelock was in any position to make a move.

Havelock now moved his 1,500 men to the village of

Mangalwar, about five miles along the road to Lucknow. There he paused to allow transport and supplies to join him. Havelock was well aware of the difficulties and dangers that confronted him. On July 28th, he wrote to the commander-in-chief from Mangalwar:

> In reply to your Excellency's telegram of the 26th, I beg to state that I should consider it certain that I must incur the risk of serious loss in an attempt to recross the Ganges to Cawnpore, even supposing that I had been reinforced by the remnant of the garrison of Lucknow. The chances of relieving that place are at the same time hourly multiplying against us. I will not now enter into all the details, but specify only that Nana Sahib has succeeded in collecting three thousand men and several guns, and is on our left flank at Fatehpur Chaurassi, with the avowed intention of cutting in upon our rear, when we advance towards Lucknow. The difficulties of an advance to that capital are excessive. The enemy has entrenched and covered with guns the bridge across the Sai at Bani, and has made preparations for destroying it if the bridge is forced. I have no means of crossing the canal near Lucknow even if successful at Bani. A direct attack at Bani might cost me a third of my force. I might turn it by Mohan, unless the bridge there also were destroyed. I have this morning received a plan of Lucknow from Major Anderson, engineer in that garrison, and much valuable information in two memoranda, which escaped the enemy's outpost troops, and were partly written in Greek character. These communications, and much information orally derived from spies, convince me of the extreme delicacy and difficulty of any operation to relieve Colonel Inglis, now commanding in Lucknow. It shall be attempted, however, at every risk, and the result faithfully reported. Our losses from cholera are becoming serious, and extend to General Neill's force as well as my own. I earnestly hope that the 5th and the 90th can be pushed on to me entire, and with all despatch, and every disposable detachment of the regiments now under my command be sent. My whole force only amounts to 1,500 men, of whom 1,200 are British, and ten guns imperfectly equipped and manned.

THE FIRST CAMPAIGN IN OUDH

Nevertheless, the next day, July 29th, Havelock moved off towards Unao, three miles away. At Unao, he found the rebels strongly posted. 'His [the rebels'] right', he wrote, 'was protected by a swamp which could neither be forced nor turned; his advance was drawn up in a garden enclosure, which in this warlike district had purposely or accidentally assumed the form of a bastion. The rest of his advance force was posted in and behind the village, the houses of which were loop-holed. The passage between the village and the town of Unao is narrow. The town itself extended three-quarters of a mile to our right. The flooded state of the country precluded the possibility of turning in this direction. The swamp shut us in on the left. Thus an attack in front became unavoidable.'

Up the road went the 78th and the Fusiliers and drove the enemy out of a bastioned enclosure, while the 64th stormed the village, destroyed the defenders and captured their guns. Meanwhile, the news came that a body of 6,000 mutineers with artillery, which had come down from Lucknow, were moving into Unao. It was now a race between Havelock and the rebels to get there first. He therefore pushed through the town and occupied a space beyond it, almost completely surrounded by swamps and commanding the road along which the rebels were moving, rapidly but in some confusion. Havelock drew up his force in line with four guns at the centre and two at either end. The rebels rushed straight into the trap and were met by heavy artillery and small-arms fire. The enemy now attempted to deploy, but their guns sank into marshy ground and they were forced to retire leaving some 300 dead and 15 guns.

Havelock, after a short pursuit, now halted for three hours so that his men might rest and eat. But the fighting was not yet over for that day. Havelock moved on to the walled town of Bashiratgunj, six miles further on, where the rebels were heavily entrenched behind earthworks overlooked, and therefore protected, by large buildings in the town. At the rear was a large sheet of water about seven feet deep over which the road was carried on a causeway. Havelock took his men around the town and so frightened the defenders that, after a short engagement, they fled. Unfortunately the 64th, harassed by fire from the walls and stopping to answer it, did not move quickly enough to cut off the retreat.

That evening the British settled down to rest, warming themselves with the satisfaction of two victories in one day. Their position, however, was still precarious in the extreme. The force was now down to 850 effectives, having lost 88 killed and wounded and many casualties from fatigue, exposure, and cholera. They occupied every piece of transport assigned to the sick. If Havelock had further casualties he would be unable to carry them. On top of this, he had used more than a third of his artillery ammunition and had still covered barely one-third of the distance to Lucknow. His intelligence reported heavy concentration of rebels across his path. Havelock decided to return to Cawnpore to leave his sick and wounded and also to receive reinforcement before going on to Lucknow. The force, greatly disturbed – as many felt that they could push on to Lucknow without much difficulty, now retired to Mangalwar which had the advantage of being on the right side of the river, within easy distance of Cawnpore and with a good natural defensive position.

In reaching Mangalwar on July 31st, Havelock sent a letter to Neill in Cawnpore, saying that he needed another battery of guns and 1,000 men before he could again take the road to Lucknow. Neill's reply was to send his chief an abusive letter which ended peremptorily. 'You ought not to remain a day where you are', he wrote. 'When the iron guns are sent to you, also the half battery, and the company of the 84th escorting it, you ought to advance again, and not halt until you have rescued, if possible, the garrison of Lucknow. Return here sharp, for there is much to be done between this and Agra and Delhi.' Neill, however, had picked on the wrong man and he received a crushing letter from Havelock in reply. 'There must be an end', said Havelock, 'to these proceedings at once. I wrote to you confidentially on the state of affairs. You sent me back a letter of censure of my measures, reproof and advice for the future. I do not want and will not receive any of them from an officer under my command, be his experience what it may. Understand this distinctly, and that a consideration of the obstruction that would arise to the public service at this moment alone prevents me from taking the stronger step of placing you under arrest. You now stand warned. Attempt no further dictation. I have my own reasons, which I will not communicate to anyone, and I alone am responsible for the course which I have pursued.'

The reinforcements Havelock expected to receive were, however, required for work elsewhere. He was informed by the commander-in-chief that he could expect nothing for several weeks. The reasons for this were that, on July 25th at Dinapur in Bihar, the sepoys, whom the local commander had made no attempt to disarm, had mutinied and, owing to inept handling, about 3,000 of them had got away almost unscathed. The reinforcements so urgently needed by Havelock had to be diverted for the protection of towns in Bihar and the Ganges valley, in case the mutineers should cut communications with Calcutta. All that was available was 257 men, barely sufficient to make up the casualties in Havelock's own force.

Although Havelock was no better off, he was determined to move on to Lucknow and on August 4th he set out once again from Mangalwar. On reaching Unao, he heard that the rebels were back in force at Bashiratgunj. Following roughly the same plan as before – only this time with more success – Havelock attacked the rebels and drove them out of the town. Again, pursuit was not possible, for Havelock was virtually without cavalry, a disadvantage which meant that the enemy was often able to take his guns with him.

The enemy now established itself at Nawabganj in some strength. Havelock did not pursue but halted to consider his next move. The prospect before him was hardly reassuring. He was, for one thing, without adequate maps of the country he was passing through. In Calcutta he had failed to find any except a 10-year-old rough sketch of the road to Lucknow and, though a survey had been made some four months before by the railway engineers, the plans had been lost at Cawnpore. Havelock's scouts reported that Nawabganj was heavily fortified and that there were fortified posts all along the road to Lucknow. A bridge over the river Sai had been broken, and the crossing was said to be defended by a force of 30,000 rebels. Havelock also heard of the mutiny of the Gwalior Contingent, which was threatening a move on Kalpi and would endanger Cawnpore and the communications with Allahabad. It was also rumoured that the rebels from Dinapur were advancing into Oudh.

The road to Lucknow would then be a fight all the way and at least a third of his force would become casualties. This would leave Havelock about 700 men with whom to attack Lucknow and its encircling canal, narrow streets barricaded and entrenched, with every house a strongpoint. The countryside was full of armed and hostile villagers led by their landlords. Above all, cholera was amongst his force and men were dying every hour. Havelock had no real alternative but to retire once again to Mangalwar. He consulted 'the only three staff officers in my force whom I ever consult confidentially but in whom I entirely confide'. They were 'unanimously of the opinion that an advance to the walls of Lucknow involves the loss of this force'.

On his return to Mangalwar, Havelock wrote to Inglis inside the Residency at Lucknow: 'When further defence becomes impossible, do not negotiate or capitulate. Cut your way out to Cawnpore', a piece of advice which, as will be seen, could not have been taken.

By now, communications with Cawnpore had improved considerably. A road had been constructed across the islands in the river and a bridge of boats established between them. Boats lashed together and covered with planks had been prepared to take over the artillery. In fact, the crossing of the river could be effected with speed and efficiency. Nevertheless, Havelock did not wish to move out of Oudh for he believed, rightly, that his presence there kept a large force of mutineers away from Lucknow and that a retreat, even for strategic

THE FIRST CAMPAIGN IN OUDH

purposes, would be considered a defeat by potential rebels.

In Cawnpore, Neill felt himself in danger and asked for a detachment to help him. The 42nd Native Infantry, which had mutinied at Saugor, was in fact within eight miles of Neill's fortified position. Havelock agreed, but it was learned that the mutineers had retired. Then, on August 11th, Neill sent Havelock the following despatch:

> One of the Sikh scouts I can depend on has just come in, and reports that four thousand men and five guns have assembled today at Bithur and threaten Cawnpore. I cannot stand this; they will enter the town, and our communications are gone; if I am not supported I can only hold out here; can do nothing beyond our entrenchments. All the country between this and Allahabad will be up, and our powder and ammunition on the way up, if the steamer, as I feel assured, does not start, will fall into the hands of the enemy, and we will be in a bad way.

Havelock consequently decided to cross the river and had, in fact, already sent across his supply train when his scouts reported a concentration of 4,000 rebels at Bashiratgunj. To cross the river with such a force in his rear would only be inviting attack. On the afternoon of the 11th, Havelock moved on Unao in heavy rain and prepared for the third time to move against Bashiratgunj. This time the situation was varied by the mutineers entrenching a village about a mile and a half in front of the town. The enemy position lay on the main road and on a mound some 400 yards from it. Both places were defended by artillery. In between was what appeared to be flat ground covered with vegetation; it was actually a marsh. The 78th Highlanders, moving up to this, were forced to attack the guns from the front. This they did under heavy fire and captured them. The rebel infantry behind the guns broke and fled and the Highlanders turned the guns on them and completed the rout. After chasing the fleeing rebels through the town, Havelock withdrew to Mangalwar and continued with the crossing of the river under torrential rain, breaking the bridges as the last men passed over on the 13th.

Cholera crossed the river with them and deaths were so high that the surgeon-general estimated that the whole force would be casualties within six weeks if they were not rested. Intelligence reports of 4,000 rebels collecting at Bithur made this impossible. Havelock now had about 335 men out of 1,415 disabled by sickness or wounds. 'But', he wrote to the commander-in-chief, 'I do not despair. I march tomorrow against Bithur, but it seems advisable to look the evil in the face; for there is no choice between reinforcements and gradual absorption by disease. The medical officers yesterday recommended repose; but I cannot halt while the enemy keeps the field, and, in truth, our health has suffered less fearfully even in bivouac than in Cawnpore.'

It was decided that the force, leaving behind only 100 men with Neill at Cawnpore, should move off in the night of August 15th/16th. Unfortunately, by the time the men were assembled it was within half an hour of sunrise. The march, and the engagement, were carried out in blinding heat and there were many casualties from sunstroke.

The enemy lay in front of Bithur, behind a plain covered with dense plantations of sugar-cane and castor-oil plants and interspersed with villages. A stream, now so swollen as to be unfordable, ran in front of the town, curved round, and joined the Ganges. The only access to the town was across a narrow stone bridge which was overlooked by high ground with buildings beyond. For some reason, instead of taking up their position behind the stream, the rebels had done so in the plain, leaving themselves only the narrow bridge over which to retreat if it should become necessary.

The attack was made by advancing in direct echelon from the right, the 78th Highlanders, the Fusiliers, and a battery facing the right wing, and the 64th, 84th, the Sikhs, and a battery facing the left. Though the rebel infantry was put to flight, the guns in well-masked entrenchments continued to pour in heavy fire. At the point of the bayonet, the enemy was finally driven across the bridge and through the town. 'I must do the mutineers justice', wrote Havelock in his dispatch; 'the

THE FIRST CAMPAIGN IN OUDH

justice to pronounce that they fought obstinately; otherwise they could not for a whole hour have held their own, even with such advantages of ground, against my powerful artillery fire.' Again Havelock's want of cavalry prevented a pursuit. Though his little band of Volunteer Cavalry, originally 18, now numbered 80, he was unwilling to risk it in an obviously too unequal contest. The force bivouacked for the night in the garden of the former British Residency.

Havelock's spies reported that a large detachment of rebels had left the main body in retreat to Fatehgarh and were now within 12 miles of Cawnpore. Havelock, fearing they might attack Neill and his tiny position, immediately moved back on Cawnpore during the morning of August 17th.

With the engagement at Bithur, the first attempt to relieve Lucknow was over. Havelock must now wait for reinforcements and rest his men. Though Havelock had consistently won victories, it was to be six weeks before a new attempt could take place. His withdrawal across the Ganges, though strategically sound, had a disastrous effect on the course of the rebellion. Many local chieftains and landowners in Oudh had, for various reasons, not joined the rebels; they now decided to do so, or were forced into unwilling support. From a military rebellion, the situation in Oudh turned into what can only be described as a national uprising. The entire province took up arms against the British.

8
The Road to Lucknow

WHEN HAVELOCK returned to Cawnpore on August 17th, he found waiting for him a copy of the *Calcutta Gazette* of August 5th announcing that he had been superseded in his command by Major-General Sir James Outram. No official communication had been made to him. Nevertheless, the appointment could hardly have come as a surprise to Havelock. He knew that Outram, who had been his superior in Persia, was following him from there. Many historians of the Mutiny have made great play of the 'supersession' of Havelock as the action of a hard-hearted government against him for not proceeding to Lucknow when he had the opportunity. Nothing could be further from the truth. As the scale of war increases, so does the rank of the commanders in the field. Havelock commanded what could barely be described as a brigade. Outram's command was to cover all troops above Dinapur – almost the entire country between Calcutta and Agra.

Outram left Calcutta on August 6th and made his way slowly up country, organizing the troops along the line. He arrived at Allahabad on September 2nd and left three days later, having despatched the 5th Fusiliers, some detachments of the 64th and the Madras Fusiliers, and a battery of artillery ahead of him. He himself travelled with the 90th Light Infantry.

While Outram was moving up country, Havelock continued his preparations for the advance on Lucknow. But his difficulties at Cawnpore were increasing. With disease taking its steady toll, his effective force now numbered fewer than 700 men. The rebel numbers were growing daily. On August 21st, he wrote to Sir Colin Campbell, the new commander-in-chief sent out from England who had assumed office four days previously:

> I find I have not sufficiently explained the danger to which I am exposed, should the enemy at Gwalior take the initiative,

and move on Kalpi with his imposing force. It is to my left rear; and a force is at the same time endeavouring to cross from Oudh to Fatehpur. This would cut in on my rear, and prevent even the advance of my reinforcements. I have sent a steamer down to destroy his boats, but have no news of its success. The Farukhabad force would also assail me in front, and this column, hitherto triumphant, would be destroyed. The Gwalior force already on the Jumna is 5,000 men with 30 guns. The force threatening Fatehpur by Dalamo ghat, may at any moment, by the fall of Lucknow, be swelled to twenty thousand, with all the disposable artillery of the province. The Farukhabad force is 12,000 men with 30 guns. If I do not get any promise of reinforcement from your Excellency by return of telegraph, I must retire at once towards Allahabad. I have no longer here a defensible entrenchment; that on the river being taken in reverse by the enemy now assembling on the right bank of the Ganges. I am for the present enabled to give [the men] shelter from the extreme inclemency of the weather, and some repose, of which they stand in need; but sickness continues to thin our ranks: we lose men by cholera to the number of five or six daily.

With 2,000 or 2,500 men, however, Havelock felt he could hold his position and defeat the enemy. Campbell immediately promised reinforcements, which Outram collected and sent up as he travelled to Cawnpore. When, in fact, they *did* arrive at Allahabad, the local commander tried to keep them to protect his position against the Dinapur mutineers but, on receipt of a peremptory telegram from Havelock, he allowed them to continue.

On August 23rd, Havelock had received a letter from Inglis at Lucknow, in reply to Havelock's suggestion that the force in the Residency should 'cut its way out':

We have only a small force. This has caused me much uneasiness, as it is quite impossible, with my weak and shattered force, that I can leave my defences. You must bear in mind how I am hampered; that I have upwards of 120 sick and wounded, and at least 220 women and about 230 children, and no carriage of any description, besides sacrificing twenty-three lakhs of treasure, and about thirty guns of sorts.

In consequence of the news received, I shall soon put this force on half rations. Our provisions will last us then till about the 10th of September.

If you hope to save this force, no time must be lost in pushing forward. We are daily being attacked by the enemy, who are within a few yards of our defences. Their mines have already weakened our post, and I have every reason to believe they are carrying on others. Their 18-pounders are within 150 yards of some of our batteries, and from their position, and from our inability to form working parties, we cannot reply to them, and consequently the damage done hourly is very great. My strength now in Europeans is 350, and about 300 natives, and the men are dreadfully harassed; and, owing to part of the Residency having been brought down by round shot, many are without shelter. Our native force having been assured, on Colonel Tytler's authority, of your near approach some twenty-five days ago, are naturally losing confidence, and if they leave us, I do not see how the defences are to be manned.

No delay could be allowed if the garrison at Lucknow was to be saved.

Because of the situation caused by the Dinapur mutineers who were reputed to be approaching Allahabad under the command of Koer Singh – who, though 80 years of age, was to prove one of the few military talents on the rebel side – Outram replied to Havelock that he would not be bringing as many men with him as he had hoped. Furthermore, he could not leave Allahabad before September 5th. Outram proposed to do the 126-mile journey in six days, but was persuaded by Havelock not to attempt it because of the heat. This advice did not reach Outram until he had begun to march, and he had lost some 40 men of the 90th disabled by fatigue and disease. In slower marches, Outram at last arrived at Cawnpore on September 15th.

On his arrival, Outram – who had been appointed chief

commissioner for Oudh, ie, the highest *civil* authority as well as military commander – did something which was both foolish and illegal. Without any authority from the government, he issued the following order:

> The important duty of relieving the garrison of Lucknow had been first entrusted to Brigadier-General Havelock, CB, and Major-General Outram feels that it is due to that distinguished officer, and to the strenuous and noble exertions which he has already made to effect that object, that to him should accrue the honour of the achievement.
>
> Major-General Outram is confident that this great end for which Brigadier-General Havelock and his brave troops have so long and gloriously fought will now, under the blessing of Providence, be accomplished.
>
> The Major-General, therefore, in gratitude for, and admiration of, the brilliant deed of arms achieved by Brigadier-General Havelock, and his gallant troops, will cheerfully waive his rank in favour of that officer on this occasion, and will accompany the force to Lucknow in his civil capacity as chief commissioner of Oudh, tendering his military services to Brigadier-General Havelock as a volunteer.
>
> On the relief of Lucknow, the Major-General will resume his position at the head of the forces.

Though this 'rare and noble act of generosity', as one historian of the Mutiny described it, was later confirmed by the commander-in-chief, the responsibility could not be passed on and Outram did in fact interfere with Havelock when he felt it necessary; but, unfortunately, he did not insist on his 'advice' being taken. It is worth pointing out that Outram was not really a soldier at all and had little experience of command in the field. During the first half of the nineteenth century (and after), many soldiers had been detached for political duties on the new frontiers as the Indian empire expanded. Outram's was such a case. He was, however, a man of considerable courage, intelligence, and decision – the qualities most required, and so often lacking, at this time.

With the arrival of Outram, the British force now numbered

3,179 men, of whom 2,388 were European infantry. The cavalry was still gravely under strength at 168, but it had at least been doubled. Havelock's original force, the 64th, 78th, 84th, the Madras Fusiliers, and the Sikhs, was now augmented by the 5th Fusiliers and the 90th Light Infantry. There were three batteries of artillery, Maude's, Oliphant's, and Eyre's, the first being of the Queen's and the other two of the Company's army. The force was divided into two brigades, one under the command of Neill and the other led by Brigadier Hamilton of the 78th Highlanders. The artillery was under the command of Major Cooper.

Havelock's preparations had included the construction of special carriages, each pulled by 20 bullocks, to transport four iron boats for use in crossing the rivers Sai and Gumti. The enemy was said to have 8,000 men and 18 guns solidly entrenched at Havelock's old position at Mangalwar, which threatened the crossing of the Ganges. It was decided, after reconnaissance, to reconstruct the bridge of boats across the islands at the site of the original crossing and this was accomplished without any attack by the rebels. On September 18th, without opposition, three guns of Maude's battery crossed the Ganges, but they were soon engaged by the enemy's guns. An artillery duel lasting three hours silenced the latter, and on the following day the force crossed over the river. On the same day a letter dated September 16th was received from Inglis inside the Regency. It was brought by a native pensioner named Ungud, and reported continued attacks by the rebels and a serious shortage of food.

Heavy rain fell on the night of the 19th and the whole of the next day was given over to preparation for the march and the crossing of the river by the heavy guns of Eyre's battery. Reconnaissance showed that the enemy was still at Mangalwar and, at 5 AM on the 21st, the force moved off in that direction. On reaching the village it was seen that the enemy right lay in the village and a walled enclosure, while their centre and left were covered by a line of breastworks behind which were sited six guns; the position was bisected by the high road.

Havelock opened fire with his heavy guns, supported by the 5th Fusiliers as skirmishers. A body of cavalry, personally commanded by Outram, charged in blinding rain on the flank and drove the enemy along the road to Bashiratgunj, killing 120 and capturing two guns.

The force moved forward and bivouacked for the night at Bashiratgunj which had been deserted by the rebels, and next day, September 22nd, marched in a deluge of rain to the banks of the Sai. In their flight the rebels had failed to destroy the bridge and had left the defensive position before it unmanned. Havelock's force crossed the river and camped at Bani, some 16 miles from Lucknow. There he fired a salvo of artillery, in the hope that it would be heard in the beleaguered Residency – but it was not, as the rebels were still shelling the defences.

The next day, food was served before the march began, as it was believed that this would be a day of intensive fighting. At 8.30 the force moved off. The rain had stopped, but the air was steaming and close, without the slightest wind. Since six o'clock the guns which had been pounding all night at the Residency had stopped, and this seemed to indicate that the heavy guns were being moved to defend the city from the invading force.

For some time, there was no sign of the enemy; then the advance force reached the vicinity of the Alambagh, the 'Garden of the World', about four miles south of Lucknow. This pleasure garden of the kings of Oudh was enclosed by a high wall with turrets at each angle. Inside was a park, with a large palace and a number of smaller buildings.

The enemy's line extended for about two miles. The left rested on the Alambagh and the right and centre were drawn up behind a chain of hillocks. Ten thousand men and 1,500 cavalry were estimated to man the enemy positions. Havelock decided to turn their right flank but the enemy was placed behind a marsh which meant a very wide circuit to avoid it. As the force moved off, a heavy battery of 24-pounders and two eight-inch howitzers shelled the enemy positions. Enemy guns, masked by trees, now opened up on the infantry and casualties were heavy until these batteries were silenced. The British guns were also turned on the enemy cavalry, which broke in confusion under a hail of shot.

The enemy was soon in full retreat. Attempting to make a stand on the walls of the Alambagh, they were driven out by the 5th Fusiliers. Outram, again leading the cavalry, pursued the rebels as far as the Charbagh bridge over the canal on the southern edge of the city but, as it was heavily defended, he withdrew to join the main force now bivouacked in the Alambagh after coming under fire from the enemy's guns.

The force now faced the city and, enlivened by the as yet unconfirmed news that Delhi had fallen to the British, prepared to relieve the Residency.

9
The Relief of the Residency

THE CITY of Lucknow covered an area of some 12 square miles. As it had been the capital of an independent state before annexation in 1856, it was full of public buildings, palaces, mosques, and temples. The buildings themselves were a mixture of East and West. The rulers of Oudh had collected Western pictures and furniture and their buildings had a European look about them. Along the right bank of the river Gumti, whose general direction was from the north-west, there was a line, with occasional branches off, of palaces and public buildings. In the centre of these lay the Chuttur Munzil, the old palace nearer to the river, and the Kaisarbagh, the new palace some distance from it. To the south-east, surrounded by parks and open ground, were the Dilkusha palace and La Martinière – a school for European boys. To the north-west was the Residency, on a raised plateau close to the river. Further up-river was the old fort of the Machchi Bhawan, in which Lawrence had had the magazine blown up before retiring into the Residency. Beyond that lay a suburb of fine houses belonging to the princes and state officials ending in a garden and country house known as the Musa Bagh. To the south and west of the line of official buildings lay the city, without walls, but bounded on the south-east, south, and south-west by a canal, across which the Charbagh bridge carried the main road from Cawnpore through Lucknow to the south-east corner of the Residency. The canal formed the curved base of a triangle with the Residency in the north-west angle and, as the other two sides, the line of palaces and the Cawnpore road. In a direct line, it was less than two miles from the Charbagh bridge to the Residency. Across the river was a smaller town joined by a stone bridge across the Gumti at the Machchi Bhawan, a little upstream from the Residency by an iron bridge, and below the Chuttur Munzil by a bridge of boats. Lucknow city itself was a warren of foetid streets whose buildings, as we have seen, flowed right up to the edge of the Residency area.

The problem before Havelock was to discover the quickest way to the Residency and one which would afford the least chance of heavy casualties. Most of September 24th was spent in considering plans for the attack. Three ways of reaching the Residency were discussed. The first led from the Charbagh bridge through the city for about a mile and a half direct to the Bailey Guard gate. But this road had been cut across with trenches and both sides were lined with loop-holed houses strongly held by the rebels. This route was abandoned because of the inescapable loss of life that would result from trying to force a way along it. The second plan of approach would be to move to the right of the Alambagh towards the Dilkusha palace and past, seize the walls and defensive positions and, under cover of them, bridge the Gumti and move round the city, crossing again by the iron bridge under the protection of the guns in the Residency. This plan had many advantages. The river would give protection as the troops moved towards the Residency, and the streets to be traversed would not be as built-up as those in the main city, nor were the houses much more than mud huts. Near the iron bridge – about 1,200 yards away – and still on the north bank of the river, stood a palace enclosed in a walled garden, known as the Padshah Bagh, which offered an admirable defensive position for the troops to assemble in before crossing the remaining 500 yards between the iron bridge and the Residency.

Unfortunately, circumstances were such as to cancel out the obvious advantages of this plan. Three days of continuous rain had so soaked into the ground that it might be impossible to move the artillery across country. Outram, forgetting that he was just a 'volunteer', insisted that the plan be abandoned. A few days' wait in the Alambagh might have made all the difference, for the rain had stopped, but the situation of the defenders in the Residency was rapidly deteriorating and any delay might mean that the native troops, loyal throughout the siege, would desert thinking that relief was hopeless.

Outram – who certainly knew the lie of the land, as he had been both resident and chief commissioner in Lucknow before the Mutiny – said that the best way was to cross the Charbagh bridge and to proceed along the left bank of the canal to the group of palaces which lay east of the Residency. This plan suffered to some extent from the same objections as the first. The rebels were well entrenched in houses overlooking the route. It was, however, the plan adopted. The baggage, sick, and wounded were to be left in the Alambagh under the protection of six officers, 42 non-commissioned officers, and 250 British soldiers. Havelock insisted that the 24-pounders should accompany the relieving force.

On the morning of September 25th, after a meal, the force was drawn up ready to move. Each man had 60 rounds of ammunition in his pouch and a similar number per man was loaded on to camels. While Havelock was breakfasting, Outram joined him and told Havelock that the plan should be modified and that the decision to divert one brigade to the right should be abandoned, and that both brigades should proceed to the Charbagh direct. As the generals sat at table, a 9-pound shot hit the ground five yards away and bounced over their heads.

Between 8 and 9 AM came the order to advance. Outram commanded the leading brigade with all the artillery and Havelock took the rear. The first brigade had scarcely moved off when it was met by heavy fire from in front and on either flank. 'The enemy', wrote Outram, 'had on that occasion flanked his road under cover of long high grass, and a murderous fire was poured on the column from a double-storeyed house, full of musketeers, and from the loop-holed walls of the large surrounding gardens, from two guns that raked the road from the right flank, and another that commanded [the] front.' But the brigade pushed through to reach the bridge. Here the rebels had decided to make a stand. The bridge was covered by six guns on the Lucknow side of the canal, one being a 24-pounder. Very heavy fire from the houses and from the walled enclosure of the Charbagh forced the brigade to a halt. Maude brought up his guns, but the breadth of the road would only allow for two and these were not enough to silence the enemy artillery. In the meanwhile, Outram with one regiment turned aside to clear the Charbagh enclosure. Neill, who commanded in Outram's absence, decided to order a charge, and one officer and 10 men of the Madras Fusiliers ran forward on to the bridge. The enemy, thinking this was the main column, fired with grape, killing almost every man, leaving only Havelock's son alone on the bridge. The main force now rushed forward and took the enemy's guns before they could reload. Outram then reappeared and crossed the bridge. The 78th Highlanders were sent forward along the Cawnpore road while the captured guns and ammunition were thrown into the canal. The remainder of the force turned to the right into a narrow lane. The 78th managed to hold their position until the remainder of the baggage, the wounded, and followers crossed the bridge and were then withdrawn to join the main body.

This, skirting the left bank of the canal, moving slowly but with little opposition, had reached a point between the Moti Mahal and the former mess-house of the 32nd. Between here and the Residency, a distance of about three-quarters of a mile, was concentrated an immense number of the enemy. At the Begum Kothi and the stables a stand was made, but the attacking force's heavy guns broke it up. Under very heavy fire from the walls of the Kaisarbagh, the force crossed a bridge and halted under the shelter of a wall so that the long column winding its way through the narrow streets could close up. The 78th, which had lost its way – and had captured the battery in the Kaisarbagh – now rejoined the column. The position of the main force was now about 500 yards from the Residency and near the Farhat Bakhsh palace.

Night was falling and the heavy guns, the wounded, the baggage, and the rearguard were still some way behind the first column. Outram prepared to call a halt and a few hours' rest. 'I proposed a halt', he wrote to Sir Colin Campbell, 'of only a few hours' duration in order to enable the rearguard to come up, by which time the whole force would have occupied the Chuttur Munzil in security, which we were then holding, and from which we could have effected our way to the Residency by opening communications through the intervening palaces; in a less brilliant manner, it is true, but with comparatively little loss.'

Havelock, however, decided on instant advance. Outram, who had interfered before, this time chose not to and Havelock had his way. Outram – though wounded in the arm – and Havelock placed themselves at the head of the column and advanced towards the Residency. As they made their way through an archway, a rebel shot Neill in the head and killed him. The loop-holed houses were full of rebels, deep trenches had been cut across the street, volley after volley was fired into the column, causing heavy casualties. 'At length', Havelock recorded, 'we found ourselves at the gates of the Residency, and entered in the dark in triumph. Then came three cheers for the leaders, and the joy of the half-famished garrison, who, however, contrived to regale me, not only with beef cutlets, but with mock-turtle soup and champagne.' The scene in the Residency was described by one of those who had waited anxiously for relief.

Once fairly *seen*, all our doubts and fears regarding them were ended; and then the garrison's long pent-up feelings of anxiety and suspense burst forth in a succession of deafening cheers. From every pit, trench, and battery – from behind the sand bags piled on shattered houses – from every post still held by a few gallant spirits, rose cheer on cheer – even from the hospital many of the wounded crawled forth to join in that glad shout of welcome to those who had so bravely come to our assistance. It was a moment never to be forgotten. The delight of the ever gallant Highlanders, who had fought twelve battles to enjoy that moment of ecstasy, and in the last four days had lost a *third* of their number, seemed to know no bounds. The General and Sir James Outram had entered Dr Fayrer's house, and the ladies in the garrison and their children crowded with intense excitement into the porch to see their deliverers. The Highlanders rushed forward, the rough, bearded warriors, and shook the ladies by the hand with loud and repeated gratulations. They took the children up into their arms, and fondly caressing them, passed them from one to another in turn. Then, when the first burst of enthusiasm was over, they mournfully turned to speak among themselves of the heavy losses they had sustained, and to inquire the names of the numerous comrades who had fallen on the way.

After five long months, the Residency had at last been relieved. But out of the 2,000 men who had marched out of the Alambagh that morning, 31 officers and 504 men had been killed or wounded, many of them because of the unwillingness of Outram to overrule Havelock on the question of the final advance through the streets of Lucknow.

10
The Second Siege

DURING the night of September 25th, several hundred of Havelock's men lay outside the Residency between the Bailey Guard and the adjacent buildings. They were moved in next day, but it was not until the night of the 26th that the rearguard also entered the Residency area. The behaviour of the relieving column had been characterized by heroism, courage, and indifferent generalship. As Maude, the artillery officer, wrote afterwards: 'It is difficult to resist the conclusion that the affair was a muddle, however gloriously conducted, from beginning to end.' It was the original intention of the government that the Residency should be evacuated, but with the loss of such a high proportion of the force such action became impossible.

Virtually the whole of the campaign to suppress the Mutiny suffered from military incompetence of one sort or another. Feeble leadership, chronic indecision, over-emotional appreciation of facts, and chaotic organization glare out from the dispatches. Inside the Residency, for example, Inglis had been appealing for help because he believed himself faced with imminent starvation. But a search by one of the relieving force discovered a huge swimming bath below the Residency packed with sufficient supplies to maintain even the enlarged garrison for two months. Lawrence had stocked it, but the commissariat officers knew nothing about it.

On September 26th, Outram – not before time – resumed military command, and the force in the Residency was reorganized. Inglis was put in command of one division centred on the Residency area proper, and Havelock assumed responsibility for the palaces and buildings to the east which now formed an extended area of defence. Troops now occupied the Farhat Bakhsh and Chuttur Munzil palaces and their enclosures. But the line was not suited for easy defence. It was 'a line of gardens, courts, and dwelling-houses, without

fortified *enceinte*, without defences, and closely connected with
the buildings of the city . . . and it was exposed to a close and
constant musketry fire from loop-holed walls and windows,
often within thirty yards, from every lofty building within
rifle range, and from a frequent and desultory fire of round
shot and grape from guns posted at various distances, from
seventy to five hundred yards'.

The garrison soon found itself isolated, cut off from the
city and from troops remaining in the Alambagh. On October
2nd, Outram was forced to write that 'his hopes of a re-action
in the city had been disappointed. The insurgent sepoys had
inspired such terror among all classes, that he had not been
able to communicate with a single inhabitant of Lucknow since
his arrival'. An attempt by the cavalry to break out and reach
Cawnpore was greeted by such heavy fire that it had to be
abandoned.

Outram was particularly concerned with the position of the
small force left in the Alambagh. An attempt to open communications with it by breaking through houses along the
Cawnpore road was given up and a semaphore signalling device
was later set up instead. The next six weeks were spent in
what can only be described as an underground war; of mine
and counter-mine. 'I am aware', wrote Outram in a dispatch,
'of no parallel to our series of mines in modern war. Twenty-
one shafts, aggregating two hundred feet in depth and 3,291
feet of gallery, have been executed. The enemy advanced
twenty mines against the palaces and outposts; of these they
exploded three which caused us loss of life, and two which
did no injury; seven have been blown in, and out of seven
others the enemy have been driven and their galleries taken
possession of by our miners.'

Despite the failure to open a route to the Alambagh,
messengers were able to pass to and fro between there and the
Residency. On October 9th came confirmation of the capture
of Delhi and on October 27th information arrived that the
column from there under Hope Grant had reached Cawnpore.
Messages were written in Greek characters to outwit the

THE SECOND SIEGE

sepoys. 'You ask me to write in English character', said Outram to one of his officers. 'So would the enemy wish me to do so. As the only security against their understanding what we write in case our letters fall into their hands, the Greek character *must* be used.' A pleasing proof that an English classical education has at least one advantage.

Days and nights of mining and counter-mining continued, interspersed with an occasional sortie against the besieging sepoys, but on November 6th it was reported that Hope Grant had crossed the Sai river and was encamped at Bani where he was to await the arrival of Sir Colin Campbell from Cawnpore. Outram had sent out to the Alambagh a dispatch for Campbell containing plans of the city and his own suggestions for the attack. It was at this stage that a semaphore signal was established between the Residency and the Alambagh. Instructions for sending a semaphore, according to Gubbins, 'were fortunately found under the head "Telegraph" in the *Penny Cyclopaedia* in my library'!

Outram was fully aware that plans and advice were no real substitute for the personal explanations which could be given by someone who knew the city and the dispositions of the sepoys at first hand. The difficulty was to find a European who could get through the lines without discovery. A clerk in one of the civil offices, one Thomas Henry Kavanagh, volunteered to make his way to Bani disguised as a native, a somewhat difficult venture as he was very tall and had golden-blond hair. Nevertheless, stained with lampblack mixed with oil, wearing suitable clothes, and accompanied by a native spy in Outram's employ, he left the Residency at nine o'clock in the evening of November 9th and reached Campbell's force the next morning. For this exploit, Kavanagh was awarded the first civilian Victoria Cross, the sum of £2,000, and a position in the civil service.

11

The Final Relief

WHILE OUTRAM and Havelock had been moving on Lucknow, Colin Campbell had remained behind to organize the forces under his command for the final suppression of the Mutiny. Much had been done before his arrival by the out-going commander-in-chief, Patrick Grant. The most important need of the new army was for horses. Large numbers of well-mounted rebel cavalry roamed the countryside and there was hardly any cavalry to oppose them. Flour, too, was scarce as the part of India producing grain was cut off from the east and west, and it had to come from overseas. Campbell had also to face the fact that, though British forces had got through to Cawnpore and were on their way to Lucknow, nothing had been done to pacify the areas they had so hurriedly passed through.

It had been Campbell's intention to deal with these problems first, before moving on Oudh, but the news that Outram was unable to break out of the Residency again made him decide to join up with the column marching from Delhi and attack Lucknow. The latest information from the Residency was that the garrison was perilously short of food. This we now know was not true, but Campbell was less accurately informed. In marching directly to Lucknow because of this, he nearly met with disaster.

Campbell was also faced with the problem of commanders. With Nicholson dead at Delhi and Havelock immured in Lucknow, only Hope Grant remained at his disposal. There was no alternative before the commander-in-chief but to take the field himself. On October 27th, Campbell with his chief of staff, Mansfield, left Calcutta and on November 3rd arrived at Cawnpore where he had previously sent General Windham to command. Windham, who had fought in the Crimea and who had the reputation of being a fighting general, was without any experience of India whatsoever. At Cawnpore, the 53rd Foot and the 93rd Highlanders were already assembling.

Campbell was a soldier of very considerable experience and achievement. He had made his way without the help of money – for he had none. He had fought in the Peninsular campaign, the Anglo-American war of 1814, China, the Sikh wars, on the North-west Frontier, and in the Crimea. In the last campaign, he had commanded the Highland Brigade and was the victor of the battle of the Alma. Though 65 years old with 49 years of service behind him, he still retained vigour of mind and body, and above all held the confidence of his men.

On November 11th, Campbell reviewed his men at camp on the Oudh bank of the Ganges. The occasion was described by an officer who was present:

> The scene was striking. The small army was drawn up in quarter-distance columns in the centre of a vast plain, surrounded by woods. On the edge of these the pickets were posted. A mere handful it seemed. The guns of the troops and batteries who came down from Delhi, looked blackened and service-worn, but the horses were in good condition, the harness in perfect repair, the men swarthy, and evidently in perfect fighting trim. The 9th Lancers, with their blue uniforms and white turbans twisted round their forage caps, their flagless lances, lean but hardy horses, and gallant bearing, looked the perfection of a cavalry regiment on active service. Wild and bold was the carriage of the Sikh cavalry, riding untamed-looking steeds, clad in loose fawn-coloured robes, with long boots, blue or red turbans and sashes, and armed with carbine and sabre. Next to them were the worn and wasted remains of the 8th and 75th, clad entirely in slate-coloured cloth. With a wearied air, they stood grouped around their standards – war, stripped of its display, in all its nakedness. Then the 2nd and 4th Punjab Infantry, tall of stature, with eager eyes overhung by large twisted turbans, clad in short, sand-coloured tunics – men swift to march and forward in the fight – ambitious both of glory and of loot. Last stood, many in numbers, in tall and serried ranks, the 93rd Highlanders. A waving sea of plumes and tartans they looked as,

with loud and rapturous cheers, which rolled over the field, they welcomed their veteran commander, the chief of their choice. It was curious to mark the difference between the old Indian troops and the Highlanders in their reception of Sir Colin. Anxious and fixed was the gaze of the former as he rode down their ranks – men evidently trying to measure the leader who had been sent to them from so far. Enthusiastic beyond expression was his reception by the latter. You saw at once that to him was accorded their entire confidence – that, under him, they would go anywhere and do anything.

In all, Campbell's force numbered 3,400 men including the Naval Brigade under the command of Captain William Peel, made up of sailors and marines of the Royal Navy armed with eight heavy guns and two rocket-launchers mounted on light carts.

With very little opposition, the force arrived at the Alambagh on November 12th. His chief engineer now advised Campbell to take the route originally suggested by Havelock – to cross the river Gumti and enter the Residency by the iron bridge – which had been abandoned because the heavy rain had made the movement of artillery impossible. Campbell, however, preferred to take Outram's advice and work through the Dilkusha park, some five miles east of the Alambagh, across the canal near the Martinière and then through the Secundrabagh and the garden close to the river. By going this way, Campbell could avoid the narrow streets in which Havelock's force had suffered so much.

With further reinforcements and the garrison in the Alambagh, Campbell now commanded nearly 5,000 men and 49 guns. These were placed under the general direction of Hope Grant. They were divided into five brigades, the first – the Naval Brigade and artillery – commanded by Brigadier Crawford; the second, cavalry composed of two squadrons of the 9th Lancers and one each of the 1st, 2nd, and 5th Punjab Cavalry, as well as Hodson's Horse, under the command of Brigadier Little; and three infantry brigades. The first of these three was commanded by Brigadier Greathed and consisted of the remnant of the 8th Foot, a battalion of detachments of regiments shut up in the Residency, and of the 2nd Punjab Native Infantry; the second, led by Brigadier Adrian Hope and the strongest of them all, consisted of the 93rd Highlanders and a wing of the 53rd, the 4th Punjab Native Infantry, and a weak battalion of detachments; and the third was made up of the 23rd Fusiliers and a detachment of the 82nd under the command of Brigadier Russell. Hope Grant was appointed brigadier-general.

On November 14th, Campbell was ready to move. The advance guard set off at 9 AM marching to the right of the Alambagh through the fields, crossing several roads leading to the city, until they came to the walls of the Dilkusha park. The rebels up to this point offered no opposition, but as the forward troops approached the wall they were met by heavy matchlock fire. Artillery brought up from the rear soon silenced this and the British moved through the park, over the crest of a plateau, to the Martinière. This operation took nearly two hours. At the Martinière a small force of rebels turned two guns on the advancing British cavalry, but before they could produce much effect were silenced by British guns hurriedly brought forward. A battalion of British infantry then moved up and the rebels hastily evacuated the Martinière and retreated across the canal with cavalry in pursuit.

Campbell now proceeded to garrison the Martinière with the fourth brigade commanded by Adrian Hope and a troop of horse artillery, and the fifth brigade was posted in front of the Martinière on the left, while the cavalry brigade and battery of guns occupied a line from the canal to the wall of the Dilkusha. Later in the afternoon two villages on the canal were occupied to cover the left of the British position. At this stage the rebels appeared to be massing for an attack and the enemy, creeping down to the canal, opened fire on the two newly occupied villages. But shots from the battery drove them back to the city. The cavalry now withdrew to the Martinière and the whole force was ordered to bivouac for the night. At 5 PM the rebels attempted another assault but this was repulsed and the bridge over the canal at Hazratgunge was taken and a post placed on the city side. The British then settled down for the night, which was undisturbed.

The following day was spent in bringing up the heavy baggage and stores to the Dilkusha park and all the heavier effects of the soldiers themselves were left there so as not to impede the advance to the Residency. The baggage convoy of the 93rd Highlanders was under constant attack as it moved, and it was not until the 18th that it was able to make its way to the camp at the Dilkusha though it had started off at roughly the same time as the other troops.

With the aid of a semaphore on the roof of the Dilkusha palace, Campbell informed Outram that he would move on the 16th and Outram made preparations to open his defences and advance to join him. Early on the 16th Campbell crossed the dry bed of the canal, moved along without opposition for a mile along the bank of the Gumti through thickly wooded enclosures, and approached the Secundrabagh. Until now, the rebels had been diverted by a number of feinting movements and artillery fire into believing that the attack would be at quite another place, but as the British approached the huts surrounding the Secundrabagh the enemy observed them and opened fire.

The Secundrabagh, Campbell reported in his dispatch, was 'a high-walled enclosure of strong masonry, of 120 yards square, and carefully loop-holed all round'. He went on:

> Opposite to it was a village, at a distance of a hundred yards, which was also loop-holed and filled with men. On the head of the column advancing up the land to the left of the Secundrabagh, fire was opened on us. The infantry of the advanced guard was quickly thrown in skirmishing order to line a bank to the right. The guns were pushed rapidly onwards, viz: Captain Blunt's troops, Bengal horse artillery, and Captain Travers's royal artillery heavy field battery. The troop passed at a gallop through a cross fire from the village and Secundrabagh, and opened fire within easy musketry range in a most daring manner. As soon as they could be

THE FINAL RELIEF

pitched up a stiff bank, two 18-pounder guns under Captain Travers were also brought to bear on the building. While this was being effected, the leading brigade of infantry, under Brigadier the Honourable Adrian Hope, coming rapidly into action, caused the loop-holed village to be abandoned, the whole fire of the brigade being directed on the Secundrabagh. After a time a large body of the enemy who were holding ground to the left of our advance were driven by parties of the 53rd and 93rd, two of Captain Blunt's guns aiding the movement. The Highlanders pursued their advantage and seized the barracks, and immediately converted it into a military post, the 53rd stretching in a long line of skirmishers in the open plain, and driving the enemy before them. The attack on the Secondrabagh had now been proceeding for about an hour and a half, when it was determined to take the place by storm through a small opening which had been made. This was done in the most brilliant manner by the remainder of the Highlanders, and the 53rd, and the 4th Punjab infantry, supported by a battalion of detachments under Major Barnston. There never was a bolder feat of arms, and the loss inflicted on the enemy, after the entrance of the Secundrabagh was effected, was immense – more than 2,000 of the enemy were afterwards carried out.

The Highlanders, according to Sergeant Forbes-Mitchell of the 93rd, had their pipers with them who, as the assault took place, 'struck up the Highland Charge, called by some *The Haughs of Cromdell* and by others *On wi' the Tartan* – the famous charge of the great Montrose when he led his Highlanders so often to victory'. 'When all was over', Forbes-Mitchell adds, 'and Sir Colin complimented the pipe-major on the way he had played, John said, "I thought the boys would fecht better wi' the national music to cheer them".'

The shortest road to the Residency from the now captured Secundrabagh ran directly westwards across a plain about 1,200 yards wide. 'About 300 yards along this road there is a small village, with garden enclosures round it; while about 250 yards further on, and 100 to the right of the road stood the Shah Najaf, a large mosque, situated in a garden enclosed by a high loop-holed wall. This wall is nearly square and very strong. Between it and the plain is a thick fringe of jungle and enclosures, with trees, and scattered mud cottages, which make it impossible to get a distinct view of the place until you come close on it. Between it and the Secundrabagh, amidst jungles and enclosures, to the right of the little plain, was a building on a high mound called the Kaddam Rasal.' Campbell now decided that, as the sun was beginning to set, the Shah Najaf must be taken. This was a difficult and dangerous task. Campbell recorded in his dispatch:

> The Shah Najaf is a domed mosque with a garden, of which the most had been made by the enemy. The wall of the enclosure of the mosque was loop-holed with great care. The entrance to it had been covered by a regular work in masonry, and the top of the building was crowned with a parapet. From this and from the defences in the garden, an unceasing fire of musketry was kept up from the commencement of the attack. The position was defended with great resolution against a heavy cannonade of three hours. It was then stormed in the boldest manner by the 93rd Highlanders, under Brigadier Hope, supported by a battalion of detachments under Major Barnston, who was, I regret to say, severely wounded, Captain Peel leading up his heavy guns with extraordinary gallantry within a few yards of the building to batter the massive stone walls. The withering fire of the Highlanders covered the naval brigade from great loss, but it was an action almost unexampled in war. Captain Peel behaved very much as if he had been laying the *Shannon* alongside an enemy's frigate.

While all this was going on, the garrison in the Residency had not been idle. A battery had been established in a garden a few hundred yards from the Shah Najaf. The battery was concealed from the rebels on two sides by a high wall and it was intended to blow down the wall by letting off a mine under it as soon as the time came for the battery to open up. Unfortunately, the powder was damp, having been laid three days before, and the wall was not properly destroyed – some of it had to be knocked down by hand. When this was completed, the battery blew holes in the walls of two buildings, the Harn-

Hindu Rao's House after the Siege

Bastion held by rebels at Delhi

Sir Henry Lawrence

Brigadier-General James Neill

Lieutenant-General
Sir James Outram, Bt

Major-General
Sir Henry Havelock, Bt

Major-General
Sir Archdale Wilson

Sir Hugh Rose

The Nana Sahib

The Rani of Jhansi

The execution of two mutineers

The interior of the Secundrabagh and the remains of the rebels slaughtered by the 93rd Highlanders and the 4th Punjab Regiment

THE FINAL RELIEF

Khana and the steam-engine house, both strongly held by the enemy. As soon as a breach had been made, the two places were occupied by men of the garrison. But though the two parties were now only a short distance apart, there was considerable opposition to be met in between and Campbell decided to bivouac for the night. The rebels were still operating in strength around Campbell's force and his outposts. They had attacked the Martinière and the Dilkusha and had deployed in considerable numbers near the Alambagh. They could also be seen moving along the opposite bank of the Gumti. Without doubt, Campbell did the right thing by waiting for daylight.

The following day, November 17th, Campbell's men were awakened by the sound of bells and the noise of the enemy's drums. It looked as if an enemy attack was under way. But the threat did not materialize and Campbell was able to follow his own plan at his own time of choosing.

This was first to carry the Mess House, a large stone building defended by a ditch 12 feet wide, about midway between the Shah Najaf and the Kaisarbagh. After capturing this, the force would move on to the Moti Mahal, due north on the direct road from the Shah Najaf to the Residency. The taking of the Moti Mahal would make it possible to meet up with Outram and the garrison from the Residency. The success of this plan would not, of course, mean the end of the battle. There still remained strong enemy emplacements in the Kaisarbagh – protected by guns in the Tara Kothi – and also in the Begum Kothi. In the city itself, there still lurked a force of rebels estimated at about 30,000 in number. Campbell intended to evacuate the Residency as he had insufficient troops to hold the city.

Campbell's first act was to secure his left flank by occupying a number of houses between the barracks and the Dilkusha. This would prevent the rebels from moving out of the Kaisarbagh and threatening the British rear. Campbell then ordered the heavy guns of the Naval Brigade under Captain Peel to bombard the Mess House. 'I determined', he wrote in his dispatch, 'to use the guns as much as possible in taking it. About 3 PM, when it was considered that men might be sent in to storm it without much risk . . . it was carried immediately with a rush.'

The attackers now pressed on to the Moti Mahal but were stopped by its solid walls which had to be breached by the sappers. An open space nearly half a mile wide separated Campbell from Outram. Across it, under heavy fire from the Kaisarbagh, Outram and Havelock – dodging the bullets – ran to meet Campbell. Eight officers and one civilian – Kavanagh – made the dash, only five arrived uninjured. After discussion, they made their way back but Havelock, who was ill, could not run and, with the support of Dodgson, the deputy adjutant-general, he walked slowly across under a hail of bullets to arrive unscathed.

The final relief of the Residency was now accomplished but, as one officer later wrote, 'a most difficult and dangerous task still remained. The garrison, with women and children, sick and wounded, guns and stores, had to be withdrawn; and to effect this in the face of the vast force of the enemy was no easy task. One narrow winding lane alone led to the rear, and through it the whole force had to be filed. To protect the march of the convoy, the whole of the immense line, extending from the ruined walls of the Residency to the wooded park of the Dilkusha, required to be held, and this gave a most hazardous extension to our forces – far too weak for the maintenance of so extended a position. To keep any considerable reserve in hand was impossible.'

12

Withdrawal from the Residency

THE EVACUATION of such a large number of sick, wounded, women, and children obviously presented a problem to Campbell and his officers. Outram and Havelock urged Campbell to drive the rebels from the Kaisarbagh and then to continue to hold the city with as many troops as he could spare. Campbell, however, had decided, quite rightly, otherwise – 'a strong division outside the town, with field and heavy artillery, in a good military position was the real manner of holding the city of Lucknow in check'. Ammunition was low and the Gwalior Contingent of mutineers was threatening Cawnpore; to regarrison the Residency was militarily unsound. Campbell decided that the British force should concentrate at the Alambagh, near the city and commanding the road to Cawnpore, and admirably placed for the final capture of Lucknow when it became possible.

On November 19th, the evacuation of the women and children began. Gubbins, one of the civilians in the Residency, described the movement.

> Most of them were conveyed in carriages closely packed, every description of vehicle being pressed into service on the occasion. Many were seated on native carts, and not a few walked. They were conducted through the Bailey Guard gate, the Farhat Bakhsh and Chuttur Munzil palaces, and emerging near our advanced battery, crossed the line of fire from the Kaisarbagh to Martin's house [the Martinière]. Thence they entered and passed through the court of the Moti Munzil, on the further side of which they gained the highroad leading to the Secundrabagh. Here, and near Martin's house, they were exposed to the fire of the enemy's guns placed on the farther side of the river. Screens formed of the canvas walls of tents, or doors placed on each side of the way they traversed, as far as the Moti Munzil, concealed the march of the fugitives from the enemy, and on one side of this a ditch or traverse had been

dug, along which, dismounting from their carriages, they walked past all the exposed places. All most fortunately reached the Secundrabagh in safety.

The movement was not as well organized as Gubbins pretends, and it was really only by luck that the operation was carried out with nothing worse than discomfort for the women and children. It was yet another example of the bad staff work that characterized every aspect of the campaigns against the mutineers.

Inside the Residency, preparations were being made for the evacuation of the garrison, and the Kaisarbagh was being bombarded. Campbell wrote:

> Upon the 20th, fire was opened on the Kaisarbagh, which gradually increased in importance, till it assumed the character of a regular breaching and bombardment. The Kaisarbagh was breached in three places by Captain Peel, and I have been told that the enemy suffered much within its precincts. Having thus led the enemy to believe that immediate assault was contemplated, orders were issued for the retreat of the garrison through the lines of our pickets at midnight on the 22nd. The ladies and families, the wounded, the treasure, the guns it was thought necessary to keep, the ordnance stores, the grain still possessed by the commissariat of the garrison, and the state prisoners had all been previously removed (two Delhi princes, and some other leading natives arrested on suspicion). Sir James Outram had received orders to burst the guns which it was thought undesirable to take away; and he was finally directed silently to evacuate the Residency at the hour indicated. The dispositions to cover the retreat and resist the enemy should he pursue were ably carried out by Brigadier the Honourable Adrian Hope; but I am happy to say the enemy was completely deceived, and he did not attempt to follow. On the contrary he began firing on our old positions many hours after we had left them. The movement of retreat was admirably executed, and was a perfect lesson in such combinations.

At four in the morning of the 23rd, the whole force had

reached the Dilkusha. During that day, Havelock, who was already weak and ill, was struck with severe dysentery and died on the following morning. His body was carried to the Alambagh and buried there on November 26th.

At the Alambagh, Campbell was faced with three major problems – the transport of the women and children to Cawnpore, the garrisoning of the Alambagh, and the action he must take against the Gwalior Contingent. The last was the most worrying as nothing had been heard from the commander in Cawnpore, General Windham, for four days. The first of the problems to be tackled, however, was the make-up of the force to be left at the Alambagh. About 4,000 men of all arms with 25 guns and 10 mortars, under Outram, were to remain there until Campbell's return and the resumption of the offensive against Lucknow. To keep up the communications with Cawnpore, the detachment of Native Infantry at the Bani bridge was reinforced with Europeans.

13

The Saving of Cawnpore

ON NOVEMBER 27TH, Campbell, with the women and children, the sick and wounded – some 2,000 in number, and convoyed by about 3,000 troops – set out for Cawnpore and reached the bridge over the river Sai the same evening. There he learned that a cannonade had been heard the previous day from the direction of Cawnpore. Without further information, Campbell decided to hurry on in case his way across the river Ganges was threatened. 'At every step', one of his officers recalled, 'the sound of a heavy and distant cannonade became more distinct; but mile after mile was passed over and no news came.' But just before midday, a native delivered a message to a staff officer with the advance guard. 'He had a small rolled-up letter in the Greek character, addressed "most urgent, to General Sir Colin Campbell, or any officer commanding troops on the Lucknow road". The letter was dated two days previously, and said that unless affairs shortly took a favourable turn, the troops would have to retire into the entrenchment; that the fighting had been most severe; and that the enemy were very powerful, especially in artillery. It concluded by expressing a hope that the commander-in-chief would therefore see the necessity of pushing to their assistance with the utmost speed.'

Campbell endeavoured to move the force forward as fast as possible but, encumbered by the women and children, the sick and the wounded, he could not move fast enough. He therefore left his infantry to protect the convoy and moved forward with his cavalry and horse artillery. On reaching Mangalwar, he halted and fired salvoes from his artillery to announce his arrival to Windham and galloped forward to see whether the bridge of boats, whose destruction would have cut him off from Cawnpore, was still intact. Fortunately, the bridge still

THE SAVING OF CAWNPORE

stood, though it was obvious that the city and a large part of the cantonments had fallen to the rebels. On November 28th Campbell crossed the bridge.

The dangerous situation he was to discover had developed in the following way. It will be remembered that when Campbell left Cawnpore on November 9th, he left behind about 500 Europeans and a few Sikhs under the command of Major-General Windham, a Queen's Officer with no Indian experience. His instructions, contained in a memorandum dated November 6th, were to occupy and improve the entrenchments near the bridge of boats, keep a watchful eye on the movements of the Gwalior Contingent and, unless he felt himself threatened, pass on reinforcements into Oudh. If there was any notable movement of rebel troops in the direction of Cawnpore, he was to make a show of force to give the impression that he had a large body of troops under his control, but in no circumstances was he to attack unless to save the entrenchment. Windham was, in fact, supplied by Campbell before he left with minutely detailed instructions covering practically every conceivable permutation of events.

Windham immediately began to strengthen the entrenchment but meanwhile the rebel general, Tantia (or Tatya) Topi, was also acting. His intelligence was good, and he knew in some detail the movements of Campbell's force. On November 9th he arrived with the Gwalior Contingent at Kalpi, a town on the river Jumna some 46 miles to the south-west of Cawnpore. Tantia Topi, leaving at Kalpi a garrison of 3,000 men and 20 guns, crossed the river on November 10th and, hoping that rebel troops in Lucknow would be able to hold Campbell' moved slowly with about 6,000 men and 18 guns in the direction of Cawnpore, leaving garrisons in the towns taken on the way. By November 19th, communications between Cawnpore and the west and north-west were dominated by Tantia Topi and supplies to the city were cut off. Windham's appreciation of this move was that the rebels intended to attack Cawnpore while Campbell and the main force were engaged in Lucknow. He therefore asked Campbell for permission to retain reinforcements for his own protection. This permission he received on November 14th.

With more troops at his disposal, Windham felt rather less anxious and made a show of his force, as he had been instructed to do by Campbell. On November 20th Windham heard of Campbell's success at the Secundrabagh and the Shah Najaf, but after that date his communications with Lucknow ceased, although on November 22nd he received information that the garrison at the Bani bridge had been captured by the rebels. Without confirmation or denial of this, Windham decided that he must do something about it or Campbell's forces might be hindered in their retirement. He therefore sent forward a detachment of Native Infantry and two guns manned by Europeans, with orders to reoccupy the bridge.

Still without communication with Campbell and with such precise instructions that he was left without field for manœuvre, Windham decided that he must disregard them and use his own judgement. He decided to meet the rebels before they reached the entrenchment. Windham's action was the subject of a great deal of argument in the nineteenth century. Some critics maintained that he should have remained in the defences as they were unassailable. Unfortunately, they were not really defensible, even though a great deal had been done in the attempt to make them so.

On November 24th, leaving a small force to guard the entrenchment, Windham moved out with 1,200 infantry, 12 guns, and 100 cavalry to a bridge over a canal on the way to Kalpi. The rebels now moved forward to attack Windham and on the 26th some 2,500 rebel infantry with 500 cavalry and six heavy guns reached the Pandu Nadi. Windham moved forward and attacked, capturing three of the guns and putting the rebels to flight. Unfortunately, as Windham now discerned, the main body of the rebels was nearer than he had at first supposed. 'I at once decided', he wrote in his dispatch, 'on retiring to protect Cawnpore, my entrenchments, and the bridge over the Ganges.' The retreat, however, was not easy as Tantia Topi had now come up with about 20,000 troops and 40 guns; by midday of the 27th, Windham was forced back into the entrenchment. The rebels then proceeded to destroy the stores of tents and other baggage which had been left outside the entrenchment in a building on the Bithur road. The rebels now threatened the bridge of boats.

Such was the story Campbell heard when he reached the entrenchment on November 28th. His first act was to secure the bridge and to bring his force over it from the Lucknow side. These operations were described in his dispatch: 'All the heavy guns attached to General Grant's division, under Captain Peel RN, and Captain Travers RA, were placed in position on the left bank of the Ganges, and directed to open fire and keep down the fire of the enemy on the bridge. This was done very effectively, while Brigadier Hope's brigade, with some field-artillery and cavalry, was ordered to cross the bridge and take position near the old dragoon lines. A crossfire was at the same time kept up from the entrenchment to cover the march of the troops. When darkness began to draw on, the artillery-parks, the wounded, and the families were ordered to file over the bridge, and it was not till 6 PM the day of the 30th that the last cart had cleared the bridge.'

This being completed, it was urged upon Campbell that he should drive out the enemy from the city, but Campbell's first duty – and the most sensible one from a military point of view – was to evacuate his civilians and sick down-river to Allahabad, leaving himself free from non-combatant encumbrances. The enemy was in an extremely strong position. 'Their left', according to an eye-witness, 'was posted among the wooded high grounds, intersected with nullahs [dry watercourses], and thickly sprinkled with ruined bungalows and public buildings, which lie between the town of Cawnpore and the Ganges. Their centre occupied the town itself, which was of great extent, and traversed only by narrow winding streets, singularly susceptible of defence. The portion of it facing the entrenchment was uncovered; but from the camp of our army it was separated by the Ganges canal ... Their right stretched out behind this canal into the plain, and they held a bridge over it, and some lime kilns and mounds of brick in its front. The camp of the Gwalior Contingent was situated in this plain, about two miles in rear of the right, at the point where the Kalpi road comes in.' The total number of the enemy was estimated at about 25,000 men with 40 guns, but it seems in reality to have been more in the region of 14,000, still overwhelmingly superior in number to Campbell's force. It was therefore essential to move the convoy of civilians and sick as soon as possible. By December 3rd the transport was assembled and that night the convoy set off for Allahabad.

Relieved of at least one of his responsibilities, Campbell could now turn to the attack. The rebels had not left him alone and on December 4th had even attempted to destroy the bridge of boats by floating fire-boats down the river on to it. On the afternoon of the next day, they opened up with artillery on the British position at the left and then spread their fire over the whole position. The British retaliated and managed to resist a sudden attack by enemy infantry.

The rebels' main position lay, as we have seen, along the canal. It appeared to Campbell that 'if his enemy's right were vigorously attacked, it would be driven from its position without assistance coming from other parts of his line, the wall of the town which gave cover to our attacking columns on our right being an effectual obstacle to the movement of any portion of his troops from his left to right. Thus the possibility became apparent of attacking his division in detail.'

Campbell's actions were as follows:

> Orders were given to General Windham on the morning of the 6th to open a heavy bombardment at 9 AM from the entrenchment of the old cantonment and so induce the belief in the enemy that the attack was coming from the general's position. The camp was struck early, and all the baggage driven to the river side under a guard, to avoid the slightest risk of accident. Brigadier Greathed, reinforced by the 64th regiment, was desired to hold the same ground opposite the enemy which he had been occupying for some days past ...

and at 11 AM the rest of the force . . . was drawn up in contiguous columns in the rear of some old cavalry lines, and effectually masked from observation of the enemy. The cannonade from the entrenchment having become slack at this time, the moment had arrived for the attack to commence. The cavalry and horse artillery having been sent to make a detour on the left and across the canal by a bridge a mile and a half farther up, and threatened the enemy's rear, the infantry deployed in parallel lines fronting the canal. Brigadier Hope's brigade was in advance in one line, Brigadier Inglis's brigade being in rear of Brigadier Hope. At the same time Brigadier Walpole, assisted by Captain Smith's field-battery, RA, was ordered to pass the bridge immediately to the left of Brigadier Greathed's position, and to drive the enemy from the brick kilns, keeping the city wall for his guide . . . The advance then continued with rapidity along the whole line, and I had the satisfaction of observing in the distance that Brigadier Walpole was making equal progress on the right. The canal bridge was quickly passed, Captain Peel leading over it with a heavy gun, accompanied by a soldier of Her Majesty's 53rd, named Hannaford. The troops which had gathered together resumed their line of formation with great rapidity on either side, as soon as it was crossed, and continued to drive the enemy at all points, his camp being reached and taken at 1 PM and his rout being complete along the Kalpi road. I must here draw attention to the manner in which the heavy 24-pounder guns were impelled and managed by Captain Peel and his gallant sailors. Through the extraordinary energy with which the latter have worked, their guns have been constantly in advance throughout our late operations, from the relief of Lucknow till now, as if they were light field-pieces, and the service rendered by them in clearing our front has been incalculable. On this occasion there was the sight beheld of 24-pounder guns advancing with the first line of skirmishers. Without losing any time, the pursuit with cavalry, infantry, and light artillery was pressed with the greatest eagerness to the fourteenth milestone on the Kalpi road, and I have reason to believe that every gun and cart of ammunition which had been in that part of the enemy's position which had been attacked, now fell into our possession.

While these operations were in progress, General Mansfield had moved on the rebels' left and routed the forces of the Nana Sahib. The pursuit continued with a rest for the pursuers on the 6th, until they reached Bithur on December 7th and there discovered the Nana Sahib's treasure packed in ammunition boxes and sunk in a well.

The saving of Cawnpore and the rout of Tantia Topi formed the turning point in the Mutiny, though much was still to be done. As Sergeant Forbes-Mitchell of the 93rd Sutherland Highlanders wrote in his memoirs: 'From the defeat of the Gwalior Contingent, our star was in the ascendant and the attitude of the country people showed that they understood which was the winning side. Provisions, such as butter, milk, eggs, and fruit, were brought into our camp by the villagers for sale the next morning.' The British soldiers also managed to get some new clothes but – and this will sound very familiar to soldiers of a later time – 'we even had to pay from our own pockets for the replacement of our kits which were taken by the Gwalior Contingent when they captured Windham's camp'!

14

A Time of Preparation

THE DEFEAT of the Gwalior Contingent and the saving of Cawnpore from the rebels ensured that Campbell's main communication line, that of the river Ganges, was held. Without this, the final suppression of the rebellion and the pacification of Oudh would not have been possible. It was now Campbell's plan to open up communications between Cawnpore and the Punjab. Having done this, he could turn once again to Lucknow. Oudh, however, was not just occupied by a huge force of rebels – the whole country was in arms. Campbell badly needed reinforcements before he could attempt an attack.

Here the situation was not encouraging. The British troops that had already arrived had come from Burma, Ceylon, Mauritius, and from Persia. A military expedition on its way to China had also been diverted. Back in Britain, the units home from the Crimea had almost all been demobilized, and of those that remained many had already been taken for the Chinese expeditionary force. What remained of the army in England was seriously under-strength and under-armed. There was also the problem of transporting reinforcements to India. Considerable criticism was levelled at the home government for not sending troops overland to India, but the problems involved would have taken too long to solve. All reinforcements therefore – the Suez Canal not yet having been dug – had to go round the Cape. Certain troops had in fact been moved from the Crimea overland, but this was an experience that did not invite repetition.

Campbell had no alternative but to wait until he was strong enough for an all-out campaign, although this did not mean that he could remain idle. To open communications with the Punjab he must first clear the Doab, as the tract of land between the Ganges and the Jumna was called. Holding Allahabad, Agra, and Delhi did not mean that the British held the river Jumna itself, and on the Ganges only Cawnpore was in British hands. Campbell was still acutely short of transport, having sent much of it down with the convoy from the Residency, and it was not until December 24th that he was able to make his first move. This was to capture Fatehgarh, about midway between Allahabad and Delhi.

Brigadier Seaton had moved down from Delhi with a force of about 1,900 men, consisting of carabineers, Hodson's Horse, the 1st Bengal Fusiliers, and a Sikh regiment. With him was an immense convoy of ammunition, tents, carts, and camels – all the things that Campbell was short of. Seaton had now reached the town of Mainpuri and Campbell sent a column under Walpole to meet him. The combined force would then march on Fatehgarh. The two columns joined at Bewar, 15 miles from Mainpuri along the road to Fatehgarh, on December 31st. Seaton had fought an engagement at Aligarh, on the way, during which the commander-in-chief of the Nawab of Farukhabad's force had been killed.

Meanwhile, Campbell himself was also moving on Fatehgarh, clearing the rebels from the country on both sides of the main road as he went. The rebels, fleeing from Seaton and Walpole, now concentrated on a suspension bridge across the Kali Nadi which led to Fatehgarh. On December 31st, they attempted to destroy the bridge but were unable to break the main chains or the supporting piers. On the morning of January 1st, 1858, Campbell detached a brigade under Adrian Hope with three guns and engineers, sappers and cavalry, and instructions to drive away the enemy and repair the bridge. When Hope appeared, the rebels fled and by seven o'clock that night the bridge was in use again.

A little later, rebel artillery began to shell the reconstructed bridge and Campbell, who had arrived on the scene, called up his main body, ordering Hope to hold the bridge in the meanwhile but not to attack the enemy. When the main force arrived, a sharp engagement routed the rebels who fled to Fatehgarh. There they picked up their easily portable baggage and moved into Rohilkhand.

That night Campbell halted 12 miles from Fatehgarh and,

next morning, occupied the fort and town without incident. Next day he was joined by Walpole's column, now reinforced by Seaton's. Campbell then had under his command some 10,000 men.

Campbell now proposed to the government in Calcutta that it would be profitable to pursue the enemy in Rohilkhand and pacify the north-west while other forces might be similarly engaged in western and central India. Oudh, he maintained, could wait. He would virtually surround the province with troops. The Gurkhas, who had come from Nepal to the aid of the British, would hold the north, and British troops – whom he did not wish to waste on a summer campaign – would remain in various stations to the south and east. Then, in the following cold weather, with the rest of India quiet, he could turn to Oudh, and in such strength as to ensure a quick victory.

But there is always more to a war than just military strategy. Political considerations weighed heavily with the government of India. Oudh, the governor-general insisted, should be reconquered *before* the hot weather of 1858. Many soldiers had doubts, at the time and afterwards, of the wisdom of the government's decision but, as Lord Canning wrote, it was the time when 'every eye is upon Oudh as it was upon Delhi. Oudh is not only the rallying point of the sepoys, the place to which they all look, and by the doings in which their own hopes and prospects rise or fall; but it represents a dynasty; there is a king of Oudh "seeking his own".' Furthermore, there was no doubt that the rulers of native states, and even the king of Burma, were watching what would happen in Oudh and would take their cue from the outcome.

Again, too, from the purely military point of view, there was the position of Outram in the Alambagh to be considered, threatened daily by growing numbers of mutineers. In fact, between November 1857 and February 1858, Outram's position was attacked six times by very large numbers of rebels. The road to Cawnpore, however, remained open and he did receive reinforcements, but their numbers were large enough only to cover his casualties. Of the attacks, the second – which took place on January 12th – was mounted by about 30,000 rebels whom Outram managed to put to flight, and each succeeding attack involved even larger numbers. By February, however, Outram had received substantial reinforcements, including cavalry, and was able to rout the enemy with heavy losses. Outram had hoped that his very presence in the Alambagh would have a stabilizing effect on the Oudh nobles, but the situation was too far gone for this. Oudh again had a king on the throne and sentiment buttressed the actions of the rebels.

With all this in mind, the governor-general ordered Campbell to return to Cawnpore and wait until he had sufficient strength to attack the rebels in Oudh. Campbell's position was favourable. The control of Fatehgarh, situated as it was on the Ganges at the south-western extremity of the border between Oudh and Rohilkhand, barred the way to any rebel force which might attempt an attack from Bareilly (see map, page 49), from north-western Oudh, or from Lucknow. The river line between Fatehgarh and Cawnpore was strongly held and the road between Agra and Cawnpore had been cleared of rebels so that the siege-train which had been moved from Delhi to Agra could join Campbell's force for the attack upon Lucknow.

While Campbell was waiting for reinforcements, he continued to harass the rebels as much as possible. In particular he wished to convince the mutineers in Oudh that he intended to attack Bareilly. To this end, he sent a force under Walpole to a place on the Ramgunga river about eight miles from Fatehgarh, where there was known to be a concentration of rebels. Walpole's instructions were that he was to give the impression of an advance force preparing to cross the river. Walpole was successful, and the rebel force – believed to number 15,000 men – stayed where it was. Finding, however, that Walpole made no attempt to cross, they detached 5,000 men and mounted an attack across the Ganges at Shamsabad, about 12 miles from Fatehgarh. Here they were met by Adrian Hope's brigade and put to flight back into Rohilkhand.

A TIME OF PREPARATION

In order to relieve the pressure on the small force which was to be left behind under Seaton in Fatehgarh, it was arranged that a column from the Punjab should cross into Rohilkhand from the north-west about February 15th. On that date Campbell himself left Fatehgarh for Cawnpore in order to make the final preparations for crossing the Ganges once again into Oudh. Hope and Walpole followed rather more slowly than their commander-in-chief, who made the journey in three days.

By February 23rd, Campbell's army was across the Ganges. On the sandy plain between Unao and Bani were massed engineers, artillery, cavalry, infantry, baggage trains, camp followers, and all the impedimenta felt necessary for an army in those days.

15

The Capture of Lucknow

CAMPBELL'S ARMY was made up of 17 battalions of infantry, all but two of which were British, 28 squadrons of cavalry, of which four were British – in all, about 20,000 men – and 54 heavy and eight light guns and mortars. The commissariat and supply organization was, yet again, insufficient and incompetently administered. The system, if it can be given such a title, had been inherited from the Mughal emperors. Each unit was responsible for its own transport, which could be of any size. The number of camp followers, blacksmiths, and other artisans and their families was enormous. The men were fed from a vast travelling bazaar. With the number of draft animals required to pull everything, the army had the appearance of some vast menagerie which ate up the land as it went, like a plague of locusts.

The plan of campaign was straightforward. Lucknow was to be attacked from the east, blockaded from the south, and enveloped on the north, while the west was to be left open. For this, large forces of cavalry were of paramount importance. Brigadier Franks, with whom was the Nepalese contingent of 9,000 men, had been moving through the country between the river Gogra and the Himalayan foothills. Franks's instructions were to move on Lucknow via Faizabad. The main attack, however, was to be made by Campbell whose force was split into three divisions under Outram (to be joined at the Alambagh), Lugard, and Walpole, with the cavalry division commanded by Hope Grant. Against this was ranged a force of rebels conservatively estimated at over 100,000 men.

Since the British evacuation of the Residency, the rebels had made great efforts to prepare the defences of Lucknow These defences fell into three lines. The outer ran along the canal to the south of the city as far as the river Gumti, and the second and third lines were centred upon many of the buildings which had been so bothersome to Campbell in his relief of the

THE CAPTURE OF LUCKNOW

Residency in November. The rebels were well supplied with heavy artillery and ammunition. The main streets of the city had been barricaded and all the important buildings had been loop-holed and fortified. However, the rebels had not chosen to defend the northern approaches to the city on the assumption, perhaps, that Campbell would follow his own previous plan of attack.

Campbell, who had reached the Alambagh on March 1st, decided to send part of his force across the river Gumti to take the rebels from the undefended north, while the main body would move by the Hazratgunge on the Kaisarbagh. The plan was not in fact of Campbell's own devising, but came from Brigadier Napier, the chief engineer.

Early on the morning of March 2nd, Campbell marched on the Dilkusha park and seized the palace. Rebel artillery, however, made things very uncomfortable for him and he was unable to move up the main body of his infantry until his own batteries were established late in the evening. The next day, under heavy fire, the enemy was forced to withdraw his guns. The line now held by the British touched the river on its right at the village of Bibiapur, intersected the Dilkusha, and stopped about two miles short of Jallalabad. Between the last-named place and the end of the line, a cavalry force of 1,600 men was deployed. In preparation for the crossing of the Gumti, the construction of two pontoon bridges was begun on March 4th. Next morning Brigadier Franks arrived with the Nepalese contingent. These reinforcements brought Campbell's force up to nearly 31,000 and 104 guns, Franks's force constituting a fourth division.

By the evening of the 5th, the two bridges – made out of beer casks, rope, and planking – were completed, and earthworks had been erected at both ends to defend them. Campbell's orders were that on the following day at two o'clock in the morning, the division commanded by Outram would cross to the other bank of the Gumti. The crossing was delayed, but before daybreak Outram's force was across the river. Once across, Outram drew up his force in three lines and marched up the river bank for about a mile, then left the river and moved straight on in the direction of the city. A brush with enemy cavalry was the only incident of the day and, by evening, the force was camped four miles from the city and half a mile from Chinhut. The 7th and 8th were spent mainly in skirmishing operations, though Outram gradually increased the area covered by his piquets. On the 8th, on instructions from Campbell, he sent back a troop of horse artillery and a squadron of Lancers and received in exchange 22 siege-guns which, during the night, were erected facing the Chakar Kothi, which had been the grandstand of the king of Oudh's racecourse.

On March 9th, after a heavy bombardment, an infantry column under Walpole* attacked the rebel left while Outram mounted an assault on the Chakar Kothi. The operation was completely successful and Campbell was informed of the result by the hoisting of the colours of the 1st Fusiliers on the roof of the Chakar Kothi. After its capture, Outram pressed forward, driving the rebels through the old cavalry lines and suburbs to the Padshahbagh. There he joined up with Walpole and occupied the houses and breastworks in front, keeping up a heavy fire of musketry on the enemy lining the walls of the garden. Under cover of this, three heavy guns and a howitzer were placed in position to enfilade the works in the rear of the Martinière, and another battery was erected near the river to keep down the fire from the city.

While Outram was moving steadily forward, Campbell remained in the Dilkusha until March 9th. Early on the morning of that day the batteries on the Dilkusha plateau opened heavy fire on the Martinière. This continued until about 2 PM when the Fusiliers' colours were seen flying on the Chakar Kothi. Without delay, Campbell launched an attack on the Martinière. The artillery bombardment, both from the Dilkusha and from

---

* It should be noted that during the operations some units from one division served in another, and one commander of division led a brigade under another commander. I have tried to reduce the confusion by mentioning as few names as possible.

Outram's batteries, had caused the rebels to abandon most of the defences, and the place was taken with very few casualties apart from the serious wounding of Captain Peel, commander of the Naval brigade. The British pushed on and, reaching the river, moved down it and captured Banks's house early on the 10th. On that day Outram's batteries directed their fire on Hazratgunge and the rebel stronghold of the Kaisarbagh, and those erected at Banks's house opened on the Begum Kothi.

The time was now ripe for the main attack – to force the line between Banks's house and the Kaisarbagh. Campbell ordered Outram to continue the bombardment of the Kaisarbagh and its outer defences during the night of the 10th and, on the following day, to move forward and attack earthworks protecting the two bridges across the Gumti – the iron bridge leading to the Residency and the stone one near the Machchi Bhawan. Outram was to take control of the end of the iron bridge on his side of the river. This operation was carried out successfully. The houses around the end of the iron bridge were occupied and two 24-pounder guns erected to defend the new position at the head of the bridge. The stone bridge, however, was in range of the rebel artillery and musket fire from the other side of the river, and Outram fell back on his camp in the Padshah Bagh. These positions he occupied during the following four days. His artillery had been augmented and Outram was able to increase his bombardment of the Kaisarbagh and so substantially assist the attack upon the place. He and his force would have been able to achieve more if he had not been prevented from doing so by a curiously stupid order from Campbell – one of a number of serious mistakes made by the commander-in-chief – which materially contributed to the prolongation of operations against the rebels. The first mistake was made when, on March 14th, Outram requested permission to cross the iron bridge and launch an attack from the north to coincide with Campbell's attack on the Kaisarbagh. The reply Outram received was that 'he was not to do so if he thought he would lose a single man'. Of all the extraordinary orders given by commanders during the Mutiny –

and there were many – this must surely rank high in the list. Why, in fact, Outram accepted such an outrageously unwarlike prohibition is not known. When asked by his officers for orders to cross the bridge, Outram replied, 'I am afraid, gentlemen, you will be disappointed when I tell you that I am not going to attack today'!

Meanwhile Campbell's position on the evening of the 10th was established along the city side of the canal on a line stretching from the Gumti to Banks's house. Heavy fire from the latter was now concentrated on a block of palaces known as the Begum Kothi. Lugard, without opposition, occupied the Secundrabagh and then prepared to move forward to the Shah Najaf which was also captured without a fight. The bombardment of the Begum Kothi had, by about three o'clock in the afternoon, opened a small breach in the walls. Unaware of the strength of the inner defences of the palace, the order was given for a storming-party to make an entry. The troops chosen were the 93rd Highlanders and the 4th Punjab Rifles.

The Begum Kothi was made up of a number of palaces and courtyards, all surrounded by a breastwork and a deep ditch. Despite the bombardment, some of the inner walls still stood undamaged. It was estimated after the attack that the place was held by about 5,000 rebels. Fighting was brisk, but the garrison seemed mainly concerned with getting away. It was, nevertheless, in Campbell's words, 'the sternest struggle which occurred during the siege' – some 600 or 700 rebels were killed, though British casualties were low. One of the dead was the cavalry leader, William Hodson. His murder of the princes at Delhi had only reinforced the bad opinion that some people of influence had of him, and the story was soon going the rounds that he had been killed while looting. Sergeant Forbes-Mitchell of the 93rd, who was an eye-witness, had a different story to tell. While leading a party, Forbes-Mitchell had discerned a group of rebels in a room in one of the buildings, 'well armed with swords and spears, in addition to firearms of all sorts, and, not wishing to be either killed myself or have more of the men who were with me killed, I divided my party, placing some at each side of the door to shoot every man who showed himself, or attempted to rush out. I then sent two men back to the breach, where I knew Colonel Napier with his engineers were to be found, to get a few bags of gunpowder with slow-matches fixed, to light and pitch into the room. Instead of finding Napier, the two men sent by me found the redoubtable Major Hodson who had accompanied Napier as a volunteer in the storming of the palace. Hodson did not wait for the powder-bags, but, after showing the men where to go for them, came running up himself, sabre in hand. "Where are the rebels?" he said. I pointed to the door of the room, and Hodson, shouting "Come on!" was about to rush in. I implored him not to do so, saying, "It's certain death; wait for the powder; I've sent men for powder-bags." Hodson made a step forward, and I put out my hand to seize him by the shoulder to pull him out of the line of the doorway, when he fell back shot through the chest. He gasped out a few words, either "Oh, my wife!" or, "Oh, my mother!" – I cannot rightly remember – but was immediately choked by blood. I assisted to get him lifted into a dooly (by that time the bearers had got in and were collecting the wounded who were unable to walk), and I sent him back to where the surgeons were, fully expecting that he would be dead before anything could be done for him. It will thus be seen that the assertion that Major Hodson was looting when he was killed is untrue. No looting had been commenced, not even by Jang Bahadur's Gurkhas.' After Hodson had been taken away, the 'men who had gone for the powder came up with several bags, with slow-matches fixed in them. These we ignited and then pitched the bags in through the door. Two or three bags very soon brought the enemy out, and they were bayoneted down without mercy.'

By the evening of March 11th the next stage of advance was in preparation. Before the main rebel stronghold of the Kaisarbagh could be stormed, the Mess House, Hazratgunge, and the Imambara must be taken. The Gurkha contingent under Maharaja Jang Bahadur now arrived and took up its position close to the canal and, covering the left, allowed the

British to mass towards the right and concentrate an attack. On the 12th the engineers continued their mining operations and Campbell rearranged his dispositions, taking Lugard's division from the front and replacing it with that under Franks. The following day, too, was mainly one for the engineers who pressed on with their work of blasting a way through the houses and walls towards the next rebel line of defence. Artillery was sometimes used to breach the walls. The rebels kept up a steady fire on the engineers but were considerably restricted by the bombardment from both sides of the river. The same day, March 13th, the Gurkha contingent crossed the canal and moved against the buildings to the left of Banks's house. By the evening a way had been broken through the buildings on the left as far as the Imambara, and artillery had opened a breach in the walls of the buildings which, it was hoped, would be big enough to allow of an assault the next morning.

The following day the guns were still pounding the walls from a distance of about 30 yards. '8-inch shot at this distance' battered through three or four thick masonry walls in succession 'as if they had been so much paper'. By nine o'clock the storming-party was ready to move. After a short, sharp engagement, the Imambara was taken and the garrison hotly pursued to the shelter of the Kaisarbagh. A palace overlooking the Kaisarbagh was occupied and heavy musket fire brought to bear on the rebel forward artillery which was finally abandoned. At this stage it was decided to halt and continue sapping operations but the Sikhs, who had driven the rebels from the Imambara, could not be restrained and managed to force their way into a courtyard adjoining the Kaisarbagh. Reinforced by a detachment of the 10th Foot, the Sikhs penetrated the Chini Bazaar, to the rear of the Tara Kothi and the Mess House, thus turning the rebel defence line at this point.

The 6,000 rebels in the Tara Kothi and the Mess House evacuated those buildings and tried to get into the Chini Bazaar, but they were prevented by heavy musket and artillery fire. At this stage, Franks pushed forward with every available man to reinforce the advance posts so unexpectedly captured. The original intention that day had been only to take the Imambara, but it was decided that, as the enemy was on the run and enthusiasm was high, an attempt should be made on the Kaisarbagh itself.

Orders were given to the troops in the Secundrabagh and the Shah Najaf to push forward. Soon, the Moti Mahal, the Chuttur Munzil, and the Tara Kothi on the left were occupied, while Franks's men, moving through the courtyard of the mosque of Sadat Ali, penetrated the Kaisarbagh itself. It was at this stage that Outram, who had been kept informed of Franks's advance, asked for permission to cross the iron bridge and received what Lord Roberts was later to describe, with some justice, as 'the unaccountably strange order' from Campbell not to advance if it meant losing 'a single man'.

The Kaisarbagh was a rectangular enclosure made up of a series of courtyards and gardens, in which were a number of small marble buildings. There was still a large number of rebels inside the palace. It was, however, soon taken. Then began a nightmare scene of looting. The soldiers went crazy. William Howard Russell, correspondent of *The Times*, was present and described it vividly.

> The scene of plunder was indescribable. The soldiers had broken up several of the store rooms, and pitched the contents into the court, which was lumbered with cases, with embroidered cloths, gold and silver brocade, silver vessels, arms, banners, drums, shawls, scarfs, musical instruments, mirrors, pictures, books, accounts, medicine bottles, gorgeous standards, shields, spears, and a heap of things which would make this sheet of paper like a catalogue of a broker's sale. Through these moved the men, wild with excitement, 'drunk with plunder'. I had often heard the phrase but never saw the thing itself before. They smashed to pieces the fowling-pieces and pistols to get at the gold mountings, and the stones set in the stocks. They burned in a fire, which they made in the centre of the court, brocades and embroidered shawls for the sake

of the gold and silver. China, glass, and jade they dashed to pieces in sheer wantonness; pictures they ripped up or tossed on the flames; furniture shared the same fate . . . Oh the toil of that day! Never had I felt such exhaustion. It was horrid enough to have to stumble through endless courts which were like vapour baths, amid dead bodies, through sights worthy of the Inferno, by blazing walls which might be pregnant with mines, over breaches, in and out of smouldering embrasures, across frail ladders, suffocated by deadly smells of rotting corpses, of rotton *ghi*, or vile native scents; but the seething crowd of camp followers into which we emerged in Hazratgunj was something worse. As ravenous, and almost as foul as vultures, they were packed in a dense mass in the street, afraid or unable to go into the palaces, and, like the birds they resembled, waiting till the fight was done to prey on their plunder.

By that evening, March 14th, the city was practically in Campbell's hands, but with comparatively little loss to the rebels who were escaping from the city virtually unhindered. Outram's advance across the bridge would certainly have prevented many from leaving. Furthermore, Campbell sent his cavalry to chase those who had already left instead of spreading a net to catch the rebels who had not yet fled the city. The consequences of this inept handling were briefly stated by Lord Roberts: 'The campaign which should have then come to an end, was protracted for nearly a year by the fugitives spreading themselves over Oudh and occupying forts and other strong positions, from which they were able to offer resistance to our troops until towards the end of May 1859.'

After the successes of March 14th, the following day was spent in consolidating the British gains and preparing for the bombardment of the next rebel line of defence. On this day, Campbell sent Hope Grant with 1,100 cavalry and 12 guns, to pursue the rebels along the Sitapur road, and Brigadier Campbell with 1,500 cavalry and some infantry guns to the Sandila road. Neither discovered any rebels, who had, of course, broken up and disappeared into the countryside.

On March 16th Outram was ordered to cross the Gumti at

the Secundrabagh over the bridge made of beer casks and join Campbell's force in the Kaisarbagh, leaving behind him Walpole's brigade to guard the iron and stone bridges. While Outram was on his way, Campbell rode out of the Kaisarbagh and gave his instructions. These were for Outram to push on through the Residency, take the iron bridge, and then storm the Machchi Bhawan and the Husainabad Imambara beyond. Outram marched through the Kaisarbagh to the Residency where, by a piece of irony, his previous role was reversed and he found himself storming the Residency which was now defended by the rebels. The siege was short, and in less than half an hour the defenders were on the run. The rebel batteries between the heads of the two bridges were the next to be taken, and artillery brought up on to the Residency plateau began to shell the Machchi Bhawan, which soon fell, followed closely by the rebel evacuation of the Husainabad Imambara.

While these operations were in progress, the rebels driven from the Residency crossed the stone bridge and attacked Walpole's piquets, but they were repulsed, while at the Alambagh a strong rebel force had moved in to attack the depleted garrison; after a three-hour battle, they were also driven off.

On March 17th and 18th Outram continued his advance, clearing the houses and the streets as he moved. It was then reported to Campbell that a large force of rebels, believed to be nearly 10,000 strong, was in the Musabagh, a large palace with garden and courtyards in open wooded country about four miles north-west of Lucknow near the river. It was rumoured that the Begum of Oudh, Hazrat Mahal, and her son whom the rebels had declared king were also there. On the morning of the 19th, Campbell instructed Outram to march on the Musabagh while Hope Grant, from the opposite side of the river, was ordered to bombard the palace. At the same time Brigadier Campbell and his force were to take up position near the Musabagh in order to intercept the rebels should they try and break away under Outram's attack.

After some difficulty in breaching a wall that barred his path, Outram opened fire on the walls of the Musabagh. The rebels fled in the direction of Brigadier Campbell. Unfortunately the Brigadier, though a cavalryman of some years' standing, made no attempt to stop them, while Hope Grant was prevented from acting by being on the other side of the river. Campbell afterwards maintained that he had lost his way and this became the official explanation, but one officer recorded his opinion that 'his error appears to have partaken of wilfulness. He moved his force in utter disregard of the statement of his guides, in opposition to the protestations and explanations of all to whose information and advice he was bound to listen.' Most of the rebel force escaped.

The city was still not cleared of rebels. In fact, in the very heart of Lucknow, one of the rebel leaders, the Maulvi of Faizabad, occupied a building with two guns. On March 21st the house was carried by assault but the Maulvi escaped. The following day a rebel concentration was reported at the small town of Kursi, about 25 miles from Lucknow on the Faizabad road. A force under Hope Grant, arriving on the 23rd, drove the rebels, believed to number 4,000, from the town.

With this action, the operations in Lucknow and its environs ended. Losses on the British side had been small – 127 officers and men killed, and 595 wounded. Certainly Campbell's determination to keep casualties down had been successful, overwhelmingly successful, in fact, if a comparison is made with the casualties before Delhi when, between September 8th and 20th, 1,674 were killed and wounded. Unfortunately, Campbell only saved lives so that they might be uselessly lost later, for in the hot-weather month of May 1858, for example, though only 100 men were killed in action, those who died from sunstroke, fatigue, and disease numbered not less than 1,000. They died fighting the rebels Campbell could have prevented from leaving Lucknow.

16

Chasing the Rebels

NOT ONLY had the task of pacifying Oudh been made difficult by the commander-in-chief's handling of the rebels fleeing from Lucknow; the difficulties were increased by the issue of a proclamation by the governor-general, Lord Canning. The proclamation was produced without consulting Outram who, it will be remembered, was the civil commissioner for Oudh, or Campbell. The terms of the proclamation were to the effect that all the land owned by those in rebellion against the British was to be considered forfeited. 'I have not', wrote Russell, still at Campbell's headquarters, 'heard one voice raised in its defence; and even those who are habitually silent now open their mouths to condemn the policy which must perpetuate the rebellion in Oudh.' Under complaint from Outram, a clause was inserted which qualified the arbitrary confiscation of land by offering:

> To those amongst them who shall promptly come forward and give to the chief commissioner their support in the restoration of peace and order this indulgence shall be large; and the governor-general will be ready to view liberally the claims which they may thus acquire to a restitution of their former rights.

The proclamation was repudiated by the government in London but the damage had already been done. The chance of an amnesty was gone and the campaign could only end in the final defeat of the rebels.

Campbell's first plan was to settle affairs in Oudh, or to refrain from major action during the summer months in order to rest his men for another winter campaign. Lord Canning, on the other hand, was quite sure that Rohilkhand should be occupied as quickly as possible. There, most of the population was loyal to the British – or at least friendly – and it would therefore be an easier campaign. Oudh could wait.

Campbell was now presented with three main tasks; the first to strengthen his outposts on the line of his advance towards and into Oudh; the second, to form a movable column for the pacification of north and north-western Oudh; the third, to prepare for the conquest of Rohilkhand.

On March 24th Campbell detached the force which was to garrison Lucknow under the command of Hope Grant. A considerable area of Lucknow, from the Machchi Bhawan to the Residency, was prepared as a fortified centre for the garrison and a good deal of demolition was carried out of houses and buildings to allow for an unrestricted field of fire.

On March 28th Campbell received news that the minor campaign which had been in progress against the rebels in Bihar was not going well. Franks had kept the district between Benares and the foothills of the Himalaya reasonably quiet, but on his leaving to join Campbell for the attack upon Lucknow the rebels had again taken the offensive. One of the rebel leaders, Koer Singh, had driven a small force under Colonel Milman into Azamgarh (see map, page 49) and besieged the town. To help Milman, Campbell sent off a column under Lugard on March 29th. It was hoped that the Gurkha contingent – which, having acquired all the loot it could carry, was now on its way back to Nepal by way of Faizabad – would help to relieve rebel pressure.

Lugard arrived at Sultanpur on the Gumti on April 5th. There he hoped to cross the river, but the bridge had been destroyed and there were no boats to be had. He therefore decided to march down the river to Jaunpur. A few miles from his destination, near the village of Tigra, Lugard encountered a rebel force of about 4,000 men with two guns. Though his men were fatigued from a 16-mile march, Lugard attacked and drove the rebels off, capturing their guns. By April 14th he was within seven miles of Azamgarh which was still besieged by Koer Singh and a force estimated at 13,000 men. Inside the town, Milman had in fact received reinforcements and was certainly strong enough to have broken out, but the commander of the reinforcements had received express instructions from Campbell not to act until Lugard arrived.

Koer Singh drew up his force along the banks of a small river at the head of a bridge of boats. His intention was to hold the river line while the majority of his force would evacuate Azamgarh, march to the Ganges, and cross over into the jungles of Jagdispur, the area in which he himself was a former landowner. Koer Singh held the bridge long enough for his men to move out and then retired, fighting a series of battles and inflicting heavy casualties. He finally crossed the Ganges on April 22nd and made for Jagdispur. By this time Koer Singh's army had been reduced to about 2,000 men without artillery. At that time there was a British force of some 350 men stationed at Arrah. Its commander marched off to meet Koer Singh and was defeated on April 23rd, owing, it was said, to the retreat being sounded by mistake; the force lost 133 killed, including the commander, and two guns. The next day Koer Singh also died, from shock, after amputating his own hand which had been shattered by a cannonball while he was crossing the Ganges. His brother, Amar Singh, then continued a guerrilla war, raiding and threatening towns and villages held by the British until his final defeat in October 1858, when he escaped to Nepal.

While all this was in progress Hope Grant, in Lucknow, was ordered by Campbell to march a column to Bari, 29 miles from Lucknow, and attack a body of rebels under the Maulvi of Faizabad concentrated there. He was then to march east to Muhammadabad, then, following the river Gogra, to investigate a rumour that Hazrat Mahal and 6,000 troops were at a place called Bithauli, and finally to march to Ramnagar. Hope Grant left Lucknow on April 11th with 3,000 men. As he neared Bari, the Maulvi, who was a natural tactician, tried to turn the British flank, but failed because some of his men did not stick to their orders. When charged by British cavalry, he finally withdrew into Rohilkhand to add to the rebel forces there.

Hope Grant, following instructions, now moved upon Bithauli in order to engage the rebels there, but when he arrived it was found that Hazrat Mahal had evacuated the town. Hope Grant's next task was to locate the Gurkha contingent moving through the country on its way home. He found them at a place midway between Ramnagar and Nawabgunge. In his journal, Hope Grant recorded a description of the Nepali troops: 'The European officer in command had great difficulties to contend with in marching through a country so filled with rebels. His force consisted of 8,000 men with 20 guns; yet he could only reckon on 2,000 men for actual fighting purposes. He had 2,000 sick and 4,000 carts; and each of the latter being filled with tents, private property, and loot, required according to the usages of these troops, a man to guard it.' Hope Grant next moved southwards to protect the road between Lucknow and Cawnpore which a body of rebels was threatening near Unao. In a series of skirmishes, he cleared his way to the fort of Jellalabad near Lucknow where he arrived on May 16th.

A threat now emerged from the south. An Oudh talukhdar (landowner) named Beni Madho issued proclamations warning the inhabitants of Lucknow to evacuate the city as he was preparing to attack it. Hope Grant moved out to intercept him but was unable to do so as Beni Madho sensibly preferred guerrilla tactics to fixed battlegrounds. The rebel leader was said to have the tremendous number of 15,000 men under his command. Hope Grant, realizing that he was unlikely to achieve any decisive engagement against such a force, scattered throughout a countryside they knew intimately, marched instead against another force of 15,000 men which had taken up a strong position some 18 miles from Lucknow along the Faizabad road. After making his dispositions, Hope Grant moved against the rebels on the night of June 12th.

The rebel position was exceptionally strong. They occupied a large plateau surrounded on three sides by a stream crossed by a bridge. On the fourth side was dense jungle. The British reached the bridge about half an hour before sunrise. At daylight Hope Grant crossed the bridge and attacked the

CHASING THE REBELS 141

rebel centre. Grant himself described in his journal what followed.

> Their forces appeared to be divided into four parts, each commanded by its separate leader, and of course acting without any unanimity. Still their attacks were vigorous, if unsuccessful, and we had much ado to repel them. A large body of fine daring zemindari men brought two guns into the open and attacked us in the rear. I have seen many battles in India, and many brave fellows fighting with a determination to conquer or die, but I never witnessed anything more magnificent than the conduct of these zemindaris. In the first instance they attacked Hodson's Horse, who would not face them, and by their unsteadiness placed in great jeopardy two guns which had been attached to the regiment. Fearing that they might be captured, I ordered up the 7th Hussars, and the other four guns belonging to the battery to within a distance of five hundred yards from the enemy, opened a fire of grape, which mowed them down with terrible effect, like thistles before the scythe. Their chief, a big fellow with a goitre on his neck, nothing daunted, caused two green standards to be planted close to the guns, and used them as a rallying point; but our grape shot was so destructive, that whenever they attempted to serve their pieces they were struck down. Two squadrons of the 7th Hussars under Sir William Russell, and two companies of Rifles, now came up, and forced the survivors to retire waving their swords and spears at us, and defiantly calling out to us to come on. The gallant 7th Hussars charged through them twice, and killed the greater part of them. Around the two guns alone there were 125 corpses. After three hours' fighting, the day was ours: we took six guns and killed about 600 of the enemy. Our own loss in killed and wounded was 67; and, in addition, 33 men died from sunstroke, and 250 were taken into hospital. Sun and heat are fearful scourges in this country during the hot weather; but, singular to say, the sufferers generally died during the night. The men fell asleep in their tents and never awoke – apoplexy, resulting from exposure to the sun, being the immediate cause of death. Regiments had for some time been endeavouring to obtain the special description of

headress suitable for the climate, but had only just been supplied with them.

This small victory had valuable consequences, for it drove the rebels from the vicinity of Lucknow. Grant now returned to that city and was ordered by Campbell to go to the aid of a former rebel raja who had turned his coat and joined the British. He was now being attacked in his fort at Shahganj by his former associates with some 20,000 men and 20 guns. On July 22nd Grant set off to relieve the raja. At that time the rebel forces in Oudh were estimated to number about 60,000 men and 40 guns. These were divided into nine principal bodies, and there were also, of course, many more men operating in small guerrilla detachments. More than 30,000 men were said to be with Hazrat Mahal on the river Gogra not far from Faizabad; another 20,000 were besieging Shahganj, and the rest were scattered throughout Oudh.

Grant, moving rapidly, arrived within a day's march of the fort at Shahganj when he heard that the force besieging it had fled in three columns, one going to Hazrat Mahal, and the other two – about 8,000 men – to Sultanpur. To that town Grant moved his force and, between August 25th and 27th, engaged in a number of actions against the rebels. On August 28th, the rebels abandoned Sultanpur. At this stage it became extremely difficult to find and attack bands of rebels without considerable loss to British troops through sunstroke, fatigue, and disease. Campbell therefore decided to postpone operations until the beginning of the cold weather in October.

17

The Campaign in Rohilkhand

CAMPBELL, WHO had become known as 'Old *Khabardar*' (Old Be-careful), was not taking any chances with the success of his proposed attack upon the rebels in Rohilkhand. The province, which had remained untouched by the British, held a considerable force of mutineers from Delhi as well as the local inhabitants, the Rohillas, who were of Afghan descent, under Khan Bahadur Khan, and the retainers of the Nawab of Farukhabad. They had also been joined by the Maulvi of Faizabad. Against this formidable combination, Campbell planned to send four divisions; one commanded by General Penny from Meerut, another by Brigadier Coke from Rurki, a third commanded by Walpole from Lucknow, and the fourth led by Seaton at Fatehgarh. The latter, with a small force, had prevented the rebels from crossing the river Ramgunga and once again entering the Doab, in an action near Fatehgarh on April 6th. Seaton's function was to hold the gate while the others attacked the rebel centre at Bareilly.

The column under Walpole left Lucknow on April 7th. It consisted of the 9th Lancers, 2nd Punjab cavalry, the 42nd, 79th, and 93rd Highlanders, the 4th Punjab Rifles, two troops of horse artillery, two 18-pounders, two 8-inch howitzers, and some mortars. Walpole's orders were to clear the left bank of the Ganges of rebels and reintroduce administration into the districts bordering the river. The campaign was not expected to offer much difficulty to a competent general. Unfortunately Walpole, in this his first independent command, displayed only a remarkable talent for sending men uselessly to their deaths.

For the first week of the march, Walpole's abilities remained untested, but on the morning of April 15th, after a march of nine miles, he found himself near Ruya, a small fort 51 miles south-east of Lucknow and about 10 miles east of the river Ganges. On two sides, the fort was protected by dense jungle. The fort was occupied by one rebel, Nirpat Singh, and about 200 men, though Walpole's spies reported that the number was over 1,500. A native trooper of Hodson's Horse, who had been taken prisoner by the rebels and held in the fort, managed to escape to Walpole and informed him that Nirpat Singh was prepared, after a show of resistance to satisfy his sense of honour, to evacuate the fort. Walpole refused to believe this story and, furthermore, stuck to the estimate of 1,500 for the garrison. He made no attempt at reconnaissance and would not allow any of his officers to examine the fort. If they had done so, it would soon have been discovered that, though the northern and eastern sides of the fort were protected by a dense bamboo jungle, the western and southern offered an easy way in. These faces were approached by a ditch, everywhere shallow and in some places quite dry, and the walls themselves could be jumped over. Walpole decided to attack through the jungle! Faced by such madness, Nirpat Singh decided to fight, causing very heavy casualties to the British forces and killing Adrian Hope, who was shot by a sniper at the very moment, it was later believed, when he had decided to take over command from Walpole and so stop the slaughter.

Finally, alarmed by the casualties, Walpole set his artillery to bombard the walls and ordered the retreat of his infantry. The force was in an uproar at Walpole's mismanagement. Forbes-Mitchell, who was there, wrote:

> After we retired from the fort the excitement was so great among the men of the 42nd and 93rd, owing to the sacrifice of so many officers and men through mismanagement, that if the officers had given the men the least encouragement, I am convinced they would have turned out in a body and hanged General Walpole. The officers who were killed were all most popular men; but the great loss sustained by the death of Adrian Hope positively excited the men to fury. So heated was the feeling on the night the dead were buried, that if any non-commissioned officer had dared to take the lead, the life of General Walpole would not have been worth half an hour's purchase.

THE CAMPAIGN IN ROHILKHAND

During the night, Nirpat Singh evacuated the fort, leaving Walpole to occupy it in the morning. Walpole then moved on and, on April 27th, was joined by Campbell on the Rohilkhand side of Fatehgarh. The column marched to Shahjahanpur, which was found evacuated, and finally reached Miranpur Katra and joined the troops of General Penny there on May 3rd. Penny himself had been killed in an ambush at Kukerauli on April 30th.

Meanwhile, on April 17th Coke had crossed the Ganges at Hardwar. General John Jones was in nominal command of the column but, as one historian of the Mutiny put it, though he was a brave man 'he was unwieldy in body, and incapable of very great activity. But he had no jealousy and he was gifted with rare common sense. He saw at a glance that Coke was the man for the work, and he was content to leave it in his hands. In the campaign that followed, then, and of which he reaped all the credit, he never once interfered with Coke's arrangements. That officer continued to be supreme – in all but name.' Coke, after crossing the river, routed the enemy at Bogniwala and continued his advance. On April 21st he encountered a rebel force of 10,000 infantry and 2,000 cavalry, with 15 guns, posted in a strong position on a canal at Nagina and, by the superb use of his native cavalry, put the rebels to flight. After this victory, the column met little opposition until it reached Moradabad on April 26th. In that town, spies had learned that a number of prominent rebel leaders were in hiding, including Firuz Shah, one of the princes of Delhi who had escaped from that city. Coke, placing his cavalry to guard the outlets from the town, sent his infantry to search the houses said to contain the rebel leaders. Twenty-one were, in fact, taken, but Firuz Shah again escaped. Coke continued his march on May 3rd and two days later reached Mirganj, about 14 miles from Bareilly. There he waited for news of Campbell. He had in fact been without information concerning the movements of the commander-in-chief since he had crossed the Ganges.

As we have seen, Campbell had passed through Shahjahanpur and had met up with Penny's force, now commanded by

Brigadier H. R. Jones, at Miranpur Katra. The evacuation of Shahjahanpur meant that Campbell had already failed in one of his principal intentions. Though he had planned that the columns converging on Bareilly would sweep the rebels into a net, the Maulvi of Faizabad – with whom was believed to be the Nana Sahib – had managed to break through into Oudh. At Shahjahanpur, Campbell left a small garrison of 500 men, and pushed on.

The combined force reached Faridpur on May 4th, only a day's march from Bareilly. According to Campbell's spies, Khan Bahadur Khan commanded a force of about 30,000 infantry, 6,000 cavalry, and 40 guns. Once again, these figures were heavily inflated. Nevertheless, there was still a very large force in the town. Bareilly itself was not particularly defensible, being rather scattered, but the approaches to it lay across a plain divided by a number of streams. One of these crossed the south side of the town, and the bridges across it still stood.

Khan Bahadur Khan decided to meet the British outside the town and, on the evening of May 4th, he set up artillery on some sandhills which could command the British line of advance. He placed his cavalry on the flanks and his second line of defence in the suburbs of the town. Early on the morning of the 5th, Campbell's advance parties encountered rebel cavalry, and by 6 AM Campbell had formed his force into two lines ready for the attack. In the first line he had his Highland regiments supported by the 4th Punjab Rifles and a Baluch battalion, with a heavy field-battery in the centre and horse artillery and cavalry on both flanks. The second line consisted of the remainder of his force and the baggage and the siege-train which might be threatened by the large numbers of enemy cavalry.

At seven o'clock the line moved forward and was met by artillery fire. The advance continued and the rebels abandoned their first line of defence without a fight and fell back on the town. The British now crossed the stream and the heavy guns were brought forward to bombard the rebel positions. While the bombardment was going on the remainder of the force crossed the stream.

Among the troops of Khan Bahadur Khan were a number of fanatical muslims, known as Ghazis, men who believed that to kill a non-believer would open their way to heaven. As the British line was reforming, a large body of Ghazis – 'fine fellows, grizzly-bearded elderly men for the most part, with green turbans and cummerbunds, every one of them wearing a signet ring with a long text from the Koran engraved on it' – appeared. Forbes-Mitchell recorded:

> The Sikhs and our light company advanced in skirmishing order, when some seven to eight hundred matchlockmen opened fire on them, and all at once a most furious charge was made by a body of about 360 Rohilla Ghazis, who rushed out, shouting *Bismillah!* Allah! Allah! *Din! Din!* Sir Colin was close by and called out 'Ghazis! Ghazis! Close up the ranks! Bayonet them as they come on.' However, they inclined to our left, and only a few came on to the 93rd, and these were mostly bayoneted by the light company which was extended in front of the line. The main body rushed on the centre of the 42nd; but as soon as he saw them change their direction Sir Colin galloped on, shouting out, 'Close up, Forty-Second! Bayonet them as they come on!' But that was not so easily done; the Ghazis charged in blind fury, with their round shields on their left arms, their bodies bent low, waving their *tulwars* [sabres] over their heads, throwing themselves under the bayonets, and cutting at the men's legs. Colonel Cameron of the 42nd was pulled from his horse by a Ghazi, who leaped up and seized him by the collar while he was engaged with another on the opposite side; but his life was saved by Colour-Sergeant Gardener, who seized one of the enemy's *tulwars*, and rushing to the colonel's assistance cut off the Ghazi's head. General Walpole was also pulled off his horse and received two sword cuts, but was rescued by the bayonets of the 42nd. The struggle was short, but every one of the Ghazis was killed. None attempted to escape; they had evidently come on to kill or be killed, and 133 lay in one circle right in front of the colours of the 42nd.

This attack over, the line advanced. It was now the hottest part of the day and Campbell decided to call a halt to rest his troops. The force found what shelter it could in the houses – still outside the town. Though the halt was medically wise, it was, like so many of Campbell's cautious and intrinsically humanitarian actions, militarily fatal. As night fell, Khan Bahadur Khan evacuated the town leaving only a rearguard, and made for Pilibhit, 33 miles to the north-east. When, the following morning, Campbell's artillery opened up on the town, the only sound that was heard in reply was that of Coke's guns from the other side! Without news of Campbell, Coke had proceeded on his way to Bareilly and had attacked the rebels and silenced their artillery. Coke also attempted to prevent the rebel evacuation with his cavalry, but without success.

The next day, May 7th, Coke and Campbell joined forces. It was now obvious that in the first stage of the campaign Campbell had been outmanœuvred – the Maulvi had escaped from Shahjahanpur, and Khan Bahadur Khan from Bareilly. It was now the Maulvi's turn to take the offensive. Believing perhaps that Bareilly would hold out longer than it actually did, he had decided to attack the weak British force left at Shahjahanpur. In fact, the British position there was not comfortable. Before the evacuation the Nana Sahib had ordered the destruction of as many houses as possible, so that the British would be without shelter, and Colonel Hale – left in command by Campbell – therefore moved in to the jail enclosure which, being substantially built, could be made defensible. The Maulvi, with some other chiefs who had joined him, moved against this on the night of May 2nd, but made the error of not attacking during the hours of darkness. When light came, Hale, who had received warning from spies, sent out reconnaissance parties who observed large bodies of cavalry approaching the town. Hale wisely withdrew into the fortified area of the jail enclosure. Meanwhile the Maulvi was occupying the town and squeezing money contributions from its wealthier citizens. He also placed eight guns in position to bombard the jail. The bombardment continued until May 11th, but without much weakening the defences.

News of what was taking place at Shahjahanpur reached Campbell on May 7th and he immediately ordered Brigadier Jones and a small force to deal with the Maulvi. Jones arrived at Shahjahanpur on May 11th and, by the astute use of horse artillery, managed to prevent the Maulvi from effectively using his cavalry. Jones rapidly drove the rebels into the city and, going round through the suburbs, moved on to the jail, sensibly refusing to fight in the narrow streets of the town. As Jones moved towards the jail he found the main body of rebels positioned on the parade ground with their advance positions in the main street leading to the jail. Here Jones was at a disadvantage, for the enemy cavalry could operate in the open space while he could not adequately deploy his artillery. He therefore decided to hold a defensive position while awaiting reinforcements from Bareilly. During the following three days the Maulvi's forces were augmented by those of Hazrat Mahal and Firuz Shah. On May 15th the Maulvi launched a series of heavy attacks against Jones's position. All were repulsed but Jones, lacking cavalry (he had only three squadrons), could not retaliate.

Back in Bareilly, Campbell, under the curious misconception that the campaign in Rohilkhand was over, was redistributing his forces. Walpole was appointed to command the troops left in Rohilkhand, in spite of his proved incompetence – or perhaps because of it, as the commander-in-chief believed the campaign to be over. Some regiments were ordered to garrison Bareilly, others back to Lucknow and Meerut. A powerful column, under Coke, marched off on May 12th towards Pilibhit and Khan Bahadur Khan. Campbell, having made his dispositions, now decided to move out of Rohilkhand to some more central spot and establish his headquarters there. With a small body of troops and artillery, he therefore left Bareilly for Fatehgarh on May 15th.

On reaching Faridpur the next day, Campbell received a dispatch from Brigadier Jones, and the day after, as he moved on, spies reported that the Maulvi – while still pressing Shahjahanpur – had removed the bulk of his force to Mohamdi in Oudh. On May 18th Campbell marched on Shahjahanpur and, after a minor skirmish with rebel cavalry, joined up with Brigadier Jones. With only three troops of cavalry to add to those already with Jones, Campbell was unwilling to risk a major engagement and, while keeping the rebels active, sent to Coke for further reinforcements. Coke, moving with great speed, joined the commander-in-chief on May 22nd. Two days later the whole force marched on Mohamdi, only to find that the Maulvi had evacuated the town after destroying its defences.

The campaign was now really over, and Campbell proceeded to divide his forces and place them in permanent positions for the rest of the hot weather. The Maulvi, one of the few genuine leaders on the rebel side, was killed by a 'loyal' raja – loyal, that is, in the sense that it was now obvious that the British were winning – at Parain on the borders of Oudh and Rohilkhand, when he attempted to capture the fort there. This was on June 5th. If he had lived, he would certainly have given the British a great deal of trouble, for, though without military training, he was a natural tactician, a description which could not be applied to any of the commanders opposing him.

Part Three
CENTRAL INDIA

1
The Outbreak of the Mutiny

IN 1857 the Central Indian Agency (see map, page 154) consisted of six native states in alliance with the British government. Nominally independent, they were in fact yet another example of indirect rule. Authority was exercised by a British agent, and enforced by troops paid for by the native rulers but officered by the British and taking orders only from them. The six states were Gwalior, Indore, Dhar, and Dewas, which were ruled by Maratha princes and had once been part of the Maratha Confederation which had been finally defeated by the British in 1817; and Bhopal and Jawra, which were Muslim states, and had once acknowledged the Marathas as overlords. To the north-west was the Rajputana, a collection of native states under the control of a British agent. The area under direct British administration was small, but it included three important military stations, Ajmer, Nasirabad, and Nimach.

The six states of the Central Indian Agency were in an area known as Malwa, which lies principally between the rivers Chambal and Narbada, the former a tributary of the Jumna which it joins about 80 miles below Agra. North of the Narbada lies Bundelkhand. To the south were a series of military stations, including Jubbulpur, Saugor, and Narod. The only European troops in the area were a company of horse artillery at Mhow near Indore. Between the Chambal and the Narbada flows another river, the Betwa, on which stands Jhansi, a small Maratha state annexed by the British in 1854 because there was no direct heir to the throne.

At Nasirabad, which was the administrative centre of the Rajputana Agency, were stationed the 1st Bombay Cavalry, the 15th and 30th Bengal Native Infantry, and a battery of native artillery. On June 8th, 1857, all except the cavalry mutinied and moved off to Delhi. At Nimach, 120 miles away, a wing of the 1st Bengal Light Cavalry, the 72nd Bengal

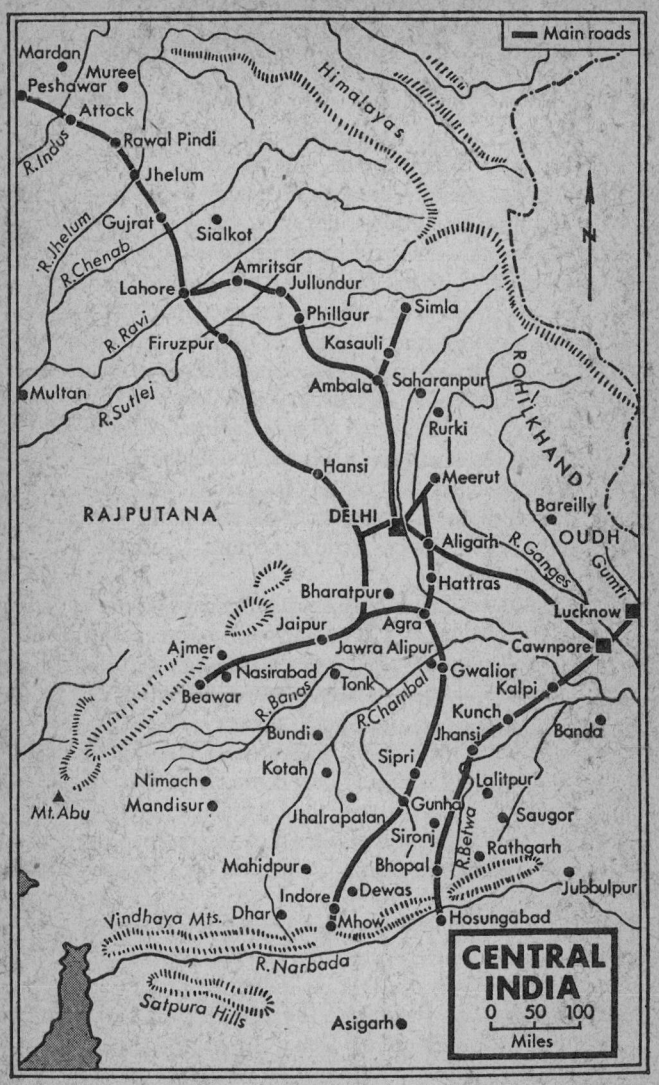

Infantry, the 7th Gwalior Contingent Infantry, and a troop of native horse artillery had mutinied four days earlier, moved off to Agra and, after defeating a British force, also marched to Delhi.

In Gwalior was a contingent raised mainly from the Bengal Army, stationed at Morar, five miles from the city of Gwalior. The contingent numbered 8,000 men, made up of two cavalry regiments, four companies of artillery, and ten infantry battalions. In addition to the main force at Morar, there were detachments at Nimach, Asigarh, Lalitpur, Sipri, Gunah, and Hattras. The mutiny at Morar took place on June 14th. After killing such of the officers and their families as they could find, the contingent remained at Morar although it later formed the bulk of the force which attacked General Windham at Cawnpore (see page 114).

At Jhansi the garrison consisted of a detachment of native artillery, a wing of the 14th Irregular Cavalry, and detachments of the 12th Bengal Infantry. These mutinied on June 5th and the British, who had taken refuge in the fort, were murdered three days later when they emerged – possibly, though this has never been proved, on the promise of a safe conduct from the Rani, widow of the last native ruler of the state.

The headquarters of the acting agent in Central India were at Indore. Mutiny did not break out there until July 1st. The acting agent, Sir Henry Durand, was not particularly sympathetic to the state ruler, who was known as the Holkar. The state army was made up of 7,500 men whose loyalty was questionable. The nearest British troops – a company of artillery – was stationed at Mhow, 13 miles from Indore, and could not be moved because their presence was the only thing that prevented the sepoys from rebelling at Mhow. Durand's first plan was to keep quiet until a column of British troops under Colonel Woodburn, known to be on its way, arrived. On July 1st, however, the Residency at Indore was attacked by the Holkar's troops and Durand was forced to evacuate Indore and retired to Sihor. Within a few hours of the outbreak at Indore, the sepoys rose at Mhow. The officer commanding the British artillery was, however, able to hold the fort and the mutineers marched off, first to Indore, then to Gwalior, and ultimately to Agra, where they were defeated by Greathed's force from Delhi (see page 42).

Durand now attempted to get in touch with Woodburn's column and finally met up with it, now under the command of General Stuart, at Asigarh on July 22nd. The column pushed on to Mhow, which was reoccupied on August 1st. At this stage, operations had to be suspended because of the heavy rains and the inadequate number of British troops at Stuart's and Durand's disposal.

2

The Campaign in Malwa

IN OCTOBER 1857, as the monsoon ended, it became obvious that some action must be taken against the various bodies of mutineers who had spent the rainy season untouched by the British. Though the situation in Indore was anything but reassuring, a more immediate danger threatened at the town of Mandisur, 120 miles away. There the mutineers were under the command of the Mughal prince, Firuz Shah, and by the end of September were believed to number 15,000 men, with 16 or 18 guns. Against this force, Stuart and Durand could muster only 1,500 men and nine guns. According to Durand's spies and to letters that had been intercepted, a general rising was planned in Malwa to coincide with the festival of Dussehra. Early in October, Firuz Shah advanced along the road to Bombay in an endeavour to cut the British force's communications with Bombay, and to attack the town of Nimach. The situation was potentially of very great danger, for, at that time, the Nana Sahib was near Kalpi with a large number of rebels and might well have attempted to join up with Firuz.

On October 12th Durand detached a body of cavalry to defend the town of Mandisur, threatened by the rebels, and sent another to the village of Gujri. Two days later he reinforced the latter with three companies of the 25th Native Infantry and some dragoons. On October 19th, with such troops as he could spare after garrisoning Mhow, he himself set off for Dhar. There the fort was occupied by a number of mercenaries, Afghans, Arabs, and Mekranis, who had for many years supplied troops to the native princes of the area. These mercenaries were said to be in communication with Firuz Shah, no doubt in the hope of employment and loot.

Durand arrived at Dhar on October 22nd. The mercenaries, made perhaps over-confident by the absence of British activity during the rains, quitted the fort in order to attack Durand in the open. With three brass cannon suitably placed on a hill to the south of the fort, the mercenaries advanced to meet the British force. An attack by the 25th Native Infantry, however, captured the guns which were then turned upon the mercenaries, while the remaining infantry and two batteries of artillery advanced against the centre and the cavalry threatened the flanks. The dragoons charged so vigorously that the mercenaries retired into the fort, leaving behind them 40 dead.

The British, sitting outside the fort, now had to wait for heavy guns to come up before beginning the siege. These guns arrived on the 24th. Durand hoped that the defenders of the fort might surrender but, after six days, there was still no sign. When, however, a storming party broke into the fort on October 31st, it was found to be empty! The main body of mercenaries had left the fort and slipped through the British cavalry piquets unobserved. Durand ordered that the fort be demolished, and continued his march through western Malwa towards Mandisur, in pursuit of the mercenaries who should not have been allowed to escape in the first place.

On November 8th the rebels attacked a native contingent under the command of British officers at Mahidpur and defeated it. A small force under Major Orr was immediately despatched to the town and arrived only to find it evacuated. Orr, pushing on, caught up with the rebel rearguard and in a sharp and bloody engagement defeated it, capturing eight guns and a large quantity of stores. Casualties on both sides were high: 100 killed and wounded in the British force, and 175 in the rebels.

Durand, delayed by the slowness of his baggage carts, reached the banks of the Chambal river on November 9th. Though his crossing was unopposed by rebels, it was resisted by nature, for the banks of the river were almost perpendicular and the water was deep and rapid and littered with vast boulders. It took two days for the guns and baggage to cross, but one eye-witness had never seen 'a more animated and beautiful picture in my life than when our brigade crossed this river. The steep, verdant, shrubby banks, covered with our varied forces, elephants, camels, horses, and bullocks; the deep flowing clear river, reaching on and on to the far east, to the soft deep-blue tufted horizon; the babble and yelling of men, the lowing of cattle, the grunting screams of the camels, and the trumpeting of the wary, heavily laden elephants; the rattle of our artillery down the bank, through the river, and up the opposite side; the splashing and plunging of our cavalry through the stream – neighing and eager for the green encamping ground before them; and everybody so busy and jovial, streaming up from the deep water to their respective grounds; and all this in the face, almost, of an enemy, formed a *tableau vivant* never to be forgotten.' But this, it must be remembered, was a picture recollected in tranquillity, and the author did not have to push the guns or pull the cattle.

By the 21st, however, Durand was within four miles of Mandisur. He encamped in a position covered to his front by rising ground, flanked on the left by a village with gardens and groves of trees and, beyond, another village. On his right were hills and villages and between them and the rising ground was a plateau, some of it under cultivation.

About mid-day on November 22nd the rebels occupied the village on the left of the British position and deployed their force in two parts about the plateau, covering the approaches to Mandisur. A brisk barrage from Durand's artillery, followed by a cavalry charge, drove the rebels from the field and into the refuge of Mandisur. Next day, Durand moved to within a mile of the town and camped there, for his spies had reported that a rebel force from Nimach was hurrying to engage the British. A cavalry reconnaissance revealed a large concentration in a village named Goraria on the road to Nimach. Durand decided to meet the rebels before they could reach Mandisur, and found them well entrenched outside the village.

Once again the better-handled artillery of the British played a vital part, but though the rebels were driven back on Goraria they could not be dislodged. While the British attacked the village, a rebel force from Mandisur attacked them in the rear, but were – with some difficulty – driven off. As night fell, the rebels still held the village. Next morning at ten o'clock

Durand's heavy artillery poured shot into the village from a range of 250 yards, setting the buildings on fire. Still the rebels held out, but at midday some 200 of them surrendered, though it was not until four o'clock in the afternoon that the remaining defenders were finally dislodged.

The stubborn defence of Goraria served its purpose. While the British were engaged there, Firuz Shah and about 2,000 men evacuated Mandisur and made for Nangarh. The British were too exhausted to follow them. Nevertheless, Durand had succeeded in holding the line of the Narbada river and prevented rebel forces from joining up with those in Indore.

Durand now felt himself free to tackle the problem of the Holkar's mutinous army. On December 14th the British force was approaching Indore ready to do battle with the rebels. But the effects of Durand's little campaign were being felt by the Holkar's troops, and the Indore army allowed itself to be disarmed.

There is no doubt that Durand had acted with intelligence and decision – two qualities in very small supply amongst officers in the Company's service at the time of the Mutiny – and prepared the way for the final campaign in Central India. He then handed over his charge to the agent, Sir Robert Hamilton, who had returned from leave, and his troops became part of the new Central India Field Force placed under the command of Sir Hugh Rose.

3

The Road to Jhansi

SIR HUGH ROSE, who assumed command of the Central India Field Force at Indore on December 16th, had had a distinguished career both as a soldier and as a diplomat. Having fought in the Turkish-Egyptian war of 1841, he had been successively consul-general in Syria, secretary to the British embassy in Constantinople, and Queen's commissioner at the headquarters of the French army during the Crimean War. His attitude to the campaign before him was simple: 'When your enemy is in the open, go straight at him and keep him moving; and when behind ramparts, still go at him and cut off chances of retreat when possible; pursue him if escaping or escaped.' He had exactly the right combination of intelligence and dash which was needed in Central India. The campaign against the rebels demanded quick decision and rapid movement; both were supplied by Rose and his men.

Rose arrived in India on September 19th, 1857, but the usual problems of supplies and organization delayed his taking field command until December. When he did so, Rose divided his force into two brigades commanded by two brigadiers of the same name which, fortunately, was differently spelt. The first brigade was led by Brigadier Stuart of the Bombay Army, and the second by Brigadier Steuart of the 14th Light Dragoons who was later forced by illness to relinquish his command. Altogether, the whole force numbered 4,500 men, of whom a large proportion were Indians. Rose's instructions were to clear the countryside and to operate towards Jhansi, but not to move forward except in concert with another column under General Whitlock which was moving up from Madras. As usual, supplies and carriage were scarce and there was a shortage of horses for the artillery. While these were being got together, Rose spent his time pacifying the countryside around Indore.

On January 6th Rose accompanied by Sir Robert Hamilton

left Mhow to join the second brigade at Sikar in Bhopal, followed by the siege-train which arrived on the 15th. Earlier, Rose had received disquieting news from the town of Saugor, where the mud fort sheltered 170 European women and children and a very small garrison of 68 European artillerymen. It had originally been intended that the relief of Saugor should be the responsibility of General Whitlock's column, but its movement was so slow that it was not expected to arrive for another two months. At Saugor were about 1,000 Bengal sepoys and 100 irregular cavalry who had so far remained loyal, but news came of a large body of mutineers moving towards Saugor and it was feared that the troops there would join them. Rose therefore decided to relieve the fort himself. On January 16th Rose and the second brigade set out for Saugor.

About 30 miles from Saugor stood the town of Rathgarh, dominated by a strong fort sited on the spur of a long, high hill. The eastern and southern faces of the fort were almost perpendicular and were protected by a deep and fast-flowing river. The north face was protected by a ditch, and the western face, which overlooked the town, was well protected by bastioned gateways. Rose arrived outside the fort on January 24th and drove the defenders' outlying piquets into the fort, and then dispersed his troops around it while he drew up a plan of attack. The rebels, once again made up of Afghan and Pathan mercenaries, reoccupied the town and attacked Rose's camp from the protection of a dense jungle. When, next morning, the British attempted to clear them from the jungle, the rebels set fire to it, forcing the British to turn back.

Meanwhile, the main body of Rose's force had driven the enemy from the town and begun to establish breaching-batteries on the hill opposite the north face of the fort. On the morning of the 27th, the batteries opened fire and continued all that day and throughout the night until, at ten o'clock on the morning of the 28th, a large breach in the walls had been made. Just as this was being reconnoitred, a rebel force was reported advancing to relieve the fort. Soon a considerable body of rebels under the leadership of the Raja of Banpur appeared with standards flying and bands playing to attack the besieging force in the rear.

Rose, however, did not slacken his fire against the fort, but in fact increased it, while detaching a body of cavalry, horse artillery, and infantry to meet the Raja. As soon as they made contact, the Raja's troops broke and fled. The failure of the relieving force had its effect on the defenders, who evacuated the fort during the following night by a route which the besiegers had believed impossible. 'The most amazing thing', wrote one who was there, 'was to see the place from whence they had escaped. To look down the precipitous path made one giddy – and yet down this place, where no possible footing could be seen, they had all gone – men and women – in the dead of night! One or two mangled bodies lay at the bottom, attesting the difficulty of the descent. Nothing but despair could have tempted them to have chosen such a way.' Despair or not, the defenders *did* get away and it was just as well that they did, for when the fort was occupied it was found to be so strong that it would have taken Rose considerable effort and loss of life to reduce it. Though some attempt was made to pursue the rebels, they had travelled too far for pursuit to be successful and it was soon abandoned.

On January 30th news came to Rose that the fleeing garrison had joined with the Raja of Banpur's troops at the village of Barodia, 15 miles from Saugor. Rose, with horse artillery, the 3rd European Infantry, most of his cavalry, and sappers, set off to engage them and, about four o'clock in the afternoon, came across the rebels drawn up along the banks of the river Bina. After some heavy fighting, Rose managed to cross the river and fought his way, step by step, to Barodia, finally putting the rebels to flight. Rose then retired to Rathgarh.

The area south of Saugor was now clear and the road to Indore reopened. Rose's next move was to march as rapidly as possible to the relief of Saugor itself. Marching directly from Rathgarh, Rose arrived at Saugor on February 3rd. One of the garrison wrote on that day:

Saugor was relieved this morning by the forces under Sir Hugh Rose. Who can imagine the gladness that then filled the hearts of the Europeans, shut up for eight weary and anxious months? For many a month and week during this period we heard of relief being near, till we grew sick with expecting and watching for its realization. It was about eight days ago that we knew Sir Hugh Rose's force had arrived in the district. It heralded its approach by the bombardment of Rathgarh, one of the strongest forts in Bundelkhand . . . At last to our joy it was reported that the fort had been taken, and that Sir Hugh Rose was close at hand . . . His troops marched right through the city of Saugor in a long line, and you can imagine the impression their number made on the natives of the place. Such a thing as a European regiment had never been seen in Saugor, and we certainly never expected to see Her Majesty's 14th Dragoons. These men, and the large siege-guns dragged by elephants, were a source of much curiosity and awe to the natives. You can hardly realize our feelings after eight months of anxiety and imprisonment.

Rose's next task was to clear the countryside to the east of Saugor. About 25 miles from the town was the fort of Gathakot, held by mutineers of the 51st and 52nd Bengal Infantry. The fort itself was a strong one, protected on one side by a river and on another by a ditch 20 feet deep. The fort itself had been constructed by French engineers and its defences were so strong that, 40 years earlier, a British force of 11,000 men with 28 guns had failed to take it by siege.

As Rose approached the fort on February 11th, he found the rebels entrenched behind earthworks outside the main defences. Driving the rebels into the fort, Rose's artillery went into action against the rebels' guns. As his force was small – he had left the majority of his men behind at Saugor – Rose was unable to surround the fort and once again the defenders slipped away during the night. After destroying the western face of the fort with gunpowder, Rose returned to Saugor.

His next objective was the capture of Jhansi. This task was held to be of great importance. Sir Colin Campbell felt himself in danger as long as Jhansi remained in the hands of the rebels. Campbell's chief of staff wrote on January 24th: 'Sir Colin will be glad to learn if Jhansi is to be fairly tackled during your present campaign. To us it is all-important. Until it takes place, Sir Colin's rear will always be inconvenienced, and he will be constantly obliged to look back over his shoulder as when he relieved Lucknow. The stiff neck this gives to the commander-in-chief and the increased difficulty of his operations in consequence you will understand.'

Rose, however, was not really strong enough to move across the 125 miles of rebel-held country which separated him from Jhansi. It was necessary for him to join up with his first brigade before marching on Jhansi, and he was also without reliable information concerning the whereabouts of Whitlock's column, which was supposed to have left Jubbulpur for Saugor. Rose was further bedevilled by problems of transport and supply, and he wrote to the governor of Bombay outlining his difficulties. 'I am unfortunately detained here by want of supplies and carriage, to the great disadvantage of the public service: I have lost nine precious days, doubly precious not only on account of lost time at a season when every hot day endangers the health and lives of the European soldiers, but because every day has allowed the rebels to recover the morale they had lost by my operations, which I had made as rapidly and efficiently as possible, knowing that any success with Orientals produces twice as good a result if one acts promptly and follows up one success with another. Nothing requires system as much as transport. Laying in supplies, as it is called, is perfectly easy in a fertile and peaceful country, but this will not do in my case, where a country has been devastated or is in the hands of the enemy.'

When news came that Whitlock had left Jubbulpur, Rose began his march to Jhansi. To get there he must first crush the rebels who had taken advantage of his enforced stay at Saugor to occupy three important passes and a number of forts. On March 3rd Rose found himself in front of the pass of Malthon, which was held by a strong rebel force. It was obvious that a frontal attack would only lead to heavy casualties and

Rose decided on an attempt to gain the tableland above the hills by going through the pass of Madanpur. On March 4th he therefore detached a small body of men to give the impression of a frontal attack while he himself led the main force against Madanpur.

The pass forms a narrow gorge between two ranges of hills thickly covered with jungle. The rebels commanded the heights with artillery and had mounted batteries in the gorge itself while deploying skirmishers in the jungles to harry the British force. The British were met by a hail of fire in which Rose's horse was shot from under him, and at one point were forced to retire. A strong infantry charge, however, drove the rebels from the heights into the town of Madanpur itself. Rose, following through the pass, now brought his artillery to bear on the town and the rebels fled to another fort at Sarai, pursued by Rose's cavalry.

The effect of Rose's victory at Madanpur was even greater than he could have expected. The rebels abandoned the Malthon pass and the fort of Narut to the rear of it; the forts at Sarai, Marowra, and Banpur, and the whole line of the Bina and Betwa rivers except for the fort of Chanderi which fell to Stuart and the first brigade on February 17th.

Rose now pressed on towards Jhansi and by February 20th his advance troops were reconnoitring the city. At this crucial stage, Rose and Hamilton received letters – one from the governor-general and the other from Campbell. Both instructed Rose to go to the assistance of the loyal rajas of Panna and Charkheri, who were being besieged by Tantia Topi and the Gwalior Contingent. 'It is the governor-general's wish', said the letter to Hamilton, 'that this object should for the present be considered paramount to the operations before Jhansi, and that Sir Hugh Rose should take such steps as may most effectually contribute to its accomplishment.'

Charkheri was 80 miles away from where Rose was encamped, while Jhansi was just over 14 miles. The problem for Rose was whether to obey orders against his better judgement or find some way of avoiding them. He decided that his opinion, formed on the spot, was better than those arrived at elsewhere however expedient they might seem to be. On March 13th Hamilton wrote to Lord Canning expressing his own and Rose's opinion on the inadvisability of bypassing Jhansi. 'To relieve Charkheri', he said, 'by this force would involve refusing Jhansi, and the suspension of the plans of operations towards Kalpi; both of which operations form the groundwork of Sir Hugh Rose's instructions. However anxious, therefore, the desire to aid the Raja of Charkheri, Sir Hugh Rose is compelled to consider the movement of his force, or of any part of it, in the direction of Charkheri at present impossible. The advance of this force on Jhansi, in the opinion of Sir Hugh Rose, is calculated to draw the rebels to assist in its defence; whilst the fall of this fortress and its possession by us will break up the confederacy, take away its rallying point, and destroy the power and influence of the Rani, whose name is prominently used to incite rebellion.' Rose wrote to Campbell in a similar vein and his decision was later approved. But before the governor-general's consent had arrived, Rose had already moved on Jhansi, arriving outside the city on the morning of March 21st.

Rose halted his force on open ground about a mile and a half from the fort of Jhansi. Between him and the town were the ruined bungalows of the European cantonment, the jail, the Star fort, and the old sepoy lines. Near the town were several large temples and groves of tamarind trees. On Rose's right, stretching to the north and east of the city, was a belt of hills; to his left were more hills; and due north lay the great fortress itself, surrounded on all sides except the north and part of the south by the walled city.

The fort, built on a high rock and completely dominating the town, was constructed of granite, its walls between 16 and 20 feet thick. There were elaborate outworks and parapets all loop-holed for muskets and artillery. Guns on the towers could play unrestrictedly on the surrounding countryside. On one turret – named the White Tower – waved the Rani's flag. The rock on which the fortress stood was almost perpendicular, and from the south face, the city wall – also loop-holed and with parapets – ran south-east to a mound on which stood a circular bastion with five guns. Around part of this bastion was a ditch 12 feet deep and 15 feet broad, of solid masonry. The walls of the city were in good repair and well defended with bastions and parapets for riflemen, and varied in height from 18 to 30 feet.

All this was observed by Rose himself during an extensive reconnaissance on March 21st. From it he learned that before he could take the fort, or even attempt a siege, it would be necessary to clear and occupy the city. That night the first brigade under Stuart joined the British camp, and the next day Rose sealed the exits from the city with his cavalry, determined this time not to let the garrison escape if it had the mind to do so. Inside the city were some 11,000 rebels.

Because of the smallness of his force – Whitlock, who was supposed to assist him, was still slowly moving on the way to Saugor – Rose divided his cavalry into seven flying columns, each with a troop of horse artillery. Each column operated from a fixed camp where bodies of artillery and native infantry were also stationed. Batteries of artillery were mounted and four of them were ready by the evening of the 24th and opened fire on the city the next day. The bombardment continued until March 29th, the rebel guns replying vigorously until, on that day, the bastion on the mound was levelled and the guns silenced. The defenders in the city kept repairing the walls as they were damaged by the British guns and, though a breach was made in the walls, the following day it was soon filled in with a stockade. When the British thought they had silenced the rebel guns, they opened fire again. Rose found himself running low on ammunition and decided that an attempt must be made to storm the city. But the attack had to be postponed, for, on the night of the 31st, the defenders in the city and the besiegers outside the walls saw the light of a great bonfire on the Jhansi side of the river Betwa. The rebel general, Tantia Topi, was hurrying to the relief of the city.

4

The Battle of the Betwa

AFTER HIS defeat by Colin Campbell at Cawnpore (see page 118), Tantia Topi had crossed the Ganges and, on instructions from the Nana Sahib, had marched to Kalpi. From there, with a small force of 900 sepoys and four guns, he had descended upon Charkheri and, reinforced by five or six regiments of the Gwalior Contingent, had taken the town, capturing 24 guns and a considerable quantity of cash. While at Charkheri, Tantia had received an urgent request from the Rani of Jhansi to come to her aid. This he did, with 22,000 men and his 28 guns.

Rose's position was hardly a happy one. Before him was Jhansi, still unconquered and understandably invigorated by the prospect of relief. Approaching was a force commanded by one of the best generals the sepoys had, and at whose hands the British had twice suffered defeat. But Rose was unshaken. He even refused to raise the siege and, as he had done before at Saugor, detached only a portion of his force to deal with the rebels. This portion consisted in all of about 1,500 men, a third of whom were British.

Rose now drew up his force in two columns, the first under Brigadier Stuart and the second under his own command. His plan was to attack the rebel force at daylight on April 1st. At four o'clock in the morning, however, Tantia Topi took the initiative and advanced on the British line. A report that a body of rebels was crossing the Betwa with the apparent intention of relieving Jhansi from the north had led Rose to send a column to intercept it. When Tantia attacked, Rose's force was less than 900 men of all arms. As the rebels advanced, Rose ordered his guns to open fire. However they did not have much effect, especially as the rebel line overlapped the British on both flanks. Rose therefore massed his horse artillery on his left, strengthened it with a squadron of cavalry, and ordered it to attack the enemy's right while he and another squadron attacked the left. Both attacks were successful. To use Rose's own words: 'the enemy poured a heavy fusillade into the cavalry; the Valaitis [Afghan mercenaries] jumped up in hundreds on high rocks and boulders to load and fire, but before they could reload their matchlocks, Captain Need, leading his troop in advance, penetrated into the midst of them, and for a time was so hotly engaged that his uniform was cut to pieces, although, singular to say, he only received a slight wound himself. The attack on the enemy's right by the fire of Captain Lightfoot's battery and the charge of the 14th Light Dragoons were equally successful; and the enemy broke and retired in confusion.'

As the flanks retired, the centre, observing British infantry advancing, broke in complete disorder, overwhelming its own second line. This line, commanded by Tantia Topi in person, occupied a position on high ground protected by jungle. As the first line collapsed, Tantia saw that Stuart with a detachment of the first brigade – which had been sent to intercept the rebels moving from the north – was also advancing, driving the enemy before him. Tantia immediately set fire to the jungle and began to retreat, hoping to make a crossing of the Betwa. This he succeeded in doing, hotly pursued by the British through the burning jungle. Tantia was forced to leave behind all his guns, large quantities of stores and equipment, and 1,500 of his force dead and wounded. Without his artillery, he decided not to try and hold a line on the Betwa and fled towards Kalpi. Rose was now free to turn his attention to the capture of Jhansi.

5

The Storming of Jhansi

WHILE THE battle of the Betwa had been going on, those left behind to continue the siege of Jhansi went on pouring shot and shell into the city. For some reason, possibly because of treachery within her own ranks, the Rani made no attempt to leave the city and attack the seriously depleted force still besieging it. British siege-guns had managed to widen the breach in the walls and, by April 2nd, it was thought to be just large enough for an attempt at assault to be made.

Rose, who had returned immediately to Jhansi after the defeat of Tantia Topi, planned to launch a false attack against the west wall of the city and, while this was in progress, the main storming party would make for the breach and attempts would be made at various places to escalade the walls. For the latter purpose, the sappers, the 3rd Bombay Europeans, and the Hyderabad Infantry were divided into two columns and a reserve. Another body, of Royal Engineers, the 86th Foot, and the 25th Bombay Native Infantry was similarly divided, one column being detailed to storm the breach and the other to attack a rocket tower to the right of it.

Three AM on April 3rd saw all the parties in position, waiting for the sound of the guns in the false attack as the signal to advance. When the sound came, the breach party under Lieutenant-Colonel Lowth moved up and through the breach, while the rocket-tower party under Major Stuart, after a sharp engagement, forced its way into the town. The two parties then joined up and made for the Rani's palace. Meanwhile the other two columns were preparing to attack one of the city gates where the defence, according to a traitor in the Rani's camp, was weakest.

As the British approached, enemy bugles could be heard and very heavy fire was brought to bear upon the advance parties carrying the scaling-ladders. However, they managed to place their ladders at three positions along the walls. But, wrote

Dr Lowe, an eye-witness, 'the fire of the enemy waxed stronger, and amid the chaos of sounds, of volleys of musketry and roaring of cannon, and hissing and bursting of rockets, stink-pots, infernal machines, huge stones, blocks of wood, and trees – all hurled upon their devoted heads – the men wavered for a moment and sheltered themselves behind stones.' Reinforced by 100 men of the 3rd Europeans, hurriedly brought up, the stormers rushed to the ladders, but many were too short and others broke as the men began to climb. But one body got over and were soon joined by more, in bitter hand-to-hand fighting. At this point a party detached by Lowth fell upon the rear of the defenders, who broke, and the British continued their movement towards the palace. Each street and house was tenaciously defended, and as the rebels retired on the palace they set fire to the houses surrounding it. A surgeon with the British force described how the stormers moved down the street to the palace which ran by the side of the fort: 'The matchlock and musketry fire on the men at this point was perfectly hellish! The bullets fell so thickly in the dusty road that they resembled the effect of hailstones falling in water when striking it, and the men fell thick and fast here. One point of the street ran quite close to the gateway of the fort and was not passed without severe loss. Here it was that most of our men fell.'

When the British finally forced their way into the courtyard of the palace, each room in the building was bitterly fought over. 'When I got into the palace', wrote an officer who was present, 'I found it crowded with our soldiery, some lying down worn out with the heat and hard work, some sauntering about with two and three puggries upon their heads and others around their waists, some lying down groaning from their wounds or the explosion, and others busily engaged extinguishing the flames in the rooms where the explosion had taken place. The whole place was a scene of quick ruin and confusion; windows, doors, boxes, and furniture went to wreck like lightning ... We had been some two hours in the palace when it was discovered that a large body of the enemy

THE STORMING OF JHANSI

had shut themselves up in the stables. The 86th and 3rd Europeans rushed in upon them and slew every man – upwards of fifty – but not before they had cut down some dozen Europeans. The wounded men came straggling out with the most terrible sword cuts I ever saw in my life.'

While the palace was being fought over, a body of rebel cavalry had attempted to force the British piquets and failing to do so had taken up a position to the west of the fort. When they were attacked, the cavalry killed themselves rather than be taken prisoner or – what was more likely – killed by the British.

Heavy street fighting continued until the following day and no quarter was given, even to women and children. 'Those [of the rebels] who could not escape threw their women and babes down wells and then jumped down themselves.' The British were not just capturing the city but were intent on destroying what was to them as much a symbol of cruelty and suffering as the city of Cawnpore. 'No maudlin clemency was to mark the fall of the city', wrote Dr Lowe. And he was right. Looting and massacre were freely allowed.

But the Rani, 'the Jezebel of India', whom the British believed responsible for the murder of white women and children, was to escape their vengeance. After leaving the palace, to which she had returned after fighting with some of her troops against the storming party, she retired into the fort. At midnight on April 4th she and a small party left the fort and made for the north gate. Passing through it she made her way through Rose's piquets and was many miles away from Jhansi before the British discovered she was gone. How she got through the cavalry piquets has never been satisfactorily explained. Rose's biographer maintained that it was 'with the connivance of a native contingent serving with Sir Hugh', which, though possible, is not probable. The more likely explanation is that Rose's troops were too busy looting and murdering to be much concerned with those escaping from the city.

When Rose heard of her flight he sent a cavalry detachment

under Lieutenant Dowker in pursuit. 'I was gaining fast', he recalled later, 'on the Rani who, with four attendants, was escaping on a grey horse, when I was dismounted by a severe wound and would have been almost cut in half but that the blow was turned by the revolver on my hip. I was thus obliged to give up the pursuit and the lady escaped for the time being.' The Rani reached Kalpi before midnight on the 5th, to be joined there by Tantia Topi who had been making his way, rather leisurely, from his defeat on the Betwa.

Rose occupied the now-deserted fort on April 5th. Once again the action had followed the general pattern of the Mutiny campaign: stiff resistance and then a sudden flight by the defenders, followed by the peaceful occupation of a fort. Some 5,000 'rebels' were claimed by the British to have been killed in the battle for Jhansi but it seems obvious that most of these were killed in the town after the British had entered it, and many were innocent women and children. The state of the city was terrible. It must have seemed like some vast charnel-house. One of the inhabitants of Jhansi who managed to escape the massacre described the condition: 'In the squares of the city the sepoys and soldiers collected hundreds of corpses in large heaps and covered them with wood, floor-boards, and anything that came handy and set them on fire. Now every square blazed with burning bodies and the city looked like one vast burning ground. By another order the people were given permission to take care of their dead, and those who could afford to give a ritual cremation took away the bodies of their relatives and friends, but the others were just thrown on the fire. It became difficult to breathe as the air stank with the odour of the burning human flesh and the stench of rotting animals in the streets. The carcases of thousands of bullocks, camels, elephants, horses, dogs, cats, donkeys, buffaloes, and cows were strewn all over the city. These were collected and removed to the outskirts of the city where a huge pit was dug into which they were all pushed and the pit covered with earth.'

British losses were comparatively small, 343 killed and

wounded. If the defenders had chosen to fight it out, Rose would probably have been unable to take the fort for, as he himself wrote in his dispatch, 'It was not till Jhansi was taken that its great strength was known. There was only one part of the fortress, the south curtain, which was considered practicable for breaching. But, when inside, we saw this was a mistake, there being at some distance in rear of the curtain a massive wall fifteen or twenty feet thick, and immediately in rear of this a deep tank cut out of the live rock.' Again it was the rebels' lack of military expertise and of dynamic leadership that gave the British their victory.

6
From Jhansi to Kalpi

AFTER JHANSI, Rose's next objective was to march on the rebel stronghold of Kalpi on the river Jumna. There the rebel forces in the area were now concentrated under the general leadership of the Rao Sahib, the Nana Sahib's nephew and one of the most energetic of the rebel leaders. Kalpi lies 102 miles to the north-east of Jhansi and 46 from Cawnpore to the south-west. The capture of Kalpi would mean that Rose's force could approach the rear line of Colin Campbell's area of operations and clear the way for a march on Gwalior (see map, page 154).

Rose, however, was in no position to leave Jhansi. His men were exhausted after 17 days of continuous action under the full weight of the Indian sun, and it was not until April 25th that he was able to begin his journey to Kalpi.

Leaving a small force at Jhansi, Rose set off with the first brigade, and left the second to follow two days later. On April 22nd Rose had sent a detachment under Major Gall to watch the rebel garrison of Kotah, which was believed to be skirmishing near the Kalpi road. Another detachment was also sent to prevent the Rajas of Banpur and Shahgarh from crossing the Betwa.

In Kalpi, the Rani of Jhansi now pressed the Rao Sahib to reorganize the rebel forces, and some attempt was made to discipline them for the coming battle. The Rani was disliked by the other rebel commanders, possibly for her good sense and certainly for her sex, and Tantia Topi was once again appointed to command the rebels against Rose. The Rani, however, did persuade the other leaders that Rose should be met outside Kalpi and the town of Kunch, 42 miles to the south, was chosen as the place to meet the British. Unfortunately, the Rani's plan of campaign – which showed some awareness of military tactics – was not accepted by Tantia Topi who, as on previous occasions, did not pay enough attention to his flanks. The choice of Kunch gave the rebels a strong series of defences, for the town was difficult to approach, being surrounded with temples, woods, and gardens. The town itself was protected by a strong wall and entrenchments were constructed in front of it.

Major Gall, who had been continually harassed by rebel skirmishers, had reached the town of Putch, 16 miles from Kunch, on May 1st, and on that day he was joined by Rose and the first brigade. Major Orr had found himself unable to cut off the forces of Banpur and Shahgarh, after attacking and dispersing them at Kotah, and most of them had managed to escape. Rose now ordered Orr to march on Kunch. The country between Putch and Kunch, in which there were a number of small forts, was evacuated by the rebels who retired on Kunch itself.

On May 5th Rose was joined by the second brigade and immediately marched to Lohari, only 10 miles from Kunch, and there prepared his plan of attack. Hearing from his spies that Tantia Topi had once again concentrated his troops in the centre in preparation for a frontal attack by the British, Rose decided to turn the rebel flank and get himself into position facing the unfortified side of Kunch. If this succeeded, the movement would also threaten the rebel line of retreat to Kalpi.

In the early hours of May 6th the British broke camp and, after a march of 14 miles, occupied a position two miles from Kunch. The first brigade formed Rose's left, the Hyderabad force his right, and the second brigade the centre. The sun was now high and a rest for a meal was ordered while Rose inspected his men and reconnoitred the town. Major Gall, after a reconnaissance, reported that the rebels had retired from the wood and temples to a position nearer the town and had with them a body of cavalry. The British artillery now began to bombard the rebel positions and drove some of the defenders out of their entrenchments and into the town itself.

Rose now decided to clear the approaches to the wall. This he did with his infantry and penetrated the north sector of the town. This action, which took about an hour, drove the rebels out along the Kalpi road. The second brigade followed in pursuit and the rebels, who had attempted to retire in good order under the protection of their cavalry, broke up into small bands which scattered over the extensive plain that lay between Kunch and Kalpi. The rebel losses were estimated at 600 men killed and 15 guns captured by the British. The casualties in Rose's force amounted to 62 killed and wounded.

The British, however, were again too exhausted to keep up the pursuit for, though their casualties in the actual fighting were small, the numbers struck down by heat exhaustion were considerable. There was no shelter from the sun and the field hospitals were full of men suffering from sunstroke. Rose, quite rightly, believed that he could have achieved a real victory if only he had been able to follow up the pursuit of the fleeing rebels. 'We should have destroyed the enemy', he wrote three days later, 'had not the dreadful heat paralysed the men. Eleven poor fellows were killed outright by the sun and many more were struck down. I was obliged four times to get off my horse by excessive debility. The doctor poured cold water over me, and gave restoratives, which enabled me to go on again. I do not think I shall stay in India to pass such another torment as 110° in the shade.'

The defeat at Kunch aroused considerable recriminations in the rebel headquarters at Kalpi. Everyone blamed someone else, but all were united in their criticism of Tantia Topi, who had fled from Kunch ahead of his men. Divisions were so deep that, when rumours reached Kalpi that Rose was on his way, many rebels left the town and dispersed into the countryside until, according to one report, only 11 soldiers remained in the whole of Kalpi.

The rumours of Rose's movements were not entirely without foundation. Though he was very short of ammunition, water, and forage, he was determined to finish the campaign before the rains began and the river Jumna overflowed its banks. By May 15th he had reached Golowli, six miles from Kalpi on the Jumna. This place was not in fact on the direct route from Kunch to Kalpi, but Rose moved there in order to meet up with a force under Colonel Maxwell which had been sent by Campbell to cooperate with him. Maxwell had reached the left bank of the Jumna opposite Golowli, and there the two forces met. The route taken also meant that the fortifications erected by the rebels to impede Rose along the main road to Kalpi were bypassed.

Rose's march was unopposed by the rebels, but the heat was far more successful than any military operation they might have mounted. 'It was 119° in the shade,' wrote Rose, 'and two hundred men out of less than four hundred of the 25th Native Infantry fell out of the ranks, stricken by the sun.' The sun's effect was even greater on the white troops. The rebels were well aware that the sun was their ally and they were ordered by their leaders not to attack the British before ten o'clock in the morning, as fighting in the sun would kill them off quickly. In spite of the heat, however, Rose was preparing for the attack upon Kalpi.

7

The Victory at Kalpi

THE SITUATION at Kalpi had now changed. The Nawab of Banda, who was a relative of the Rao Sahib and who had been forced to join the rebels, arrived unexpectedly at Kalpi with 2,000 cavalry, some infantry and guns. This sudden reinforcement revived the rebels' spirits and the sepoys began to return to Kalpi from the surrounding districts. The Rao Sahib held a council of war, and it was decided to defend Kalpi to the last man. 'We will win or perish but never will we leave the field', they swore on the sacred waters of the Jumna.

The rebel position at Kalpi was a good one. Though the town itself was without fortifications, it was approached by many miles of country split by deep ravines. In front, and in the direction of Kunch, elaborate defences had been constructed to bar the road. These outworks were made up of trenches and barricades. The rear of the town lay upon the Jumna itself and the fort was sited on a precipitous rock emerging from the river. The rebels believed that the ravines would severely hamper the movement of cavalry and guns. Should the rebels be driven out of their forward entrenchments, they could fall back on a line of temples each surrounded by walls. Behind the temples were more ravines, then the town itself, with more ravines behind and finally the fort, perched on its rock over the Jumna.

These five lines of defence were all very well, if Rose approached from the front, but the British commander had no intention of doing anything so foolish. From May 16th to 20th, the British prepared for the attack under constant fire from rebel patrols as well as the unceasing glare of the sun. The state of Rose's men can be gathered from the report of the chief medical officer. 'In the action before Kunch of the 7th instant, one regiment about 420 strong lost seven men by sunstroke, and on the march to Banda lost five men and admitted 35 into hospital; and whenever it has been exposed it has suffered very severely. Though the rest of the troops have borne exposure better, their losses have been heavy and their admissions into hospital very numerous, from the overwhelming effects of a temperature ranging from 109° to 117° in tents, and seldom falling under 100° at night. But to illustrate better the state of health of all ranks, I may mention that we have now 310 Europeans in hospital, having lost in the week twenty-one by sunstroke; and there is scarcely an officer of the staff fit for duty. The quartermaster-general, clergyman, the adjutant-general, the commissariat officer, the baggage master, the brigade major, and quartermaster-general and brigadier of the second brigade, are all sick. Several of these and many other officers will have to go to Europe, and others will have to go elsewhere for change of climate. Thus paralysed as the force already is, and with the rest enfeebled and worn out by this long and arduous campaign, I cannot refrain from mentioning my apprehensions that should the operations before Kalpi be protracted and the exposure great, the force will be completely prostrated.'

On the 19th, however, a mortar battery was established and opened fire on the town, and two days later batteries were set up on the northern bank of the Jumna by Maxwell and opened fire on the fort and the river side of the town. Rose's plan was that, while Maxwell's batteries bombarded the town, he would clear the ravines and attack the southern face of the fort. The British force occupied the ground between the river and the road from Kalpi to Banda, with its right resting on the ravines near the river and its left nearly touching the road. On May 22nd Rose received information from his spies that the rebels planned an attack in force on either himself or Maxwell. In fact, it was the rebels' intention to mount a false attack against the British left while the real attack was to be made against the right under cover of the ravines.

The rebels marched out at ten o'clock on the morning of the 22nd along the Banda road and engaged the British whilst their artillery opened fire on the centre. This force was led by the Nawab of Banda and the Rao Sahib, and, though intended only as a feint, soon developed into a full-scale engagement. Rose, however, was not taken in, and on the right and centre only replied with heavy artillery fire. That this was the wisest thing he could have done was suddenly proved when the rebels hiding in the ravines disclosed themselves with heavy musketry fire, while their batteries opened up upon the British left. The attack was so unexpected and made with such strength that the British were forced to retire. In fact, the British were weak from the effects of the sun and their rifles, which had been in constant use, were becoming difficult to load because of fouling of the barrels.

The British fell back until they reached their own gun and mortar emplacements. There they were rallied by Brigadier Stuart. The rebels, however, continued to press on and it seemed probable that they would overwhelm the artillery. An eye-witness described the situation at that moment. 'Nearly 400 of my regiment – the 86th – were *hors de combat*. The native regiment – the 25th Bengal Native Infantry – not much better, and thousands of yelling savages were pressing on while we had the river in our rear. We were well-nigh beaten when the Camel Corps came up; and about 150 fresh troops soon turned the tide, and sent the bhang-fortified enemy to the rightabout again. It was the Camel Corps that virtually saved Sir Hugh Rose's division. The enemy were within twenty yards of our battery and outpost tents, the latter full of men down with sunstroke. Another quarter of an hour and there would have been a massacre.'

Rose's counter-attack relieved the pressure on one sector. The rebels were also suffering badly on the left, where the Rao Sahib and his men were driven back as the British guns continued to strafe them. Rose and his men now moved forward and cut the Rao Sahib off from Kalpi. Those who remained in the fort soon found it too hot for them as Maxwell's guns poured shot and shell into it from the north bank of the river. Night had now fallen and Rose decided to break off action until the following day. His troops needed a rest from the sun and the enemy's attacks had almost shattered them. 'Most of the officers were sick', wrote Dr Lowe. 'But', he adds, 'in the cool of the evening we were speculating on the capture of Kalpi on the morrow.'

Before dawn the following morning, Brigadier Stuart, commanding the first brigade, led his men through the ravines and along the course of the Jumna towards the fort. The second brigade, with Rose at its head, made its way along the Banda road. Maxwell's artillery continued to bombard the fort and the buildings in front of it. From the latter there was no opposition, for the rebels had fled during the night.

When the British entered the fort they found it had been converted by the rebels into an ordnance factory and arsenal. 'The enemy had erected houses and tents in the fort, had their smiths' shops, their carpenters' shops. Their foundries for casting shot and shell were in perfect order, clean and well constructed; the specimens of brass shell cast by them were faultless . . . In the arsenal were about 60,000 pounds of gunpowder, outside it were large heaps of shot and shell ranged after the fashion of our own . . . It would appear . . . that the enemy had prepared for a long stand here.' And another eye-witness records that in the arsenal 'the uniforms were knee-deep, comprising not only sepoy clothes but coats that had been taken from Windham's slain, belonging to HM's 88th Regiment, some bearing the number 92, with the Prince of Wales' plume; also one or two ladies' bonnets, together with brass band instruments, parts of cornopeans, French horns, trumpets, and infantry bugles, military drums, flags, standards, glengarries, stocks, caps, pouches, belts, and boxes of musket cartridges.'

As it was May 24th and Queen Victoria's 39th birthday, the Union Jack was ceremonially raised over the fort and marked, so Rose believed, the end of the campaign. There is no doubt that he hoped it was, for he was prostrated with the effects of the heat and was hoping to go to England on sick-leave. After the fall of Kalpi, Sir Colin Campbell decided that the Central India Force should be broken up and distributed, and Rose issued a parting proclamation to his men, but before he could leave for Bombay on his way to England a totally unexpected development was to change the situation in Central India. The news, when it came, was almost as sensational, and what had happened was certainly as potentially dangerous, as the first outbreak of the Mutiny at Meerut.

8
The Rebels at Gwalior

AFTER THEIR defeat at Kalpi the rebel leaders held a council at which delegates of the sepoys were also present. The situation that faced them was hardly an appealing one. The rebels had lost, at Kalpi, their last stronghold south of the Jumna river, and a new field had to be found for their operations against the British. The sepoys wanted to join their comrades in Oudh, the Rani of Jhansi wanted a base somewhere in Bundelkhand, the Rao Sahib preferred the Deccan, once the heartland of the Maratha empire which he was fighting to revive. Then it was suggested, either by the Rani or Tantia Topi, that they should take the fort at Gwalior. Tantia Topi, it is believed, had visited Gwalior after his defeat at Kunch and had come to the conclusion that the Maharaja Sindhia's troops could be persuaded to revolt. The Maharaja had in fact begun to purge his army of certain officers and men whom he thought unreliable and naturally the rest of his army began to feel uneasy. Sindhia, as we have seen, had thrown in his lot with the British mainly because he felt they were too strong for him, and as he was a foreigner in his own state – he was a Maratha and the majority of subjects were Jats, Bundelas, and Rajputs – he felt that friendship with the British was his only prop against rebellion. His 'loyalty' to the British had, however, alienated his principal officers and nobles, and there was considerable sympathy amongst the majority of them for the rebel cause.

The attempt to win over Gwalior, and if possible the Maharaja, was left to Tantia Topi. If he succeeded in the first, it would mean that the rebels would have an important base with an exceptionally strong fort and, what was of more immediate importance, funds and supplies. If Tantia also succeeded in winning over the Maharaja it would be a serious blow to British prestige, and other seemingly 'loyal' princes might throw in their lot with the rebels. Tantia Topi's mission was completely successful with Sindhia's army and his principal nobles, and he received solemn promises that, if the rebels marched on Gwalior, they would meet with no resistance. The Maharaja, on the other hand, would not listen to Tantia Topi's overtures, for he believed that if he could hold out long enough, the British would come to his aid. The Maharaja had also been told that the rebel army was without supplies and in a demoralized state.

On May 30th news came to the Maharaja that Tantia Topi, the Rani of Jhansi, and the Rao Sahib, with 7,000 infantry, 4,000 cavalry, and 12 guns had reached Morar, a town not far from Gwalior. Believing reports that the rebels were not in a fit condition to fight, the Maharaja marched out on June 1st to attack them and took up a position two miles to the east of Morar. His army consisted of 1,500 cavalry, his personal bodyguard of 600 men, and eight guns. Dividing these into three bodies, with his guns in the centre, he waited for the rebels to attack. They obliged him at about seven o'clock in the morning.

The rebel advance guard consisted of cavalry and camels. The Maharaja's guns opened fire on them, but as the smoke cleared away, 2,000 rebel horsemen charged and took the guns. At this, most of Sindhia's troops, except his bodyguard, went over to the rebels, and after a bitter struggle the Maharaja and his men fled and did not stop until they reached Agra.

The rebels now moved rapidly on Gwalior itself and occupied the town and fort without opposition. No looting was permitted and most of the officials who had remained behind were confirmed in their appointments. But the Rao Sahib did plunder the Maharaja's treasury, the contents of which were used to pay his own and Sindhia's troops. The rebels' next step was to set up a government, proclaiming the Nana Sahib as the Peshwa (or chief) of the revived Maratha dominion, with the Rao Sahib as his governor of Gwalior. Celebrations were held to commemorate the capture of the town and letters were despatched to the rulers of adjoining states asking them to come to Gwalior. There is no doubt that the Rao Sahib expected the princes of the Deccan to rise in rebellion against the British. The Rani of Jhansi, however, was rather less sanguine. She knew from her experience at Jhansi that Rose would probably march immediately upon Gwalior, and she tried to persuade the rebel leaders to make preparations for the coming British attack. They appeared to be more interested in letting off fireworks and posturing about the Maratha revival. If the Rao Sahib, instead of staying at Gwalior, had pushed on to the Deccan, he probably could have raised the princes there, but for some reason he chose to stay where he was. Nor were any real preparations made for the defence of Gwalior. It was a fatal mistake, for Rose – with his characteristic dash – was already on the move.

9

The Campaign for Gwalior

BACK AT Kalpi, Rose had not been idle while awaiting his departure on sick-leave. The pursuit of the rebels had not stopped despite the fact that the rainy season was starting. A column under Colonel Robertson had pushed on to a point 55 miles from Gwalior when he learned of the attack on that town by the rebels. Robertson immediately sent a messenger to Kalpi with the news, and it reached Rose on June 1st. Rose then despatched Brigadier Stuart and what was left of his original brigade to join Robertson and march on Gwalior. Rose certainly did not expect to hear that Gwalior had fallen to the rebels. His original belief was that Sindhia would hold out and that, on Stuart's arrival, the rebels would be caught in a trap.

Rose received the news that Gwalior had fallen on June 4th, in a dispatch from Stuart. The choice that faced him was either to wait for his replacement from Bombay or to reassume command of the Central India Field Force. To Rose the situation was clear. The rains were coming, rivers would burst their banks, and the countryside become a sea of mud in which guns could not be moved. Delay was out of the question, for to wait until after the rains would not only damage British prestige but give the rebels ample time to recruit more princes and men to their banner. Rose telegraphed the governor-general and offered his services once again. His offer was gratefully accepted and he resumed command.

Leaving a small garrison behind in Kalpi, Rose and a small force made up of one troop of Bombay Horse Artillery, one squadron each of the 14th Light Dragoons and the 3rd Bombay Light Cavalry, with sappers and miners, set out on June 5th to join up with Stuart's brigade. Colin Campbell, when informed of the fall of Gwalior, had ordered a column under Colonel Riddell, then moving across the country north of the Jumna, to join Rose. A brigade of the Rajputana Field

Force under Brigadier Smith was also ordered to make for Gwalior. The Hyderabad Contingent, which had been sent home from Kalpi, volunteered to return – and did so.

Rose now made his dispositions. Major Orr, commanding the Hyderabad troops, was ordered to make for Paniar on the road between Sipri and Gwalior, in order to block any retreat to the south. Smith's column was sent to Kotah-ke-serai, five miles south-east of Gwalior. Riddell, who was escorting a large number of siege-guns, was told to move up the Agra–Gwalior road and await further orders. All troops were to be in their positions by June 19th.

Despite the terrible heat, Rose overtook Stuart on June 12th and together they reached a point five miles east of Morar by the 16th. There Rose was joined by his successor, General Napier, who had waived his right to take over the command in order to serve under Rose. Napier at once assumed command of the second brigade. At six o'clock on the morning of the 16th, a cavalry reconnaissance revealed a strong rebel force at Morar. 'My force', wrote Rose in a later dispatch, 'had had a long and fatiguing march, and the sun had been up for some time. Four or five miles more march in the sun, and a combat afterwards would be a great trial for the men's strength. On the other hand, Morar looked inviting with several good buildings not yet burnt; they would be good quarters for a portion of the force; if I delayed the attack until the next day, the enemy were sure to burn them. A prompt attack has always more effect on the rebels than a procrastinated one. I therefore countermanded the order for encamping and made ... arrangements to attack the enemy.'

The rebels had occupied the area fronting the British with strong bodies of cavalry supported by infantry and, to the right, by artillery. Rose, placing his cavalry and guns on the flanks, marched his infantry in such a direction as to turn the enemy's almost unprotected left. But a guide sent by Sindhia to help Rose, for he was completely without maps or knowledge of the countryside, lost his way and Rose found himself under fire from a concealed battery. Bringing up his own guns,

Rose pushed his infantry forward and forced the rebel gunners to retire. Meanwhile the Hyderabad cavalry endeavoured to cut off the rebels by pushing through the cantonments behind them, but the ground they had to cross was pitted with ravines, which held them up long enough for the rebels to fall back on new positions. The action now developed into a hand-to-hand struggle and the British, particularly the 71st Highlanders, suffered severely, but at length the rebels were put to flight and strongly pursued by the Light Dragoons.

Rose's success was followed by another gained by the column under Brigadier Smith. Passing through Jhansi, he reached the town of Antri and was joined there by Major Orr and the Hyderabad Contingent on June 14th. Together they marched to Kotah-ke-serai and arrived there at 7.30 in the morning of the 17th. Smith had encountered no rebel opposition on his way, but on reaching Kotah-ke-serai he found a mass of enemy cavalry and infantry occupying hilly ground between there and Gwalior. Though Smith was encumbered by a large baggage train, he decided to attack the rebels before they attacked him. A reconnaissance of the ground in front of him showed it to be intersected with small ravines making it impracticable to use cavalry. It was also discovered that enemy batteries were sited across the road to Gwalior within 1,500 yards of Kotah-ke-serai. Smith, however, determined to attack. He first sent his horse artillery forward and their fire forced the rebels to limber up their guns and retire. This was followed by an infantry charge which drove the rebels back to their entrenchments. The infantry found itself held up by a deep ditch with about four feet of water in it. Steep banks made it impossible to cross in any strength and the rebels had taken advantage of the delay to move their guns across the hills. The British infantry, after finally crossing the ditch, re-formed and pressed on. In the meanwhile Smith had moved his cavalry across a river close to Kotah-ke-serai and had come under fire from a previously unobserved battery. At the same time a body of the enemy threatened the baggage train left behind in the village. Smith, sending detachments to defend the baggage and his rear, moved on in the direction of Gwalior. As he was marching through a defile, he was heavily attacked but managed to fight his way through. Emerging from the defile, and observing the rebels in front of him, Smith ordered a squadron of the 8th Hussars to charge them. The Hussars drove the rebels towards Gwalior. In the flight, the Rani of Jhansi – who commanded the rebel troops – is believed to have been killed, though there are many conflicting stories about the place and manner of her death.

The charge of the Hussars was Smith's last effort. 'Upon the return of the squadron, the officers and men were so completely exhausted and prostrated from heat, fatigue, and great exertion, that they could scarcely sit in their saddles, and were, for the moment, incapable of further exertion.' But the rebels were still threatening and Smith decided to hold the defile until the following morning. He recalled his cavalry from the pursuit, brought up his baggage, put out piquets, and camped for the night. Smith's position was not particularly secure, and, on his request, Rose sent him reinforcements.

Next day more troops arrived from Kalpi, and Rose could make preparations for the main attack upon Gwalior. Leaving Napier at Morar, with such troops as he thought could be spared, and with orders to pursue the enemy if they retreated that way from Gwalior, Rose marched off in the afternoon of June 18th. The march was made in great heat and over 100 men of the 86th were compelled to fall out with sunstroke. Rose pushed on and bivouacked for the night between the river and the position held by Brigadier Smith.

Next morning Rose observed a rebel force estimated at about 10,000 men with cavalry and two 18-pounder guns manœuvring for position. Rose believed that his best plan was to attempt to cut this force off from Gwalior. It seemed that the rebels, who were separated from Brigadier Smith's position by a canal, were making preparations to attack him. Rose therefore ordered Brigadier Stuart, with the 86th and the 25th Bengal Native Infantry, to cross the canal and attack the rebels' left flank while the 95th regiment, under Colonel

Raines, would create a diversion by crossing the canal and attacking a hill on which was placed a rebel battery.

The 86th successfully hit the rebel left and took the guns threatening the defile. They then pushed on towards the town. Raines was also successful and cleared the heights of rebel artillery. Within a short time, the British controlled the hills overlooking Gwalior. 'The sight', wrote Rose, 'was interesting. To our right was the handsome palace of the Phulbagh with its gardens, and the old city, surmounted by the fort, remarkable for its ancient architecture, with lines of extensive fortifications round the high and precipitous rock of Gwalior. To our left lay the Lashkar, or new city, with its spacious houses half hidden by trees.' In the plain between the hills and the city, the rebel forces could be seen converging without discipline and without their weapons. Seeing this disorganized flight, Rose was convinced that he could take the city 'before sunset'.

Covering his extreme right with a troop of horse artillery and a detachment of Hussars, Rose ordered the Bombay Lancers to leave the heights and move upon the city from the south. He himself, covered by artillery and the dragoons, moved his British infantry forward. As they reached the plain, the lancers appeared and charged the retreating rebels, driving them into the new town. Before long, the British had occupied the new town and Rose was sitting in the palace of the Maharaja. Brigadier Smith, who had also moved forward, had taken the Phulbagh and cleared the rebels from the gardens surrounding it, capturing most of their guns.

That night, most of the rebels fled the city. The Rani of Jhansi was dead, 'the bravest and best military leader of the rebels', as Rose described her when he heard of her death. The Rao Sahib and Tantia Topi had gone, the former on a journey that was to end in his taking up the life of an ascetic in the forests of the Punjab before being betrayed to the British four years later. Of Tantia Topi much more was to be heard.

Though Rose had driven the rebels from the town of Gwalior, the fort still remained in their hands. Its aspect was most formidable. The fort was built upon a rock one and a half miles in length by about 300 yards wide, rising 340 feet above the plain. The sides of the rock were rugged and in some places perpendicular. The only direct approach was on the north-east side of a steep road and then steps. The outer edge of the staircase was protected by a thick wall and there were seven gateways along the road which could be commanded by artillery placed at the top. Inside the main ramparts stood a palace of massive masonry surmounted by six towers. Within the fort there was a plentiful supply of water. Guns on the ramparts had in fact maintained continuous fire on the British during the operations of June 19th. The next day they were still firing, though practically all the garrison had departed.

In the morning of June 20th Lieutenant Rose of the 25th Bombay Native Infantry was in command of a detachment at a police station not far from the main gateway of the fort. He proposed to a brother officer, Lieutenant Waller, who commanded a small party of the same regiment, 'that they should attempt to capture the fortress with their joint parties, urging that if the risk was great, the honour would be still greater. Waller cheerfully assented and the two officers set off with their men and a blacksmith ... They crept up to the first gateway unseen. Then the blacksmith, a powerful man, forced it open; and so with the other five gates that opposed their progress. By the time the sixth gate had been forced, the alarm was given, and when the assailants reached the archway behind the last gate, they were met by the fire of a gun which had been brought to bear on them. Dashing onwards, unscathed by the fire, they were speedily engaged in a hand-to-hand contest with the garrison. The fight was desperate, and many men fell on both sides. The gallantry of Rose and Waller and their men carried all before them. Rose especially distinguished himself. Just in the hour of victory, however, as he was inciting his men to make the final charge, which proved successful, a musket was fired at him from behind the wall. The man who had fired the shot ... then rushed out and cut him across the knee and wrist with a sword. Waller came up, and despatched the rebel;

too late, however, to save his friend. But the rock fortress was gained'.

While Sir Hugh Rose was occupying Gwalior, Napier – left behind at Morar in order to cut off the rebel retreat – moved off early in the morning of the 20th with his force of 560 cavalry and a battery of horse artillery to intercept and destroy the enemy. He caught up with about 4,000 rebels holding a strong position at Jawra Alipur on June 22nd. Though a reconnaissance showed their strength, Napier resolved to attack. Under rebel artillery fire, the cavalry charged accompanied by the horse artillery. 'You cannot imagine', wrote an eye-witness, 'the dash of the artillery: it was wonderful. We [the cavalry] could scarcely keep up with them.' After a brief resistance, the rebels broke and fled, hotly pursued. They lost 25 guns, all their ammunition, elephants, tents, carts, and baggage, and left behind them 300 or 400 dead.

With the defeat at Jawra and the capture of Gwalior, the main Central Indian campaign was at an end. Once again, Rose relinquished his command to General Napier, and the men of the Central India Field Force were distributed to new stations. With the death of the Rani of Jhansi and the flight of Tantia Topi and the Rao Sahib into the jungle, the men of the force could now look forward to a well-earned rest. But this was not to be. For yet again, Tantia Topi had run away only to return. A few weeks after the last little stand at Jawra Alipur, the villages and jungles of Central India were once again ringing with the name and the exploits of the rebel leader.

10

The Pursuit of Tantia Topi

WHEN TANTIA TOPI fled from Jawra Alipur with the Rao Sahib and the Nawab of Banda, a detachment of British troops was sent to Bharatpur to cut him off from the north. When the rebel leaders heard of this they moved westward in the hope of reaching Jaipur (see map, page 154) where Tantia believed he would be welcome. The disposition of British forces in the area made by Napier after Rose's departure was as follows: a fairly strong body of horse, infantry, and artillery at Gwalior; a similar body at Jhansi; Brigadier Smith's brigade at Sipri; and a force of irregular cavalry at Gunah. The commander of the Rajputana Field Force, General Roberts, from whose force Smith's brigade had been detached, took up quarters at Nasirabad. It was Roberts who was to have the first brush with Tantia.

On June 27th Roberts was informed that Tantia Topi had sent a letter to Jaipur assuring the disaffected nobles there that he was marching towards them and that they should be in readiness to join him. The next day Roberts marched on Jaipur and arrived there before Tantia. The rebel leader, hearing of this, turned southwards and attacked Tonk, where the ruler's army went over to him. By this time he was being pursued by a flying column under Colonel Holmes.

The rain was now falling heavily and the river Chambal was so swollen that Tantia could not cross it and was forced to make for Bundi, where the ruler closed the gates of the town in his face. Tantia, under the impression that the pursuit was close behind, decided not to waste time besieging Bundi. Publicly announcing that he proposed to move south, Tantia in fact moved to the west and made for the country between Nasirabad and Nimach, where the embers of rebellion still glowed. The pursuit, however, was bogged down by the rain and it was not until August 5th that Roberts was able to march on Nimach. Two days later he received news that Tantia was at Sanganir, some 10 miles away. Actually, Tantia's position was midway between Sanganir and Bhilwara, which were separated from each other by a little river. Roberts, knowing that Holmes was coming up behind Tantia's position, decided to attack though he himself was without cavalry.

The rebel position was well sited, but Roberts drove forward, crossed the river, and brought his artillery to bear on the rebels' position. During the night, however, Tantia fled. Unfortunately, Holmes was not near enough for immediate pursuit, and Tantia was able to retire to the village of Kotra in Udaipur. The next day Holmes joined Roberts and the combined force moved after Tantia. The same day they made contact with the rebel advance guard, and from prisoners taken Roberts learned that the main rebel force occupied a position on the Banas river, seven miles away. Roberts's intelligence was unusually efficient, for the British had suffered badly from the lack of reliable information throughout the campaign. His method of obtaining information 'was to have about twenty cavalry in advance close to the rebels. They left connecting links of two or three men every few miles, so as to keep up the chain of communication. The advance party was composed half of Baluch Horse, who had no sympathy with the rebels but could not communicate very well with the villagers, and half of horsemen belonging to the Raja of Jaipur, who were supposed, as Rajputs, to be on good terms and able easily to communicate with the villagers, but not to be very warm partisans of the British. By this mixed party, correct and immediate intelligence was constantly supplied.'

Roberts learned that Tantia had been forced to remain where he was as his troops refused to move because they needed rest. Again, Tantia's position was naturally strong. The river ran in front of him and also protected his right with a bend. To his left lay steep hills. On the opposite bank of the river a flat plain 800 yards wide offered no cover to his attackers. When Roberts arrived, the rebels' four guns opened up but, despite casualties, the infantry forded the river and scaled the hill while the cavalry attacked the centre. The charge broke the rebel line and the cavalry pursued for nearly 15 miles, cutting down stragglers and capturing three elephants and a quantity of baggage. The pursuit was abandoned when the rebels reached the jungle where cavalry could not operate.

Tantia now made for the river Chambal, followed by Roberts who, when he reached Punah near Chitor, met up with a brigade under Brigadier Parke who had come up from Nimach in order to cut off the rebels from the south. Roberts handed over the pursuit to Parke. Unfortunately, Parke's cavalry horses were not in good shape and he was compelled to return to Nimach for remounts. There he was told by some self-styled experts that Tantia would not be able to cross the Chambal as it was swollen by the rains. Parke chose to believe them rather than the political agent in Udaipur who assured him that Tantia would undoubtedly cross the river. When Parke actually received information that Tantia was indeed making the crossing, he arrived too late and found only 'a few disabled ponies standing on the left bank and the rebels disappearing among some mango trees in the west horizon'. Parke then returned to Nimach.

Tantia, still moving rapidly, now arrived at the town of Jhalrapatan in Jhalwar state. Here the state troops welcomed him and the Raja was forced to pay a large ransom before he was able to contrive his escape. Tantia also obtained 30 guns with ammunition horses which he badly needed, having had to abandon his artillery at the Banas river engagement. The rebels remained five days in Jhalwar, as the Chambal had risen and blocked pursuit. Jhalwar is only 50 miles from Indore and Tantia conceived the plan of making for that town and raising the rebellion there once again. However, the British had not been idle, and General Michel, commanding in Malwa, sent a force to cover Indore from a position at the town of Ujjain. At the same time a small force moved out from Mhow.

Michel himself, who had now also assumed General Roberts's command, joined the two forces at Nalkera where he received reports that Tantia was moving in a north-easterly direction. Though it was now September, heavy rain was still falling and movement was difficult. Michel, however, pushed on until he met up with the rebels near Rajgahr. Michel's men were extremely fatigued, night was coming down, and it was decided that the attack could wait until the morning. But when the next day dawned Tantia and his men were nowhere to be seen, and all that remained were the tracks of his elephants and the wheelmarks of his artillery.

Michel at once sent his cavalry in pursuit and discovered the main rebel force deployed for battle. By the time the infantry and guns had caught up with the cavalry, the rebels were already in flight. In their haste to depart they abandoned 27 guns. Tantia now disappeared into jungle country on the way to Sironj. The British began to close in. Brigadier Parke controlled the approaches to Indore and Bhopal; Smith's brigade was moving down from the north; and the column from Jhansi under Colonel Liddell was closing in from the north-east. Michel himself continued to move in from the west.

While General Michel was making his preparations and Tantia Topi was moving silently through the jungles near the river Betwa, Napier – operating out of Gwalior – had also been active. Gwalior state, though reoccupied, was not pacified and the countryside was still disturbed. In August a tributary of the Maharaja of Gwalior, named Man Singh, quarrelled with his overlord and raising an army of 12,000 followers attacked the fort of Paori, 83 miles from Gwalior along the road to Sipri. Napier ordered Smith, then still at Sipri, to march on Paori. When Smith neared the town, Man Singh sent a messenger with a letter asking for an interview and claiming that he was not in rebellion against the British but only against the Maharaja who had, he said, robbed him of his ancestral right to the little state of Narwar. Man Singh, in fact, told the truth when he claimed, 'I have no connexion with the rebels and no quarrel with the English.' Unfortunately, in such circumstances, when rebellion was rebellion, however justified the cause, the British commander informed Man Singh that he must surrender and be punished for breaking the peace.

Paori was well fortified and amply supplied with ammunition. Smith's force was too small to attempt a successful siege. He therefore sat down outside and waited for reinforcements. Napier, deciding that Man Singh was showing no inclination to surrender, gave the order that he must be attacked before others followed his example and he sent Smith the reinforcements he required. After a 24-hour artillery bombardment, Man Singh and his men quitted the fort on the night of August 23rd, leaving the British to occupy – and destroy – the fort next day. Man Singh was pursued and some of his men under his uncle Ajit Singh were caught up with and dispersed near Gunah, but Man Singh himself had disappeared.

Meanwhile, Tantia Topi had reached Sironj about the middle of September. After a few days' rest, he took and plundered a town south of Sipri and there decided upon his future plans. The result led to a decision to divide the rebel force. Tantia, with the bulk of the men and five guns, was to make for Chanderi in Bundelkhand while the Rao Sahib, who was still with him, was to take six guns and fewer men in the direction of Jhansi.

At Chanderi, Tantia found himself unable to take the fort which was held by one of Sindhia's men, and after three days of wasted effort he moved off towards the west bank of the Betwa. But Michel was close behind and caught up with him at Mangrauli on October 10th. There Tantia stood his ground and, after a short engagement, abandoned his guns and fled. Michel did not pursue him because, once again, he was without cavalry. Tantia, always a little ahead of his pursuers, stopping now and again to fight them, seemingly defeated only to appear somewhere else, finally at the end of October joined up once again with Rao Sahib, crossed the Narbada river and entered Nagpur, a former Maratha state where he expected to be joyously and actively received. A year earlier he probably would have been, and might well have been able to spread rebellion south into the territory of the Nizam of Hyderabad. Now it was too late, the British were winning and no one was prepared to join a dying rebellion. British forces were also in a position to bar a further move southwards. The rebels did receive some reinforcement at Kurgaon and, despite every effort by the British, recrossed the Narbada and made for Baroda, another Maratha state where there was considerable sympathy for the rebels. However, he was not destined to reach there for he was overtaken by Parke at Chota Udaipur, 50 miles from Baroda, and once again defeated.

From Chota Udaipur, Tantia and the Rao Sahib entered the little Rajput state Banswara and then made for Pratabgarh, where, on December 25th, he had a brush with a small British force. From there Tantia Topi moved to Mandisur and then to Zirapur, almost due south of Gwalior. But, despite his rapid movement, the British were closing in, and the rebels marched to Nahergarh where they joined up with Man Singh. Another rebel leader now reappears on the scene. Firuz Shah, after Campbell's campaign in Rohilkhand, had crossed the Ganges and made for Kunch and Kalpi. Napier moved to intercept him and did so at Ranod, a large town 50 miles north-east of Gunah. There Napier inflicted a severe defeat and Firuz, with the remainder of his force, moved away to meet up with Tantia Topi at Indargarh.

It now seemed that the rebels, whose combined force numbered scarcely 2,000 men, were caught in a trap from which it was impossible for them to escape. But escape they did, though a British force caught up with them at Daosa, between Jaipur and Bharatpur, on January 14th, 1859. And though the rebels lost a tenth of their men, the remainder with their leader managed to get away. They rested for a day or so at Sikar in Jaipur state, but the column under Colonel Holmes caught them by surprise on January 21st, and routed them – though, as usual, the leaders escaped.

After their defeat at Sikar, the three rebel leaders decided to separate and so make it easier to evade their pursuers. Tantia, with three horses and a pony, left the others for the jungles of Paron and there met Man Singh who, according to Tantia's own deposition, asked, '"Why did you leave your force? You have not acted right in so doing." I replied that I was tired of

THE PURSUIT OF TANTIA TOPI

running away and that I would remain with him whether I had done right or wrong.' The other two, avoiding all attempts to cut them off, found a safe hideout in the Sironj jungles.

The British, with four columns, were sweeping the jungle and did in fact find the rebel camp. The Rao Sahib and Firuz Shah, however, had vanished. But the rebels were no longer confident and negotiations were opened for terms of surrender. The Nawab of Banda had already taken advantage of the amnesty offered by the British in November 1858 (see page 202), and had been rewarded with a pension. On February 19th, 1859, two men had been arrested near Nimach who claimed to be envoys of the rebel leaders. They were told that the amnesty offer was still open. Negotiations through third parties continued and a final offer was made to the Rao Sahib. 'If Rao Sahib surrenders, his life will be pardoned. He will not be put into irons or imprisoned – nor suffer any indignity – a provision will be made for his maintenance. He will have to reside in such part of India as the Govt. will fix for him. These promises are made to him provided he has not with his hand or tongue incited or caused the murder of British subjects.' The Rao Sahib did not accept these terms. Firuz Shah, as befitted a Mughal prince, wanted something better and his letters to the British were written in rather offensive terms, for he still used royal styles and titles.

In April 1859, Tantia Topi was betrayed by Man Singh and the rebel leader was captured on the 8th of that month with the help of Man Singh himself, who persuaded Tantia Topi to meet him. When captured, Tantia Topi was alone, for his two remaining followers had deserted him. In his possession were a sword and a knife, three gold armlets, and 118 gold coins. On April 15th he was court martialled for 'having been in rebellion and having waged war against the British government', found guilty and hanged. The Rao Sahib was also betrayed, but not until 1862. He too was hanged. Firuz Shah escaped and died, penniless, in Mecca in December 1877.

With the capture of Tantia Topi, the last embers of the dying rebellion flickered out – the Mutiny was over.

Epilogue:
AFTER THE MUTINY

1
The Queen's Peace

As THE campaign to suppress the Mutiny progressed, other just as violent events were taking place in the field of politics. Back in Britain, it was decided that the East India Company could no longer be allowed to rule over India. The Company was, of course, an anachronism – a trading organization that virtually no longer traded, ruling a vast empire with all the advantages of patronage in its hands. Though the Company's government was strictly supervised and the governor-general appointed by the British government, the Company's responsibilities were still real. Many of its privileges had however been whittled away over the years by parliament, and the Mutiny offered a perfect excuse for those who wished to get rid of them and the Company altogether. On August 2nd, 1858, while the whole future of the British in India was still questionable, Queen Victoria signed the Act by which the government of India was assumed by the British Crown. The proclamation, which was not made until November 1st, among its numerous clauses, contained an amnesty for all who had been in rebellion against the Company 'except those who have been or shall be convicted of having directly taken part in the murder of British subjects. With regard to such, the demands of justice forbid the exercise of mercy.' Another clause guaranteed that the leaders or instigators of revolt would have their lives spared but would not escape punishment. The amnesty was only extended until January 1st, 1859.

Most of the rebels still fighting at the time of the proclamation took advantage of the offer of amnesty. But there were others besides Tantia Topi, the Rao Sahib, and Firuz Shah who would not surrender. The Nana Sahib, who would certainly have been hanged if he had been caught, did attempt to negotiate with the British in April 1859, but he would not surrender without satisfactory guarantees which were not forthcoming, and he disappears from history – for where and when he died are unknown. The old king of Delhi, Bahadur Shah, was brought to trial in Delhi on January 27th, 1858, and after a hearing lasting 40 days – in which a great deal of dubious evidence was displayed – was exiled to Lower Burma. His name once again became a symbol of revolt when, in 1944, the Japanese-sponsored Indian National Army paraded before the tomb of the last Mughal emperor in Rangoon before preparing to invade British India. The Rani of Jhansi, too, was not forgotten, for a women's brigade in the INA was named after her.

Lord Canning, the last governor-general for the East India Company and first viceroy of the Queen, officially announced the end of the Mutiny in July 1859. 'War is at an end; Rebellion is put down; the Noise of Arms is no longer heard where the enemies of the State have persisted in their last Struggle; the Presence of large Forces in the Field has ceased to be necessary; Order is re-established; and peaceful Pursuits have everywhere been resumed.'

It was now a time for reconciliation and for reconstruction. The princes who, in the main, had sided with the British or who had at least been neutral, were no longer threatened with annexation. Over the years that followed the Mutiny, every attempt was made to show the princes that their true interests lay with the British, and everything was done to give them a position, albeit one empty of real power, in the new Empire of India. Recognizing that one of the causes of the Mutiny was the fear that the British intended to make all Indians Christians, Queen Victoria's proclamation categorically stated that, though 'firmly relying ourselves upon the truth of Christianity and acknowledging with gratitude the solace of religion, we disclaim alike the right and the desire to impose our convictions on any other subjects . . . and we do strictly charge and enjoin all those who may be in authority under us that they abstain from all interference with the religious belief or worship of any of our subjects, on pain of our highest displeasure.'

Only one of the rebel leaders replied to the Queen's proclamation. The Begum Hazrat Mahal of Oudh, refusing the offer of a pardon and pension, stayed in Nepal to which she had escaped and from there issued her reply. The Begum's 'proclamation' is an unusual document. It dissected Queen Victoria's text, paragraph by paragraph, and in its rather prolix way it enshrines the fears and misunderstandings that led to the sepoy revolt. Her criticism of the clause guaranteeing freedom of religious worship is worth quoting, for behind its words lies the truth of the tragedy of 1857. 'In the proclamation it is written that the Christian religion is true, but no other creed will suffer oppression, and that the laws will be observed towards all. What has the administration of justice to do with the truth or falsehood of a religion? That religion is true which acknowledges one God and knows no other. Where there are three gods in a religion, neither Mussulmans nor Hindus – nay, not even Jews, sun-worshippers or fire-worshippers – can believe it to be true. To eat pigs and drink wine, to bite greased cartridges, and to mix pig's fat with flour and sweetmeats, to destroy Hindu and Mussulman temples on pretence of making roads, to build churches, to send clergymen into the streets and alleys to preach the Christian religion, to institute English schools, and pay people a monthly stipend for learning the English sciences, while the places of worship of Hindu and Mussulman are to this day entirely neglected, with all this how can the people believe that religion will not be interfered with? The rebellion began with religion, and for it millions of men have been killed. Let not our subjects be deceived; thousands were deprived of their religion in the north-west and thousands were hanged rather than abandon their religion.'

But the rebellion was dead. The Queen's Peace now lay over India. The next rebellion was to come from neither the soldiers nor the princes, but from the middle classes who, in 1857, supported the British, and though their revolt took longer it was they who 90 years after the Mutiny were to be successful in making Britain give up her Indian empire.

2

The Reform of the Army

THE SUPPRESSION of the rebellion and the assumption of power by the Crown raised the problem of what was to happen to the old Bengal Army, the mutiny in which had formed so large a part of the uprising. In 1857 the Company's armed forces had been almost entirely Indian, 10 regiments of cavalry, 74 of foot, a large force of artillery, and 18 regiments of irregular horse. Of the 74 infantry regiments, 45 had mutinied and all except five of the remainder had been disbanded or disarmed in case they were going to mutiny too. Against this mass of native troops were set three European regiments. In addition to these there were various units of Queen's troops, but there was no fixed number detailed for service in India.

Late in 1857, while the East India Company still ruled, it had been suggested to the governor-general by the directors in London that a mixed commission of Queen's and Company's officers and civil servants should be set up to consider the future of the Bengal Army. Canning's reply was that he could not spare officers for the commission, but instead he appointed a soldier to make an inquiry. The person selected, Sir Henry Durand, began his researches in May 1858. In England, with the decision to transfer power to the Crown, a royal commission had been established and it presented its report in March 1859. Two issues were of outstanding importance: what should be the proportion of white to native troops, and how were the white troops to be recruited?

The governor-general had sent his own proposals to London with Sir Henry. Canning envisaged an army of 45 white regiments for Bengal, 15 coming from England and 30 raised for service in India only, 20 regular native regiments, and 30 irregular (ie, with a smaller number of white officers). The cavalry units he wished made up of 3 Queen's regiments and 10 locally raised. For the separate armies of Bombay and Madras he suggested 12 and 15 white regiments respectively.

New recruiting for the native regiments, Canning proposed, should be for larger numbers of Hindus, as the army had now a preponderance of Sikhs.

When the Queen's proclamation was made in November 1858, it produced an unexpected reaction from the white troops of the Company's army, who now found themselves soldiers of the Queen, without having been asked whether they wanted to be or not. Their not unreasonable request for the right to claim their discharge or a bounty on re-enlistment in the Queen's forces was refused by the home government. The result was considerable unrest amongst white troops and, on May 2nd, 1859, there were reports from Meerut – a name with a sinister ring to it – of mutinous behaviour. At Allahabad the general commanding the station even requested permission to disarm European troops. But it was not granted. All through the summer of 1859 there were outbursts of disorder throughout the military stations of northern India, and courts of enquiry were set up. They revealed that discontent was widespread and it was finally decided, after a change of government in Britain, that NCOs and men would be allowed to take their discharge if they wished and be given free transport back to England. Re-enlistment, however, would not be permitted and anyone who took his discharge would not be allowed to re-enlist into any regiment in India.

As this was being announced to the troops, news came that the men of the 5th European Regiment stationed at Berhampur had 'refused to do any duty and are in a state of mutiny'. A force of 500 white troops with two guns was sent to remind the them of their oath of allegiance.

The affair at Berhampur was the end of what has been called the 'white mutiny', but it was followed by a steady demand for discharge by the men of the old Company's regiments. In fact, out of 15,000 men, 10,116 claimed their discharge and returned to England. Their transport cost the government over £250,000. Indiscipline continued amongst those who remained and when, in June 1860, Sir Hugh Rose became commander-in-chief, he decided that harsh measures were necessary. Once again, the

5th European Regiment, now at Dinapur, responded with a near mutiny and one soldier was sentenced to death, though with a recommendation for mercy. Rose went personally to Dinapur and refused to commute the sentence. 'The state of the 5th is quite hopeless', he wrote. 'All the elements of order and discipline are the wrong way in them ... Fancy, the 5th, last year, in May 1859 after the order was read stating that they were not to get their Discharges, giving "Three cheers for the Company and three groans for the Queen"! Nothing will stop the mutinous and insubordinate conduct of the 5th but capital punishment. They do not seem to care for Penal Servitude, even for life. I fear that the Army at large has a very erroneous impression of it.' On December 12th the sentence of death was carried out and the regiment subsequently disbanded.

This sorry business, which could have been avoided by the payment of a modest bounty, had considerable effect upon the deliberations of the royal commission. Practically all military opinion, including that of Sir Colin Campbell and Sir Hugh Rose, was now strongly against the recruitment of a local European force in India. Canning, however, still preferred a force committed to serve only in India. Discussion continued until in June 1860, the final decision was made for amalgamation. White troops in India would not be permanently stationed there. The proportion of native to white troops was not to exceed two to one, and all the artillery was to be exclusively in the hands of Europeans.

The reconstruction of the native element in the Indian forces was one of extreme complexity. In the Bengal Army the number of infantry regiments was reduced from 146 in 1857 to 72 and similar reductions took place in the Bombay and Madras armies. The number of men in each regiment was also reduced to 600. In 1861 there were about 70,000 white troops to 135,000 native troops. All the arsenals and the principal forts were now held by white soldiers. In spite of modifications, which included the abolition of the separate armies of Bengal, Madras, and Bombay, the basic form laid down by the

THE REFORM OF THE ARMY

royal commission was maintained until the end of British rule.

Many other lessons were learned from the Mutiny, and slowly the changes that they demanded took place. The most revolutionary, perhaps, and certainly the least remembered by historians, were concerned with the welfare of British troops and in particular with their health, for the campaigns of the Mutiny had proved that there was a greater enemy than the rebellious sepoys. The casualty figures that emerge after a battle are always instructive for they are often used as the yardstick by which generalship is measured. During the Mutiny, 2,034 white officers and men were killed in action or died of wounds, but no fewer than 8,987 succumbed from the effects of sunstroke and sickness! There are no reliable figures for native casualties, but many thousands are known to have died from the rigours of climate and disease.

The reforms that followed the Mutiny left one factor basically unchanged: the British still depended for their power upon native soldiers. In fact, they could not have defeated the rebels without them. Before Delhi, for example, out of 11,200 effectives, no fewer than 7,900 were Indians. Even if the British had not had the service of loyal sepoys, they could not have moved an inch without the vast army of non-combatants – of whom there were 20 to every white soldier. Indians cooked the food, Indians brought water, and Indians carried the wounded away from the battlefield. Though the British could not do without the native portion of their Indian army, and despite its gallant performance in the two world wars, never again would they wholly trust it. There is no doubt that fear of another, and greater, Mutiny had its effect upon the negotiations that ended with India's independence in 1947.

Appendix:
THE COURSE OF THE MUTINY

1857

January — Rumour of 'greased cartridges' started in Dum Dum.

February 25th — Mutiny of the Nineteenth Native Infantry at Berhampur.

March 30th — Disbandment of the Nineteenth Native Infantry in Barrackpur.

April — Unrest and incendiarism in Ambala.

May 3rd — Mutiny in Lucknow prevented by Sir Henry Lawrence.
Disbandment of Seventh Irregular Cavalry.

May 6th — Disbandment of Thirty-fourth Native Infantry in Barrackpur.

May 10th — *Mutiny and Massacre at Meerut.*

May — Meerut Mutiny followed by outbreaks in Delhi, Ferozepur, Bombay, Aligarh, Mainpuri, Etawah, Bulandshar, Nasirabad, Bareilly, Moradabad, Shahjahanpur, and many smaller stations. Disarming of sepoys in Lahore, Agra, Lucknow, Peshawar, and Mardan.
Delhi Field Force advanced to Karnaul.
Death of General Anson, British commander-in-chief.

June — Mutinies at Sitapur, Hansi, Hissar, Azamgarh, Gorakhpur, and Nimach. Surviving Europeans besieged in Nimach fort.
Mutinies at Gwalior, Bharatpur, and Jhansi.
Mutiny at Cawnpore, then siege of European survivors (June 4th–25th) and massacre.
Mutiny in Benares forestalled; sepoys and

APPENDIX

doubtful Sikh battalion dispersed by gunfire.

Mutinies at Jewanpur, Allahabad, Jullundur, Phillaur, Nowgong, Rhoni, Fatehgarh, Aurungabad (Deccan), Fatehpur, and Jubbulpur. Aurangabad mutiny suppressed after a few days; rebels fled.

Forcible disarming of Indian units at Nagpur and Barrackpur.

Mutinies at Faizabad, Sultanpur, and Lucknow. Order was restored in the latter, but the city and surrounding neighbourhood remained disturbed. Europeans sheltered in the Residency.

British defeated at Chinhut (June 30th), near Lucknow.

Siege of Lucknow began.

Also in June:

Battle of Badli-ke-serai (June 8th). Delhi Field Force took up position on the Ridge and began operations against Delhi.

Throughout June, the revolt spread through the Ganges plain, the Rajputana, Central India, and affected parts of Bengal.

July

Mutinies at Indore and Mhow, Auggur, Jhelum, Saugor, Sialkot, Dinapur, and Agra. Europeans concentrated in fort of Agra.

Siege of Lucknow Residency continued throughout July; as did Delhi Field Force operations against the city of Delhi. General Barnard, commanding at Delhi, died of disease (July 5th).

General Havelock's force, advancing from Allahabad to the relief of Cawnpore, arrived on July 17th, one day too late to save the women and children from massacre.

Indian units in Rawalpindi disarmed. Sialkot mutineers defeated by General John Nicholson at Trimmu Ghat (July 16th).

August	Mutinies at Kolhapur (Bombay Presidency), Poonamali (near Madras), Jubbulpur, Bhopawar (near Indore), Mian Mir (near Lahore). During August, rebellion spread through Saugor and Narbada districts. Also in August: Surprise disarmament of Indian units in Berhampur (August 1st). Continuation of siege of Residency at Lucknow; Havelock's first attempt to relieve it failed.
September	Outbreak forestalled in Karachi (September 14th). Further outbreaks in Saugor and Narbada districts. Beginning of siege of Saugor. *Delhi assaulted and recaptured* (September 14th–20th). *Lucknow relieved by Havelock and Outram* (September 25th); new siege of the reinforced garrison began.
October	Mutiny at Bhogatpur (near Dinapur). Unrest in Bihar, North Bengal, and Assam. Mutiny in Bombay city forestalled (October 15th). Revolt in Kotah state (October 15th); Major Burton, the political agent, murdered.
November	*Lucknow relieved by Sir Colin Campbell* (November 17th); garrison evacuated, and Residency and city temporarily abandoned. General Windham defeated outside Cawnpore (November 28th); line of retreat from Lucknow threatened by mutineers.
December	*Decisive battle of Cawnpore* (December 6th); armies of the Rao Sahib – nephew of the Nana Sahib – and of Tantia Topi routed by Sir Colin Campbell. Campaign in the Doab. Capture of Fatehgarh.

APPENDIX

1858

January	Beginning of Sir Hugh Rose's Central Indian campaign.
	Sir Colin Campbell began campaign to recapture Lucknow.
	Gurkha army of Nepal came to assistance of British in Lucknow campaign.
February	Saugor relieved by Sir Hugh Rose (February 3rd).
	Assembly of Sir Colin Campbell's 'Army of Oudh' along Cawnpore–Lucknow road to await arrival of Gurkha army under Jang Bahadur.
March	*Lucknow recaptured* (March 21st) and rebel armies dispersed into Oudh.
	Continuation of Sir Hugh Rose's campaign.
April 1st	Battle of Betwa; Tantia Topi defeated.
April 3rd	*Jhansi stormed.*
April 4th	Rani of Jhansi fled.
April 6th	Final capture of Jhansi.
	Azamgarh recaptured and garrison relieved.
April 25th	Sir Hugh Rose resumed advance on Kalpi.
	Also in April:
	Sir Colin Campbell began reconquest of Rohilkhand.
	Fresh rising in Bihar, led by Koer Singh; after campaign against him, Koer Singh retreated wounded to his stronghold of Jagdispur, where he died of his wounds.
May 5th	Battle of Bareilly.
May 7th	Bareilly recaptured.
	Battle of Kunch; defeat of Tantia Topi.
May 10th	Jagdispur recaptured.
May 23rd	Kalpi reoccupied by British.
May 24th	Battle of Mohamdi. End of resistance in Rohilkhand.

May 27th	Rebels began guerrilla warfare in jungle. Tantia Topi and Rani of Jhansi at gates of Gwalior.
June 1st	Gwalior army deserted to rebels. Tantia Topi and Rani of Jhansi seize Gwalior by surprise.
June 6th	Sir Hugh Rose marched from Kalpi.
June 16th	Arrival of Sir Hugh Rose at Gwalior.
June 17th	Battle of Kotah-ke-serai; this date is also supposed to be that of the death of the Rani of Jhansi.
June 19th	*Battle of Gwalior.*
June 20th	*Capture of the fortress;* flight of Tantia Topi. Also in June: Continuation of suppression of scattered guerrilla forces in Oudh, Bihar, and along Nepalese frontier.
July–December	Guerrilla bands gradually suppressed everywhere except in the Rajputana and Central India, where Tantia Topi remained free and continued active resistance.
1859	
April 7th	Tantia Topi betrayed by Man Singh, and captured.
April 15th	Trial of Tantia Topi.
April 18th	Execution of Tantia Topi.

Bibliography

The number of published and manuscript materials about the Indian Mutiny is enormous. The manuscript sources are mainly in the National Archives of India, New Delhi, and the India Office Library, London. Of the many hundreds of books on the subject, most have been out of print for years. The basic standard work is J. W. Kaye's *History of the Sepoy War* (3 vols, 1880), and its continuation, G. B. Malleson's *History of the Indian Mutiny* (3 vols, 1878–80). There is no satisfactory modern history of the Mutiny, but that of the Indian historian, S. N. Sen, *Eighteen Fifty-Seven* (New Delhi, 1957), is valuable for its attempt to free the story from the not unnatural bias of nineteenth-century British writers.

Of personal memoirs, my own editions of the London *Times* correspondent William Howard Russell's journal, published under the title of *My Indian Mutiny Diary* (London, 1957), Maria Germon's *Journal of the Siege of Lucknow* (London, 1958), and William Forbes-Mitchell's *The Relief of Lucknow* (London, 1962) are useful as contemporary accounts. For other works, the reader will find the extensive bibliography printed in Sen's book extremely helpful.

Index

Afghans, 157, 162, 170
Agra, 6, 41, 121, 155, 186, 210, 211, relief of, 42, 43
Ajmer, 153
Alambagh, the, *see* Lucknow
Aligarh, 210
Alipur, 23, 194
Allahabad, 48, 51, 52, 59, 67, 77, 211; 6th Native Infantry mutiny at, 52, 211; Europeans killed and quarters looted, 53, 211; ruthlessly pacified by Neill, 53, 71; Commandant wishes to disarm European troops, 207
Amar Singh (rebel leader after death of Koer Singh), 139
Ambala, 13, 210
Anderson, Major (R.E.), 78
Anson, General George (1797–1857), C.-in-C. Bengal Army (1856), 6, 13; death of, 14, 210
Antri, 190
Arabs, 157
Army, reform of after the Mutiny, 206ff.
Arrah, English garrison of, defeated by Koer Singh, 139
Asigarh, 156
Auggur, 211
Aurungabad, 211
Azamgarh, 59, 139, 210

Badli-ke-serai, battle of, 14, 24, 211
Baghpat, 14
Bahadur Khan (Khan of Rohilkhand), 143, 146; escapes from Bareilly, 148
Bahadur Shah (King of Delhi) exiled to Burma, 203
Bakht Khan (rebel C.-in-C.), 41
Banda, Nawab of, 180, 182, 201
Bani, 78, 91, 101, 113, 116, 125
Banks, Major, 66
Banpur, Raja of, 163, 176
Bareilly, 59, 124, 210, 213; Bahadur Khan's defence of, 146

Barhat, Ahmad, 62
Barnard, General Sir Henry, 14ff., 211
Barnston, Major, 107, 108
Barrackpur, 6, 210, 211
Barter, Richard (*qu.*), 31
Bashiratgunj, Havelock takes, 79, and retakes, 81; rebels reassemble at, 83; Havelock takes for third time, 83; and for last time, 91
Benares, native troops disarmed at, 52, 210; mutiny at, 59
Bengal Army, 4, 5, 206, 208; *see also* British forces, *and* Indian (Mutineer) units
Beni Madho (Oudh rebel leader), 140
Berhampur, 6, 210; 5th European Regiment mutinies, 207, 208
Bertrand, 31
Betwa, battle of the, 169ff., 213
Bharatpur, 195, 210
Bhogatpur, 212
Bhopal, 153, 198
Bhopawar, 212
Bibighur, the, 56, 72, 75
Bihar, failure of minor campaign in, 138, 213
Bithauli, 139, 140
Bithur, 48; rebels assemble at, 83, 84
Blunt, Captain, 106
Bogniwala, 145
Bombay, 206, 210, 212
Brind, Major, 39
British and loyal Indian forces:
  Artillery, 51, 71, 90, 119, 143, 169, 189
  Baluch battalion, 30, 146, 196
  Bengal Fusiliers:
    1st, 13, 23, 30, 36, 122
    2nd, 13, 30
    3rd, 42
    5th, 13, 86, 90
    23rd, 105
  60th Bengal Infantry, 13
  Bombay Horse Artillery, 188

INDEX

British and loyal Indian forces—*cont.*
  3rd Bombay (European) Infantry, 171
  25th Bombay (Native) Infantry, 157, 171, 179, 182, 191
  56th Bombay (Native) Infantry, 54
  Bombay Lancers, 192
  3rd Bombay Light Cavalry, 188
  Camel Corps, 182
  Carabineers, 122
  3rd European Infantry, 163, 171
  5th European Infantry, 207
  Foot Regiments:
    8th, 30, 103, 105
    32nd, 47, 50, 58, 59, 61, 62
    37th, 51
    42nd, 143, 144, 147
    52nd, 30
    53rd, 51, 103, 105
    61st, 23, 24, 30
    64th, 51, 67, 68, 73–5, 79, 86, 90
    71st (Highlanders), 190
    75th, 13, 30, 103
    78th (Highlanders), 51, 67, 68, 73–5, 79, 83, 84, 90, 96, 146
    79th, 143
    84th, 51, 52, 67, 68, 73–5, 84, 90
    86th, 173, 182, 191
    88th, 183
    92nd, 183
    93rd (Highlanders), 103–8, 130, 143, 147
  Hodson's Horse, 104, 122, 141
  Horse Artillery, 13, 143
  7th Hussars, 141
  8th Hussars, 191, 192
  Hyderabad Infantry, 171, 177, 189, 190
  4th Irregular Cavalry, 13; disarmed, 70
  Kashmir Contingent, 30, 34, 39
  Kumaon Battalion, 30
  9th Lancers, 13, 24, 104, 143
  9th Light Cavalry, 13
  14th Light Dragoons, 157, 170, 188, 190
  90th Light Infantry, 86, 90
  Madras Fusiliers, 51, 52, 67, 68, 71, 73, 74, 79, 84, 86, 90
  Multani Horse, 24
  Naval Brigade, 104, 109, 129
  Oudh Irregular Cavalry, 61
  Punjab Cavalry:
    1st, 104
    2nd, 24, 104, 143
    5th, 104
  Punjab Infantry:
    1st, 24, 30
    2nd, 24, 30, 105
    4th, 30, 105, 107, 130, 143, 146
  Royal Artillery, 51, 69, 90
  Royal Engineers, 171
  Sikh cavalry, 103
  Sikhs, 122, 132, 147
  4th Sikhs, 30, 67, 68, 71, 73, 74, 76, 84, 90
  Sirmur Battalion, 30
  Volunteer Cavalry, 61, 68, 71–4, 85
Bulandshar, 210
Bundelkhand, 153, 185
Burton, Major, 212

Calcutta, 5, 7, 77
Cameron, Colonel (42nd Foot), 147
Campbell, General Sir Colin (1792–1863), 86, 87, 96, 101, 164, 208; his dilemma over command, 102; takes the Alambagh and enters Lucknow, 104, 105; signals Outram that he will reach the Residency by 16 Nov., 106; captures the Secundrabagh and Shaf Najaf Mosque, 107, 108; relieves the Residency and decides on evacuation, 109, 112, 212; advances on, and takes Cawnpore, 114–20; defeats Tantia Topi, 119; forced to await reinforcements, 121; captures Fatehgarh, 122; joined by Seaton and Walpole, 125; plans final attack on Lucknow, 126ff.; orders Outram not to attack, 129, 133; his inept handling of campaign, 129, 133; leaves Bareilly for Fatehgarh, 149; decides to disband the Central India Field Force, 183
Campbell, Colonel (later Brigadier), 28, 30, 31, 34, 135; fails to stop rebels fleeing from Musabagh, 136

INDEX

Canning, Charles John, Earl (1812–62), Governor-General, 17; decides against Campbell's wishes that Oudh must be reconquered first, 124; issues proclamation that all rebels' lands will be forfeit, 137; first Viceroy, 203

Casualties, 36, 37, 80, 84, 98, 136, 158, 174, 175, 178; *see also* Indian (Mutineer) units

Cawnpore, 42, 47ff., 155; outbreak of mutiny and siege, 54, 59; massacre of women and children, 57; Havelock sets out to relieve, 68; defeats Nana Sahib at, 72ff.; taken by Havelock, 75; Hope Grant reaches, 101; Lucknow survivors set out for, 114; Campbell's capture of, 114–19

Central Indian Agency, 153

Chamberlain, Neville (Adjutant-General), 18, 19, 20

Charkheri, 166, 167

Chinese Expeditionary Force, 121

Chinhut, 128; Lawrence defeated at, 63, 211

Cholera, 19, 78, 80, 82, 84

Coke, Brigadier, 143; routs rebels at Bogniwala and Nagina, 145; attacks Bareilly, 148; moves to attack Bahadur Khan at Pilibhit, 149

Colvin, John (Provincial Lieut.-Governor), 42

Cooper, Major (R.A.), 90

Crawford, Brigadier, 104

Dalhousie, Lord (Governor-General, 1848–56), 1

Daosa, 200

Deccan, 185

Delhi, 3, 11ff., 54; captured by the rebels, 11; preparations for the siege of, 20ff., 211; storming of, 33ff.; casualties, 37; capture of, 38ff.; King surrenders to Hodson, 41; British treatment of the population, 41

Dewas, 153

Dhar, 153, 157

Dinapur, 6; sepoys mutiny and escape from, 81, 88; 5th European Regiment mutinies at, 208, 211, 212

Doab, the, 47, 212

Dodgson (Deputy Adjutant-General), 110

Dowker, Lieutenant, 174

Dum Dum, 210

Durand, Sir Henry (1812–71), (Acting Agent-General for Central India), forced to evacuate Indore, 155; defeats rebels at Dhar, 157, 158; crosses Chambal River, 158; captures Goraria after stubborn defence, 159, 160; disarms Holkar's army at Indore, 160; hands over command to Sir Robert Hamilton, 160; appointed as Commissioner to enquire into the future of the Bengal Army, 206

East India Company, 5, 203; armed forces of, 5; *see also* British forces *and* Indian (Mutineer) units

Enfield rifle, 3

Etawah, 210

Eyre, Captain (East India Co. Artillery), 90

Faizabad, 59, 126, 211; Maulvi of (rebel leader), 136, 139, 143, 146–9; killed, 150

Faridpur, 146

Farukhabad, Nawab of, 143

Fatehgarh, 56, 143, 211, 212

Fatehpur, 211; Havelock joins up with Renaud at, 68; Battle of, 69

Ferozepur, 210

Firuz Shah (rebel leader), 145, 149, 157, 160, 200, 201, 202–3

Flagstaff Tower, 15

Forbes-Mitchell, Sergeant (93rd Highlanders) (*qu.*), 107, 120; his account of Hodson's death, 130–1; on Walpole's mismanagement and unnecessary casualties, 144; on the bravery of the Ghazis, 147

Franks, Brigadier Thomas, 126; joins Campbell at Lucknow with Nepalese contingent, 127

INDEX

Gall, Major, 176, 177

Ganges, 48, 52; Havelock ferries his army across, 78

Gardener, Colour-Sergeant (42nd Foot), saves life of Col. Cameron, 147

Gathakot fort, 164

Ghazis (fanatical Muslims), 147

Golowli, 179

Gorakhpur, 210

Goraria, rebels' stiff resistance at, 159, 160

Grand Trunk Road, 15, 52, 69

Grant, Brigadier Hope, 35, 102, 105, 117; sent to pursue rebels fleeing from Lucknow, 134; drives rebels from Kursi, 136; to garrison Lucknow, 138; sends detachment to attack Bari, 139; his campaigns at Bithauli, Jellalabad, and Nawabgunge, 140; sent to relieve Shahganj, 142

Grant, General Patrick, 102

Graves, Brigadier, 17

Greathed, Brigadier, 42, 43, 104, 118, 156

Gubbins (Residency civilian in Lucknow) (*qu.*), 101, 111

Gumti River, 90, 129

Gunah, 155, 195

Gurkhas, 123, 127, 131, 132, 140

Gwalior, 87, 154, 155, 156, 185, 210, 214; Army sides with mutineers, 185, 186; remains unpacified, 198

Gwalior Contingent threatens Cawnpore, 111, 113, 115, 117; threatens the Ganges pontoon bridge, 118; besieges Charkheri, 166

Hale, Colonel, 148

Hamilton, Colonel, 74, 90

Hamilton, Sir Robert (Agent for Central India), takes over from Durand, 160; informs Canning that Jhansi must be retaken and Charkheri left for later action, 167

Hannaford, Private (53rd Foot), 119

Hansi, 210

Hattras, 155

Havelock, Brigadier-General Sir Henry (1795–1857), 43, 44; assumes command, 67; at battle of Fatehpur (*qu.*), 68–70; sends to Neill for reinforcements, 72; takes Cawnpore, 75, 211; crosses Ganges into Oudh and defeats rebels at Unao, 79; and at Bashiratgunj, 79, 80; sends to Neill for further reinforcements 80; retakes Bashiratgunj, 81; retires to Mangalwar, 82; takes Bashiratgunj for third time, 83; marches against Bithur, 84; takes it but has to retire to Cawnpore, 85; superseded by Outram but left in command for final attack on Lucknow, 89; defeats rebels at the Alambagh, 92; relieves the Residency, but surrounded, 93ff.; joins up with Campbell outside the Residency, 110

Hayes, Captain Fletcher, on the situation at Cawnpore (*qu.*), 50, 54

Hazrat Mahal, Begum (rebel leader), 139, 140, 142, 149; her criticism of Queen Victoria's Proclamation, 204

Highlanders, *see* British Forces

Hinduism, 2

Hindu Rao's House, 15, 18, 29, 35

Hissar, 210

Hodson, Major (1821–58), accepts surrender of King of Delhi, 41; and murders the three princes, 41; killed, 130, 131

Hodson's Horse, 104, 122, 144

Holkar, the, *see* Indore

Holmes, Colonel, 195, 196

Home, Lieut., 34

Hope, Brigadier Adrian, 105; in charge of La Martinière garrison, 105, 112; commands advance against rebels before Kalpi, 119; killed at Ruya, 144

Humayun, Tomb of, 41

Hyderabad contingent, 171, 189, 190

Indargarh, 200

INDEX

Indian (Mutineer) units:
  Bengal Infantry:
    12th, 155
    15th, 153
    30th, 153
    72nd, 153, 155
  1st Bengal Light Cavalry, 153
  Gwalior Contingent, 82, 155
  7th Irregular Cavalry, 210
  14th Irregular Cavalry, 155
  2nd Native Cavalry, 54, 70
  Native Infantry:
    1st, 54
    6th, 52
    19th, 210
    34th, 210
    41st, 59
    42nd, 83
    53rd, 54
  7th Oudh Irregulars, 47; see also British Forces
Indian National Army (1944), 203
Indore, 153, 155, 197, 211; army submits to being disarmed, 160; Holkar of, 155
Inglis, Colonel, 58, 62; takes military command at Lucknow, 66, 78; Havelock advises him to break out from Lucknow, 82; replies that such is impossible, 87, 88; his ignorance of hidden supplies in the Residency, 99; commands rear brigade in battle for Kalpi, 119
Inglis, Lady (qu.), 62

Jaipur, 195
Jang Bahadur, Maharaja (Ghurka leader), 131
Jawra, 153
Jawra Alipur, 194
Jellalabad, 140
Jewanpur, 211
Jhalrapatan, 197
Jhalwar State, 197
Jhansi, 1, 153, 165, 195, 210; battle for, 166ff.; massacre and looting at, 173
Jhansi, Rani of, 169; flees to Kalpi, 174, 185; tries to persuade rebels to prepare for British attack on Gwalior, 185; killed at Kotah-ke-serai, 191, 192, 214
Jhelum, 211
Jones, General John, 145
Jones, Brigadier H. R., 30, 33, 35; takes command of column after Penny's death, 145–6; sent to relieve Shahjahanpur, 149
Jubbulpur, 153, 165, 211, 212
Jullundur, 211

Kalpi, 82, 87, 116, 119, 169, 200; Tantia Topi and Rani of Jhansi take refuge in, 169, 173; to be defended to the last man, 180; captured by Rose, 183, 213, 214
Karnaul, 14, 210
Karachi, 212
Kashmir Gate, the blowing-up of the, 33, 34
Kavanagh, Thomas Henry, clerk, awarded V.C. for gallantry, 101, 110
Kaye, J. W. (historian) (qu.), 38
Koer Singh (rebel commander), 88, 138, 139, 213
Kokrail, 61, 62
Kolhapur, 212
Kotah, 176
Kotah-ke-serai, 189; Battle of, 190–1, 214
Kotrah, 196
Kudsia Bagh, 29, 33
Kunch, rebels mass at, 177; Rose captures, 178, 213
Kursi, Hope Grant drives rebels from, 136

Lahore, 20, 210
Lalitpur, 155
Lawrence, Sir Henry (1806–57), Chief Commissioner of Oudh, brother of John, 47, 210; sends troops to aid Wheeler at Cawnpore, 50; prepares for trouble at Lucknow, 61; sallies out but defeated at Chinhut, 63; prepares Residency for siege, 64; killed, 65, 77
Lawrence, Sir John (1811–74), 20
Lawrence, Captain Richard, 35

INDEX

Liddell, Colonel, 198
Lightfoot, Captain (R.A.), 170
Little, Brigadier, 104
Lohari, 177
Lohunga, 68, 71
Longfield, Brigadier, 30
Looting, 133, 173
Lowe, Dr (*qu.*), on the storming of Jhansi, 171–3; on the fight for Kalpi, 183
Lowth, Lieut.-Colonel, 171, 172
Lucknow, 6, 43, 93, 210, 211, 212, 213; capture of, 126ff.; Alambagh, the, 91, 94, 100, 111, 123, 124, 127; Campbell's forces arrive at (12 Nov.), 104; rebels attack in force (16 March), 135; Bailey Guard and Water Gate, 65; Cawnpore and Redan Batteries, 65; Charbagh Bridge, 93, 94, 95; Dilkusha Palace, 93, 94, 105, 127, 128; Hazratgunge, 131; Imambara, 131, 132; Kaisarbagh, 109, 110, 112, 131–3, 135; Machchi Bhawan, 64; Martinière, La, 93, 105; Mess House, the, 132; Musabagh Palace, 135; Padshah Bagh, 94, 129; Residency, the, 93; siege of, 64; second siege, 99ff.; final relief of, 105, 110; withdrawal from, 111; Secundrabagh, the, 106, 130; Shah Najaf, 108, 130
Ludhiana, 20
Ludlow Castle, 15, 22, 29, 30, 32
Lugard, General, 126, 130; sent to relieve Milman in Azamgarh, 138

Madanpur, 166
Madras, 161, 206
Maharajpur, 72
Mahidpur, rebels' victory at, 158
Malthon Pass, 166
Malwa, the, 153; campaign in, 157ff.
Mandisur, 157, 200; evacuated by Firuz Shah, 160
Mangalwar, 80; Havelock retires to, 82; and again, 83; halts on way to Cawnpore, 114
Mansfield, General (Campbell's Chief of Staff), 102; routs Nana Sahib, 120

Man Singh, 198–200; betrays Tantia Topi, 201
Maps, lack of adequate, 81
Marathas, 153
Mardan, 210
Marowra Fort abandoned by rebels, 166
Maude, Captain (R.A.), 90; his criticism of the Lucknow Campaign, 99
Maulvi, *see* Faizabad
Maxwell, Colonel, 179, 181–3
Meerut, 11, 14, 143, 210; mutinous behaviour of white troops at, 207
Mekranis, 157
Mercenaries, 157, 162, 170
Metcalfe House, 15, 22, 28
Metcalfe, Sir Theophilus, 23
Mhow, 153, 155, 157, 162, 197, 211
Mian Mir, 212
Michel, General, 197–8; defeats Tantia Topi at Mangrauli, 199
Milman, Colonel, driven into Azamgarh by Koer Singh's troops, 138
Mirganj, 145
Mohamdi, 150
Moradabad, 210
Morar, 155, 186, 189
Mughal Empire, 3, 5, 12
Muter, Captain, 35

Nagpur, 1, 199, 211
Nahergarh, 200
Najafgarh, battle of, 22ff.
Nalkera, 197
Nana Sahib, 48, 51, 146, 169; offers terms to besieged Cawnpore, 55–6; his dispositions near Cawnpore, 72, 74; his defeat, 75; proclaimed chief of revived Maratha dominions, 186
Nangarh, 160
Napier, Brigadier Robert (Chief Engineer), 127, 131; succeeds Rose as C.-in-C., 189; but agrees to serve under him, 189; left at Morar to pursue rebels fleeing from Gwalior, 191; defeats rebels at Jawra Alipur, 194
Narbada, 153, 199, 200, 212
Narod, 153

INDEX

Narut fort, 166
Nasirabad, 153, 195, 210
Nawabganj, enemy in force at, 82
Nawabgunge, 51, 60, 140
Need, Captain, 170
Neill, Colonel, disarms native troops at Benares, 52; reaches Allahabad, 53; joins Havelock at Cawnpore with reinforcements, 76; sends abusive reply to Havelock when asked for further reinforcements, 80; threatened by rebels in Cawnpore and asks Havelock for aid, 83; commands brigade in final march on Lucknow, 90, 96; killed, 97
Nepalese contingent, see Gurkhas
Nicholson, Brigadier John, 20ff., 211; killed, 37
Nimach, 153, 155, 159, 195, 197, 210
Nirpat Singh (rebel leader at Ruya), 143–5
North, Major (78th Highlanders) (qu.), 74
Nowgong, 211

Oliphant, Captain (R.A.), 90
Orr, Major, 158; disperses rebels at Kotah and marches on Kunch, 177; commands Hyderabad troops and is sent to Paniar to block rebel retreat from Gwalior, 189
Oudh, 1, 3, 7, 47, 93, 134; general uprising against the British, 85; pacification of, 121; Canning's view of the importance of reconquering quickly, 123; his efforts nullified by his proclamation about land forfeiture, 137
Oudh, Begum of, see Hazrat Mahal, King of, 123, 135
Outram, Major-General Sir James, 67; supersedes Havelock, 86; arrives at Allahabad, 87; and at Cawnpore, 88; issues order that Havelock is to have the honour of relieving Lucknow, 89; his plan for relief of the Residency, 95; resumes overall command, 99; moves to join Campbell, 106, 111; remains to defend the Alambagh, 124; crosses Gumti River on pontoon bridge, 127; receives strange order from Campbell, 129, 133; ordered to cross the Gumti bridge, 134

Pandu Nadi, 71, 116
Panna, 166
Paori, 199
Parke, Brigadier, 197, 198; defeats Tantia Topi at Chota Udaipur, 200
Pathans, 162
Peel, Captain William, R.N. (C.O. of Naval Brigade), 104, 108, 109, 112, 117, 119
Penny, General, 143; killed at Kukerauli, 145
Peshawar, 6, 20, 210
Phillaur, 211
Pilibhit, 148, 149
Poonamali, 212
Punah, 197
Punjab, 20ff., 121
Putch, 177

Raines, Colonel, 191–2
Rajputana, 153, 211
Rajputana Field Force, 188–9, 195
Ramgunga River, 124
Ramnagar, 140
Rao Sahib (rebel leader), 176, 185; vows to defend Kalpi to the last man, 180, 182; takes Gwalior, 186; flees from Gwalior, 192; joins Tantia Topi, 199; and Man Singh, 200; refuses amnesty, 201; betrayed and hanged, 201
Rathgarh, 162
Reed, General, 19
Reid, Major, 29, 30, 34, 35
Reinforcements from England, difficulties in obtaining, 121
Renaud, Major, 67–71
Rhoni, 211
Riddell, Colonel, 188–9
Roberts, Frederick (later Earl), 26, 43, 133
Roberts, General H. G., 195; occupies Jaipur, 195; his Intelligence system, 196
Robertson, Colonel, 188

Rohilkhand, 59, 124-5; Canning insists on the conquest of, 137; Maulvi of Faizabad joins forces at, 139; campaign in, 143ff., 213

Rose, Lieutenant (25th Bombay Native Infantry), 193

Rose, Sir Hugh (1801-85), C.-in-C. Central Indian Field Force, 160, 213-4; Rathgarh and Barodia, 162, 163; takes Gathakot fort, 164; plans advance on Jhansi, 164; takes Madanpur, 166; bypasses Charkheri and takes Jhansi by storm, 169-75; his plan for capture of Kalpi, 180; takes Gwalior, 191, 192; refuses to commute death sentence on white mutineer, 208

Rurki, 143

Russell, Sir William (C.O. of 7th Hussars), 141

Russell, William Howard (*The Times* correspondent) (*qu*), on the looting in Lucknow, 133

Salkeld, Lieutenant, 34

Sarai fort abandoned by rebels, 166

Satara, 1

Saugor, 153, 163, 211, 212; relieved by Rose, 164, 213

Seaton, Brigadier, moves from Delhi with men and stores for Campbell, and defeats Nawab of Farukhabad at Aligarh, 122; left to garrison Fatehgarh, 125; campaign against Rohilkhand, 143

Selimgarh fort, 40

Shahjahanpur, 59, 145, 210; the Maulvi escapes from and attacks the British left there, 150

Shahgarh, Raja of, 177

Showers, Brigadier, killed, 23

Sialkot, 211

Sihor, 155

Sikar, 162

Sikhs, *see* British forces

Simla, 6

Sindhia, Maharaja (of Gwalior), 185; remains loyal to British but routed by rebels, 186

Sipri, 155, 195, 198

Sitapur, 59, 210

Smith, Brigadier, 189; defeats rebels at Kotah-ke-serai, 190; defeats Man Singh at Paori, 198, 199

Smith, Major Baird, 18, 19, 26

Smith, Captain (R.A.), 119

Sterling, Major (64th Foot), 75

Steuart, Brigadier (14th Light Dragoons), 161

Stuart, Brigadier (Bombay Army), 156, 161; takes Chanderi fort, 166; commands column at Jhansi, 169; rallies troops at Kalpi, 182, 183; reaches Morar, 189; attacks left flank before Gwalior, 192

Subzimundi (the Green Market), 15

Sultanpur, 59, 138, 142, 211

Sunstroke casualties, 136, 178, 179, 180

Sutherland Highlanders, *see* 93rd Highlanders (British forces)

Suttee (widow burning), 2

Tantia (Tatya) Topi (rebel general), leaves garrison at Kalpi and moves on Cawnpore, 115; threatens Ganges crossing and the bridge of boats, 117; routed by Campbell, 119; takes Charkheri and comes to the relief of Jhansi, 169; defeated on the Betwa and retreats to Kalpi, 170, 213; blamed for the debacle of Kunch, 178; after fall of Kalpi tries to win over Gwalior, 185; flees from Gwalior, 194; the pursuit of, 195ff.; flees to Jhalwar State, 197; joins with Rao Sahib and enters Nagpur, 199; betrayed and executed, 194, 201, 214

Taylor, Alexander, 28

Thuggee, 2

Tonk, 195

Travers, Captain (R.A.), 106, 117

Trimmu Ghat, 211

Tytler, Colonel, 71, 88

Udaipur, 196

Ujjain, 197

Unao, 125; battle of, 81

Ungud (native pensioner), 90

INDEX

Valaitis (Afghan mercenaries), 170
Victoria, Queen, signs Act assuming government of India, 202; proclaims freedom of worship, 203-4

Waller Lieutenant, 193
Walpole, Brigadier, 119; sent to meet Seaton and to take Fatehgarh, 122; sent to make feint attack near Fatehgarh, 125; commands division for final attack on Lucknow, 126, 128; left to guard Lucknow bridges, 135; ordered to clear left bank of Ganges: his incompetence, 143; joins up again with Campbell and with Penny's Division, 145; left to command Rohilkhand garrison, 149
Wheeler, Major-General (C.-in-C. of Oudh and Doab region), 47-8, 50-1
Whitlock, General, 161, 165, 168
Wilson, General Archdale, 14, 19, 20, 26, 28, 37, 38
Windham, Major-General, 102, 113, 114-16, 155, 183, 212
Woodburn, Colonel, 155

Zirapur, 200

BRITISH BATTLES SERIES (illus.)

BATTLES OF THE '45 (30p) 6/–
Katherine Tomasson and Francis Buist
The story of the fiercely fought engagements which took place between the royal army and the Jacobites, led by Prince Charles Edward.

THE SPANISH ARMADA (25p) 5/–
Michael Lewis
'A brilliantly clear picture of the campaign'—BRITISH BOOK NEWS.

TRAFALGAR (25p) 5/–
Oliver Warner
'A stirring picture of the battle in which Nelson died destroying Napoleon's power at sea'—NEW YORK TIMES.

BATTLES OF THE ENGLISH CIVIL WAR (30p) 6/–
Austin Woolrych
Covers the three decisive engagements which sealed the fate of King Charles I.

BATTLES OF THE BOER WAR (30p) 6/–
W. Baring Pemberton
Belmont, Modder River, Magersfontein, Colenso and Spion Kop. 'Admirable with an intimate picture of many of the commanders involved'—THE OBSERVER.

BATTLES OF THE CRIMEAN WAR (30p) 6/–
W. Baring Pemberton
'The best Crimean "primer" ever'—THE DAILY TELEGRAPH.

THE BATTLE OF THE ATLANTIC (25p) 5/–
Capt. Donald Macintyre
Extracts from the log-books of both warship and U-boat commanders help tell the gripping story of those crucial months from 3rd September, 1939, to 24th May, 1943.

CORONEL AND THE FALKLANDS (30p) 6/–
Geoffrey Bennett
The story of the first major sea battles of World War I.

THE BATTLE OF MATAPAN (25p) 5/–
S. W. C. Pack
'Told with a skill and vividness which recreate the picture in all its gallant and striking colours—THE TIMES.

BRITISH BATTLES SERIES (cont.)

THE BATTLE FOR NORMANDY (30p) 6/–
Eversley Belfield and H. Essame
'The last great set-piece of the Western World'—
THE OBSERVER.

CORUNNA (30p) 6/–
Christopher Hibbert
The battle in the Peninsular War which saved a British Army from annihilation.

AGINCOURT (25p) 5/–
Christopher Hibbert
'A straightforward and absorbing account of this astounding battle and the campaign that so improbably led up to it'—THE OBSERVER.

WATERLOO (25p) 5/–
John Naylor
'No commanders were ever better served by their men, British, French and Prussian'—BRITISH ARMY REVIEW.

THE SOMME (30p) 6/–
Anthony Farrar-Hockley
One of the most bloody and protracted battles in history.

YPRES 1914: Death of an Army (30p) 6/–
Anthony Farrar-Hockley
A magnificent and moving story of the old British Regular Army.

BATTLES OF THE INDIAN MUTINY (35p) 7/–
Michael Edwardes
'Lucknow relieved ... Cawnpore avenged, Delhi stormed ... all excellently recounted using much unpublished material'—THE SUNDAY TIMES.

THE BATTLE FOR THE MEDITERRANEAN
Capt. Donald Macintyre   (30p) 6/–
Achieves an excellent balance between the strategic and the operational features of the campaign'—RUSI JOURNAL.

(To be published 6th November, 1970.)

COLES NOTES
the world's finest revision aids.

Are you taking G.C.E. 'O' or 'A' levels this year? If so, you will be interested in Coles Notes. Coles Notes are examination revision aids which cover all aspects of G.C.E. examinations.

If you are studying Shakespeare, we publish a study aid for almost every play that Shakespeare wrote.

You are still trying to understand what James Joyce means in his masterpiece PORTRAIT OF THE ARTIST AS A YOUNG MAN? Then once again Coles Notes on that title will be of considerable help.

In addition, nearly all the classics of English Literature are covered in our extensive list. If your problem is poetry, you almost certainly will need a Note on the author you are currently studying and you should find one on our list.

Apart from subjects already mentioned, Coles Notes also publish books on History, Geography, Maths., General Science, Physics, Chemistry, Geometry, Algebra, French, German, Latin. You name it—we publish a Note on it.

Also available for the first time is our new series called Forum House. These are in the main critical analyses of English Literature, Anthropology, Politics and Psychology written with University and College students in mind. Amongst authors discussed at length in this excellent new series are E.M. Forster, T.S. Eliot and D.H. Lawrence.

For further details and free list please apply to

**Coles Notes Division,
Pan Books Limited,
33 Tothill Street,
London, S.W.1.**